Structural Existential An

Structural Existential Analysis (SEA) is a qualitative research method which uses an existential-phenomenological framework that has been developed through decades of therapeutic and research practice. This book describes the method of SEA and how to apply it to qualitative research.

The book starts with a detailed description of the existential underpinnings of SEA, drawing on a range of phenomenologists, to demonstrate the need for a phenomenology of interiority. The method is described in full, explaining the use of a specific form of self-reflection (SOAR) and of the Existential Research Dialogue. The second part focuses on the analysis of the research data. A full description is given of each of the filters, in terms of their origin, their meaning and the specific ways in which they are applied. The text is enlivened by ample examples demonstrating how the filters can be used and how the analysis can draw out different aspects of human experience throughout the process.

The book will be essential reading for all those involved in education, training or research in existential therapies, clinical psychology and counselling psychology.

Emmy van Deurzen is a philosopher and psychologist who has practiced as an existential therapist for over 50 years. She is the author of many well-known books and Co-Founder and Director of the Existential Academy, London, UK.

Claire Arnold-Baker is a counselling psychologist and existential therapist and Principal of NSPC, London, UK. She specialises in researching and working with mothers and supervising doctoral research in this and other related areas.

This innovative and inspiring new text provides a comprehensive guide to *structural existential analysis*: a research method that – as a stand-alone approach or in combination with other methods – can help to develop a deep, rich, and vivid understanding of participants' lived-worlds. Philosophical foundations for the approach are clearly explained, with practical guidance and illustrations throughout to show their application. A valuable resource for qualitative researchers in the counselling and psychotherapy field and beyond.

Mick Cooper, *Professor of Counselling Psychology, University of Roehampton, UK*

Grounded in existential literature, theory and practice this timely book wonderfully articulates the qualitative research method of Structural Existential Analysis (SEA) where the key focus is on how people actually experience human existence. The application of SEA is beautifully articulated and how it can offer more depth and richness of meaning through the use of the Existential Research Dialogue (ERD). The authors describe SEA research as a passionate research enterprise, and they certainly articulate that passion as they both challenge and engage the reader to share in the essential quest for knowledge of the human condition. The book offers a significant opportunity to what the authors describe as therapist-researchers in facilitating a different and informed choice of qualitative research method.

Alistair McBeath, *BPS Chartered Psychologist and Associate Fellow; he is also a UKCP registered Psychotherapist and Senior Lecturer on the DC Psych programme at the Metanoia Institute, UK, and co-author of* Enjoying Research in Counselling and Psychotherapy

Structural Existential Analysis

An Existential-Phenomenological Method for Researching Life

Emmy van Deurzen and
Claire Arnold-Baker

LONDON AND NEW YORK

Designed cover image: MirageC/Getty Images

First published 2025
by Routledge
4 Park Square, Milton Park, Abingdon, Oxon OX14 4RN

and by Routledge
605 Third Avenue, New York, NY 10158

Routledge is an imprint of the Taylor & Francis Group, an informa business

© 2025 Emmy van Deurzen and Claire Arnold-Baker

The right of Emmy van Deurzen and Claire Arnold-Baker to be identified as authors of this work has been asserted in accordance with sections 77 and 78 of the Copyright, Designs and Patents Act 1988.

All rights reserved. No part of this book may be reprinted or reproduced or utilised in any form or by any electronic, mechanical, or other means, now known or hereafter invented, including photocopying and recording, or in any information storage or retrieval system, without permission in writing from the publishers.

Trademark notice: Product or corporate names may be trademarks or registered trademarks, and are used only for identification and explanation without intent to infringe.

British Library Cataloguing-in-Publication Data
A catalogue record for this book is available from the British Library

ISBN: 978-0-367-70794-1 (hbk)
ISBN: 978-0-367-70793-4 (pbk)
ISBN: 978-1-003-14804-3 (ebk)

DOI: 10.4324/9781003148043

Typeset in Times New Roman
by Apex CoVantage, LLC

This book is dedicated:

To all those who seek to understand human existence better and who are committed to searching for truth and clarity

Contents

List of Figures	ix
List of Tables	x
Abbreviations	xi
Acknowledgements	xii
Introduction: Why Structural Existential Analysis?	1

PART ONE
Theory — 9

1	Existential Philosophy and Its Importance for Research	11
2	The Phenomenological Attitude in Structural Existential Analysis	21
3	Designing Structural Existential Analysis Research	40
4	Designing, Conducting and Recording an In-Depth Existential Research Dialogue	59

PART TWO
Application — 79

5	The Filter of TIME	81
6	The Filter of SPACE	97
7	The Filter of PARADOX	114
8	The Filter of PURPOSE	128

9	The Filter of PASSION	144
10	Synthesis	164
11	Returning to Phenomenological Principles	178

Bibliography — *195*
Appendix — *204*
Index — *209*

Figures

2.1	The intentional arc	34
5.1	Structural Existential Analysis diagram	82
5.2	Eugène Minkowski: All time exists in the present	86
5.3	Double figure eight	88
5.4	Movement around time (Deurzen, 2025)	89
5.5	The dialectics of time (Deurzen and Arnold-Baker, 2018)	89
8.1	Layers that a person is engaged with in the world (Deurzen, 2025)	137
9.1	Compass of emotions	148
9.2	Four kinds of emotions	149
9.3	Threat to value: fight with pride, jealousy, anger	149
9.4	Loss of value: flight in despair, fear, sorrow	151
9.5	Promise of value: from freeze to shame, envy and desire	152
9.6	Gain of value: find hope, love, joy	153
9.7	Emotional compass (Deurzen, 2025)	155
9.8	Olga's emotional experience of freedom	160
9.9	Luke's emotional experience of freedom	162
10.1	The emotional aspects of Bonnie's experience of freedom	171
10.2	The filter of PASSION	176
11.1	Landenberg's (2020) diagram of how to blend SEA and IPA	180

Tables

5.1	Summary of Olga's temporal themes	95
5.2	Olga's experience of freedom over time	96
6.1	Summary of the four dimensions and their main concerns	103
6.2	Example of working with meaning units in SEA research	109
6.3	Example of a full analysis of the four dimensions	112
6.4	Summary of Bonnie's experiences of freedom in the four dimensions	112
7.1	Dimensions and tensions of human existence (Deurzen, 2010: 141)	119
7.2	Paradoxes and tensions	119
7.3	Olga's paradoxes of freedom	123
7.4	Bonnie's paradoxes of freedom	124
7.5	Luke's paradoxes of freedom	125
7.6	Overall paradoxes of freedom	126
8.1	Positive purposes and negative concerns and minimal and optimal goals on the four dimensions (adapted from Deurzen, 1998)	138
10.1	The filter of TIME	165
10.2	The filter of SPACE	166
10.3	Bonnie's experiences of freedom	168
10.4	The filter of PARADOX	169
10.5	Themes for the filter of TIME	175
10.6	The filters of SPACE and PARADOX	175
11.1	Feigin's (2021) consolidated 16-point table	179

Abbreviations

ERD   Existential Research Dialogue
HMS   Her Majesty's Ship
IS   Information Sheet
PRISMA   Preferred Reporting Items for Systematic reviews and Meta-Analyses
PTSD   Post-Traumatic Stress Disorder
SEA   Structural Existential Analysis
SOAR   State of Mind, Orientation, Attitude, Reaction

Acknowledgements

We would like to thank the three participants, Olga, Bonnie and Luke (pseudonyms), who took part in the research into total freedom that we conducted in order to illustrate the application of the Structural Existential Analysis method. The research was granted ethics approval by the NSPC/Middlesex University ethics panel, and care and consideration has been given to ensure that informed consent, anonymity and confidentiality have been closely adhered to. All the participants were informed at the outset of the research that the research would be appearing in this publication and they gave us further permission to publish once they had read the sections that related to them in the book.

We would also like to thank our graduates who gave us permission to include aspects of their own research in this book to further illustrate the application of the method. We are indebted to the many students who have adopted this methodology for their research which has helped us to develop and further refine the approach. We are also grateful to our NSPC research supervisors who have engaged with the methodology and have provided rich feedback over the years.

As always, we are deeply grateful for the love and support of our spouses, Digby and Will, who, sometimes unknowingly, contribute to our work in myriad ways.

Introduction
Why Structural Existential Analysis?

Structural Existential Analysis (SEA) is a qualitative research method that is particularly appropriate for the investigation of deeply personal ideas, feelings and experiences. More than any other available research method it focuses directly on the most intimate and most deeply personal aspects of a person's existence. It combines some aspects of narrative work, hermeneutic work and phenomenological methodology, but it always keeps these in the background. The focus remains firmly on the human experience that is being made sense of and the method always seeks to connect with what is most meaningful in people's experiences with the human condition.

SEA is unique amongst qualitative research methods in having this focus on a very subjective, meaningful understanding of a person's experience. In this respect it is perhaps most true to the original intentions of Husserl's phenomenological project (Husserl, 1927, 1931, 1969, 1970b, 1983), which was to bridge the gap between objectivity and subjectivity, by making observations that are, as Kierkegaard (1940, 1980) would say, a form of subjective objectivity or objective subjectivity.

SEA has been developed as a clinical method over many decades and has the advantage of having been filtered meticulously by this clinical experience (Deurzen-Smith, 1984, Deurzen 2010, 2012, 2014a and b, Deurzen and Arnold-Baker, 2005, 2018, Deurzen and Adams, 2016, Deurzen and Kenward, 2005, Deurzen et al., 2019, Du Plock and van Deurzen, 2015), so that it has become fine-tuned to the things that really matter to ordinary people who find themselves in a difficult situation. It developed organically to provide a complete map and compass for clinical work, but this same thoroughness makes it eminently suited to organising a person's experience of their existence in a clinical case study or in a research project where the life phenomena stand out.

This adherence to the psychotherapeutic project is not by chance. Indeed, a 'practice-led model of psychology' (Strawbridge and Woolfe, 2003: 14) has been a central paradigm of counselling psychology research and knowledge for some time. A position which emanated from Polkinghorne's (1992) post-modern stance that academic psychology, and we would argue traditional philosophy too, can establish general laws or ontological aspects of human existence, but to fully understand the ontic experience of people we need to draw on the expertise and interactions of those who work most closely with these individuals. Therefore, instead of producing general theories this practice-led knowledge produces 'little narratives' (Polkinghorne, 1992: 14) or 'local knowledges' (McLeod, 2003: 75), in-depth understandings of the meanings and subjective experience of specific groups of people. These 'little narratives', can then become interwoven into the ever-evolving understanding of the rich tapestry of human existence.

Therefore, it is logical that existential forms of therapy should develop their theoretical instruments for understanding and categorising human experience carefully. Indeed, this is what we have seen happening historically with the work of Binswanger (1963), Jaspers (1963, 1971) and Boss (1957, 1979), who all sought to find a more truthful way of accounting for the experience of psychiatric patients than a psychoanalytic or behavioural model could provide (Spiegelberg, 1972). Later, this project blossomed further with the logotherapeutic work of Frankl (1964 [1946]) and the existential humanist work of Bugental (1981) and May (1983, 1977 [1950], 1967, 1969a and b). Additionally, authors like Laing (1961, 1959, 1967) and Yalom (1980, 1996, 2001, 2005, 2008) did a lot to focus attention on the richness that could be obtained from paying close attention to the suffering human being in action. There is now a rich global patchwork of existential theorising in existential therapy (Deurzen et al., 2019) and with this it has become more desirable to organise our understanding and to adopt a research method that can cope with the wide range and variety of life phenomena that are revealed in that process.

When we look at other qualitative research methods, especially one of the well-established ones, such as grounded theory (Glaser and Strauss, 1967), we see that they have shown that categories emerge from observations, provided we keep making these observations without pre-conceptions until there is saturation of the data. Such saturation is arrived at in the field of psychotherapy by many therapists, speaking with many different clients about the same kinds of ideas and problems until a theory about the origin, meaning and function of such problems is arrived at. Philosopher and psychiatrist Karl Jaspers (1997) already suggested a century ago, in his magnum opus on psychopathology, that our observations about mental and emotional phenomena should be organised like the colours of the spectrum, after careful observation of how they fit together organically, instead of trying to impose a structure on them.

In these circumstances where better to turn than to a form of qualitative research that directly connects our understanding of human existence to the observations of therapist researchers? Existential therapists specialise in the field of human existence, aiming to understand it as it is experienced, in praxis by their clients and themselves. They have created a wealth of methods, for the collection of data, for the cataloguing of data and for the interpretation and understanding of these data. They have also developed careful and respectful methods for engaging with the participants of this research, in order to find out what makes people tick and what makes human beings inspired or despairing. We shall show in the following pages how we can revolutionise this research by building greater understanding in using these therapeutic methods and instruments systematically. They are finely tuned and attuned to the individual who is expressing a deeply personal understanding of existence to the researcher. They allow researchers to intensify their investigation and get a much more thorough connection with the subject they are exploring. When we work with SEA, we first learn to pay careful and meticulous attention to the being-in-the-world of the people we work with. They are not just research participants, but partners in our quest for a systematic and structured investigation that is always pointed towards the heart of the matter: the experience of the human beings in question. R. D. Laing once remarked that psychotherapy is a form of research, as it is a search to get a better grasp of the way in which we have lived our lives. He said: 'Psychotherapy must remain an obstinate attempt of two people to recover the wholeness of being human through the relationship between them' (Laing, 1967: 45).

For him the process of psychotherapy was an essential and vital form of human research, which could give unique access to new understanding, not just for the person examining their existence, but for humanity in general. This process was about uncovering what had remained unsaid, unseen and unknown about life. Laing said:

> The psychotherapeutic relationship is therefore a research. A search, constantly reasserted and reconstituted for what we have all lost.
> (Laing, 1967: 47)

When we research people's experiences carefully, we find that they live their lives in a multi-dimensional field of forces and tensions, both conjunctive and opposing ones. We also find that human beings inevitably work hard at making sense of their experiences. They do so in many ways, not just by creating structures of meaning and making sense of things in the outside world, but also by paying attention to their inner resonance with what happens in their existence, both emotionally and intuitively. Therefore, we cannot just pay attention to how the person is situated in space, at all levels, but we must also pay attention to how they come to the question they reflect on in terms of their historical and genetic progression. Furthermore, we must pay heed to their emotional state of mind and the quality of their connection to the world they are part of. In this respect we shall not just borrow from the practice of existential therapists, but we shall also turn to some of the existential philosophers who have applied such ideas to matters of the heart. Outstanding amongst these is Simone de Beauvoir (1953, 1966, 1969, 1984, 1996), who has applied her own capacity for resonance and clarity to making sense of human existence, theoretically and practically, emotionally and intellectually. Maurice Merleau-Ponty (1962, 1964, 1968, 1992) has equal merit in this respect and his work is always highly enlightening to those who seek to understand the mysteries of humanity. We can add many more authors who are similarly inspirational to those of us who wish to get transparency with regards to our own complex motivations, reactions and objectives. Hannah Arendt (2018, 2020) and Edith Stein (1964 [1921], 2004) should definitely be amongst them. We have already mentioned the nineteenth century Danish philosopher Kierkegaard, but should also mention Friedrich Nietzsche (1982 [1881], 1974 [1882], 1961 [1883], 1969 [1887]), because he too, tried to see into his own heart and that of the other people around him to come to a much more real and true grasp of the contradictions of the human condition.

We cannot pass over the work of the giants of existential theory, Martin Heidegger (1957, 1961, 1962, 1966, 1968, 1969) and Jean Paul Sartre (1956, 1962 [1938], 1962 [1939], 1963, 1968, 1982, 1992), both of whom spent their entire lifetime trying to refine their personal take on human existence. All too often they are seen as the gurus or the wise men of existential philosophy, but it is important that we keep their contribution in perspective. Going back to Husserl's work is always important (Husserl, 1931, 1973, 1977), and Michel Henry's work on a more interior phenomenology is an excellent complement to this (Henry, 1975, 2008). What Structural Existential Analysis allows us to do is to investigate thoroughly how people actually experience human existence, instead of taking Heidegger's or Sartre's word for it. It helps to read widely in philosophy and literature, and we could do a lot worse than to read people like Camus (1955 [1942], 2000 [1942], 1948 [1947], 1954 [1951], 1955 [1942]) or Dostoyevsky (1999 [1880], 2003 [1866]) and many other existential novelists to develop our own perspective on the world. And when we work with our research participants, or indeed in psychotherapy, our windows of the soul will not be quite as tainted or distorted as they might be otherwise. We can then allow the individuals we are in conversation with to speak their own minds and to tell us, as best they can, what it is that truly matters to them on the topics under investigation. Thus, we shall come to know much more about human existence than any single philosopher could ever aspire to decree is the case.

It is this focus on understanding the human condition in all its uniqueness and predicaments that forms the basis of this research method. Although SEA's methodology is grounded in existential philosophy and therapy, potential researchers do not need to be either a philosopher or an existential therapist. All that is required is for the researchers to have the desire to gain a deeper understanding of human experience and to have some skills in conducting an in-depth therapeutic dialogue. The method goes beyond other qualitative research methods in its scope and reach, making it ideally suitable for psychological, therapeutic or other human or social science research which aims to capture the richness and paradoxical aspects of human experience. Moreover, it is the very fact that this method is grounded in, and has emerged from, years of understanding human experience in all its complexity through therapeutic practice which makes this methodology most suited to human science research.

It is unsurprising then that Structural Existential Analysis shares many similarities with other qualitative research methods, particularly those which are founded on phenomenology. Yet it also combines heuristic, hermeneutic and existential elements and each form a cornerstone of the methodology. Research is a passionate endeavour, and most qualitative research arises from the passion of the researcher. Researchers typically choose topics that they are interested in either because they want to investigate an experience that they have had themselves or an experience that they have become passionate about through their clinical practice or everyday lives. Therefore, there is always an implicit heuristic element to research as it involves our connection to the subject matter, which is an inescapable element of our *being-in-the-world* (Heidegger, 1962). SEA explicitly acknowledges this heuristic element and actively incorporates it into the research method as it provides essential knowledge of the subject area enabling a more holistic and robust research design. It allows the researcher to both tune into the subject in a way that aids the design of the procedure and the interview or dialogue schedule and at the same time to feel encouraged to explicitly reflect on their own biases and assumptions, checking their own position in the research reflexively.

The cornerstones of phenomenology provide the method of data collection for Structural Existential Analysis, but they also inform the SOAR attitude which the researcher needs to develop during the whole research process, and this will be discussed further in Chapter 2 of this book. Phenomenology allows for a rich description of an individual's experience and involves an in-depth exploration with the aim of getting to the essence or essential qualities of an experience.

Although phenomenology is an important element of SEA, the methodology does not purport to be a pure phenomenological project. Our experience of supervising doctoral research projects over the years has highlighted the limitations of such an approach, particularly for human science research, as at times the method can be quite constraining. Most researchers have noted that a pure phenomenological method as expounded by Husserl focuses on developing a descriptive account of experience and through the three reductions that Husserl explicated researchers are able to uncover the meaning and essence of the experience. Whilst this is an important aspect of SEA, and phenomenological research in general, there is a question of how realistic it is to maintain a non-interpretative position. Both Heidegger (1962) and Ricoeur (1974) argued that existence always involves an element of interpretation, and it is not possible to completely suspend our biases and assumptions. We are relational beings, Heidegger argues, and it is through our relationships and how we relate to the things that we experience which enables us to make sense of our world. Interpretation is therefore an embedded element of our meaning creation and sense making, and therefore hermeneutics plays an important part in SEA. Our bias is, in some ways, our leading edge, as Deurzen has argued (Deurzen, 2010).

However, what makes SEA stand out is its focus on bringing into existential awareness an experience alongside a phenomenological description and hermeneutic understanding. It is this emphasis on the existential dimension that allows researchers to move beyond a purely descriptive account of their observations, drawing out the multi-dimensional and paradoxical aspects of human existence that are contained within. An existential dimension to research allows for the experience under investigation to be placed into the context of human existence. Which by its very nature is complex, paradoxical, multi-layered, dynamic and temporal. Our focus on these existential dimensions of human experience will enable these elements to emerge in the research.

More than any other qualitative research method, SEA attends to the personal, psychological or the emotional aspects of human existence. It is somewhat surprising that other research methods have not overtly focused on the emotional experience of individuals. Our experiences are not just determined by how we think about or grasp what is happening to us but also how we feel about what is materialising and how we make sense of those feelings. Phenomenological methods often focus on the perception of an experience and not necessarily the emotion behind that experience. Placing an emphasis on the emotional content of experiences will also elicit a person's values (see Deurzen's Emotional Compass, 2010, 2016, Deurzen and Arnold-Baker, 2018) which in turn will uncover their intentionality and their purpose in life, adding the important onto-dynamic dimension of directionality to our observations. These are important components in understanding the world of an individual.

Whilst the method is grounded in decades of therapeutic practice, it is also through our work as the supervisors of dozens of pieces of research that the methodology has been refined to reflect the needs of those researching a variety of different areas. We shall refer to these throughout the book. Christophy (2017) describes how the rationale for him choosing SEA for his doctoral research was based on its emphasis on both the ontological structures of the phenomena but also on the existential dimensions that are inherent in experience and the interplay between feelings and thoughts.

> Using SEA facilitated a systematic and thorough exploration of the experience without altering or interpreting it and was flexible enough to be guided by the research. SEA emphasises description and meaning, and as with the technique of Imaginative Variation (Moustakas, 1994, p. 99), it is concerned with the universal structures related to the phenomenon that precipitate feelings and thoughts such as time, space, bodily concerns, materiality, relation to self and others.
>
> (Christophy, 2017: 56)

van Deurzen-Smith (2016) also emphasised that 'It is important to note that an existential approach is likely to bring out certain themes that one might not identify with other approaches' (van Deurzen-Smith, 2016: 8), highlighting how the unique lenses that SEA employs serve to draw out qualities of an experience that are often neglected in other phenomenological approaches.

An example would be the paradoxical elements which Garland (2019) wished to explore in her research on becoming a mother:

> This existential framework [The Four Worlds] can help explore the challenges, contradictions, conflicts or dilemmas experienced in multiple and manifold phenomena.
>
> (Garland, 2019: 92)

Researchers have also found that SEA's systematic approach ensures that experiences are viewed in 360 degrees, offering a holistic view. Sadia (2020) noted:

> SEA is helpful here by providing us with the structural framework for the investigation that allows the adoption of a systematic rather than arbitrary approach and allows us to ensure sufficient coverage as well as avoidance of subjective observations.
>
> (Sadia, 2020: 74)

Yet it is important not to mistake a systematic approach for a dogmatic one. The heuristics and filters that SEA utilises enable researchers to respond to the data as they emerge and allow for tensions and polarities to show themselves. These heuristics and filters should not be applied in a rigid or inflexible way, and they are not categories into which data are forced. Instead, they provide reference points or viewpoints from which deeper understandings, reflections and meanings can emerge. They open the door to a playful interaction with what we are observing.

The aim of this book is to demonstrate how you can build a productive piece of qualitative research on the intimate and most deeply felt forms of individual experience of existential issues and challenges. The cornerstone elements of this research are the phenomenological method and the philosophical methods of hermeneutics, heuristics, maieutics and dialectics, which together create the bedrock for our research. Within their safe framework we then create focal points for in-depth exploration by applying the five existential lenses of Time, Space, Paradox, Passion and Purpose, as heuristic devices to filter, sieve and clarify the existential material that has been collected. This provides us with a complete and comprehensive way of researching human experiences in the round, systematically and from a 360-degree perspective. Ample examples of the method will be included, using both previous research and the ongoing living example of a piece of research on human freedom, which we did as a pilot for this project. This will serve to enable readers to follow a research project from start to finish using SEA. Our freedom research project was conducted by us as an illustration we could use as part of this book to bring the method to life in a very direct manner.

In Part One of the book, we shall guide you through the process of doing SEA, beginning with a look at the theoretical underpinnings of the various elements of the method. This will take us on a journey through philosophical ideas, to phenomenological methodology, especially of the phenomenology of interiority. We will then show you how to prepare for a piece of SEA research and how to structure it. This will be followed by a discussion of the process of the research interview. We shall introduce you to the Existential Research Dialogue (ERD) model for the interviews of your participants. This is a more in-depth way of collecting data and experiences from your participants than you would be likely to engage with by approaching your participants with a standard semi-structured interview. The ERD interview is essential in making the most of the existential exploration you are embarking on and it is a vital part of the SEA method. It is deeply rooted in the practice of existential therapy, which it is inspired by. You may need to learn how to do this, unless you are already a trained existential therapist.

Existential research investigates the big questions that human beings struggle with, which involves using a lot of interrogative pronouns, such as why, where, how, when and what for? In Part Two of the book, we will take you through the application of each of the existential filters that will address these questions in the round. We will look systematically at a person's situatedness in space, their location in time, their sense of polarities and paradox. We will also consider where their passions, moods and emotions take them and how these are in turn directed by their sense of purpose, direction and intentionality.

Finally, we shall pull all these layers together to show you how, having unravelled a person's most intimate experiences of the world, we can now bring everything back together, with a much deeper level of understanding of the meaning of what this person was expressing about their existential experience. When this is done well, some aspects of human existence are illuminated in a new way and this may be of value in revealing the structures of life that were previously hidden.

Part One
Theory

Chapter 1

Existential Philosophy and Its Importance for Research

Introduction: Philosophical and Literary Sources

Many qualitative researchers begin their study with a statement about their epistemology and ontology. This can be a rather unhelpful practice which is confusing to those of us who are trained in philosophy. People don't *have* an 'epistemology' or 'ontology'. They pursue epistemological enquiries or ontological enquiries or indeed logical enquiries or moral enquiries. Epistemology is the philosophical study of knowledge, which addresses issues of method, theory building and the scope of what can be known. It consists of detailing the history of the human search for knowledge and checking the rationality and validity of beliefs that underpin scientific discourse with the help of another branch of philosophy called 'logic'. Logic is a branch of philosophy which studies the rules of inference and argument that are valid and those that are not valid. We cannot 'have' our own logic or our own ontology, epistemology, metaphysics or ethics. It would be a bit like making a statement about the neurology or psychology we have. These are all highly developed and very technical disciplines that most qualitative researchers do not have sufficient knowledge of to have their own version. Epistemology is particularly concerned with the limits of human knowing and with the different ways of knowing that human beings have experimented with at different periods of human history. We cannot speak of a person having their own epistemology without distorting the sense of this word and the branch of philosophy it refers to. What we can do is to speak cogently about both methodology and method. A person will certainly have their own worldview and philosophical outlook and it is useful to examine this before we engage with research, but in epistemological terms, researchers should simply share a commitment to epistemological clarity and clarification. It matters a great deal that you are engaging in a small and specific way in a search for greater understanding and truth about human subjectivity. It is excellent to describe the way in which you will carry out your research and what methods you favour and why. You will also need to ask yourself how you have come to the things you are building on. The process of self-scrutiny about how and why you are undertaking your study is certainly vital. Hopefully your research will stimulate you to think anew about many things you thought you knew but realised you did not really know that much about at all. That is what research is: opening yourself to new learning, by investigating the world you are a part of. It is crucial to be modest and to tightly determine the limits of your research project, setting boundaries to it. What are you investigating? In existential research, the methodology will generally be to elicit people's first-hand life experiences and the conclusions they have drawn from them. We can use many different methods in doing so. SEA is one of these methods.

The same restrictions apply to a researcher's declaration about their 'ontology': it would be a bit grandiose to pretend that each researcher has developed a personal ontology. Ontology, as a branch of philosophy, is the study of being and becoming, instead of knowing. It is in fact an aspect of the philosophical branch of metaphysics, which is the study of the fundamental nature of reality. It has its own specific requirements and methods to formulate ontological principles. To ask for a researcher's ontology may be a bit misleading, when what we are actually expecting the researcher to do is to explain their theoretical standpoint or position in relation to their investigation. What we would expect is for them to have a basic understanding of ontic research, since this is what they are in effect participating in, but not to have formulated their own ontology. At the very least we would expect an existential researcher to understand the basic distinction between the term ontological, meaning the study of being, and the term ontic, meaning the facts of actual practical existence. For researchers to truthfully make the claim that they can explain their ontology in any kind of meaningful way would require them to spend at least a few years studying philosophy, so as to be able to speak cogently and coherently about it. Most researchers who define their 'ontology' have very little idea about concepts like monism versus dualism, or the many varieties of pluralism, and they do not know about the wide-ranging philosophical debates about determinism versus liberalism, or materialism versus idealism. These concepts are probably not particularly relevant to them at this stage. Clearly what is intended is not to clarify an epistemology, since by definition a phenomenological research project takes phenomenology as its method. Nor is the search for an 'ontology' the search for a complete ontological theory, but rather an attempt at clarifying the researcher's worldview and philosophical standpoint.

The latter may be that of a humanistic stance, where the primacy of the human being is affirmed, or an existential stance, where existence itself is foregrounded. It may also be a more psychoanalytic or sociological perspective that guides the researcher, and there will probably be hermeneutic elements to their outlook, as they are seeking to make sense of another person's outlook on and experience of the world. It is good to have some awareness of your research philosophy. But it is often fused, as in Hans Georg Gadamer's description of the 'fusion of horizons' in his book *Truth and Method* (Gadamer, 1975), where he speaks about the importance of two people's outlooks and different horizons and prejudices coming together in dialogue to throw light on each and create a new wider horizon which benefits both. This is the very objective of existential research. Indeed, the search for dialogical truth is always about looking at life from different angles and carefully describing experience from these different perspectives, before we engage in comparing notes with each other to come to some conclusions. This is in some ways the essence of phenomenology: to consider what we are observing from many different angles in space and time and to be aware of the changing nature of any phenomenon as we become better acquainted with it. It is always about suspending our prejudice and taking time to look again at each phenomenon under the different guises through which it is revealed to us. Husserl spoke of things being genetically constituted, i.e. always being in motion and in a dynamic process of transformation. This is even more true of human experiences: these are phenomena that take place in time and that continue to be altered as time and new experiences change a person's memory of the event or the experience. This is why it is so important and productive to study the evolution of a person's experience.

Another illustration of this genetically constituted investigation is that of the work of Marcel Proust. Marcel Proust's minutely observed experiences of eating a small Madeleine cake dipped in tea, in his famous book *In Search of Lost Time* (Proust, 1973), generates a sense of the flow of time, and of the whole range of sensory experiences involved in that particular instance, which can be recalled with possibly more intensity and reality than when it first happened. The nostalgia he evokes with his descriptions touches our own inner sense of remembrance of such events. It makes it clear that the lens of memory is often more powerful than the lens of momentary experience. Out of our initial experience, sensations and feelings, we conserve certain observations with which we can create a meaningful dialogue which takes us beyond our original point of view towards a wider understanding of the reality we have lived. Because of this capacity for memorising, the narrative element of our work needs to be as refined and evocative as possible.

Socratic Dialogue

This leads naturally into the importance of dialogue in SEA research, which is discussed further in Chapter 4. Deurzen has written widely about the importance of dialogical investigation (Deurzen, 2010, 2012, 2015, Deurzen and Young, 2009, Deurzen and Iacovou, 2013, Deurzen and Adams, 2016, Deurzen and Arnold-Baker, 2018). Socratic dialogues are based in this concept of talking through our experiences, formulating definitions of our opinions, which get challenged, contradicted or amplified by other people's definitions and opinions. We discover the gaps by attending to different perspectives and facets of the issues. We seek better formulations, probing the essence of something until we can agree that we have gotten a little closer to a true grasp of the phenomenon. It is a powerful way of clarifying and refining our understanding of any concept or experience. Because of this, Socrates used to refer to his method as maieutic, which literally means the method of a midwife. In a Socratic dialogue, we don't try to prove the other person wrong. We aim to allow them to give birth to the truth that already lives inside of them.

It is pertinent to make these critical remarks about some of the rather lax tendencies in the use of such concepts in qualitative research. It is important that we do not try to reinvent the wheel, or to presume that researchers can just position themselves within their own ground rules. Ground rules are fundamental, if they are based on observations of what is the case.

In doing existential therapy or existential research it is therefore fundamental that we situate ourselves firmly on the ground of existence, as we know it. In both cases we aim at grasping and accurately capturing the reality of the people we are in dialogue with, in order to get a better sense of what their human existence entails. We seek to explore the aspects of life that are most important to the person we are to speak with. We also ensure that we make as many connections as possible between their worries and objects of concern and their general life priorities, so that their framework of reference becomes increasingly clear. Therefore, we need to consider the aspects of life that stand out as mattering to people. The trouble is that there is no certain knowledge about these experiences. Human beings have wide-ranging experiences that vary from day to day and from year to year. One person's experience is very different to another person's experience and we cannot come up with rules about it, in the way we can come up with rules about measuring a triangle or a square.

As we were remarking earlier, we can learn much from the philosophers, the novelists and even the artists, because they constantly try to adhere closely to their own observations of people's lives. When Maurice Merleau-Ponty introduced his book *Phenomenology of Perception* (1962) he compared phenomenology to the painstaking work of authors like Balzac, Proust, Valéry, or artists like Cézanne, because we show the 'same kind of attentiveness and wonder, the same demand for awareness, the same will to seize the meaning of the world of the history as that meaning comes into being' (Merleau-Ponty, 1962: xxiv).

Normally the trouble with philosophers is that they harden their view, in order to shape a theory that looks solid. They wish to come across with certainty and confidence and launch fully formed hypotheses that they affirm through argumentation, but that never get checked empirically. Heidegger's work is a good example of this. Like Freud, Heidegger wrote volumes about his personal understanding of human existence, creating a theory about human consciousness, without checking any of it by speaking to people and asking them whether this made sense to them or whether it was different for them. Existential freedom is a good example of this need to check with people. Simone de Beauvoir's writing about freedom, as a woman, in her book *The Second Sex* (de Beauvoir, 1953) was considerably different to that of Heidegger or Sartre, as she pointed out the reality of a woman's existence, as an existence of 'the other', an existence in which freedom was limited. Frantz Fanon's writing from a Black existential perspective (Fanon, 1963, 2021 [1952]) on freedom was very different again, as it showed up the privilege of those who speak from a position of power. Freedom changes according to how much one is deprived of it.

The existential research done by students and researchers of existential psychotherapy and counselling is a painstaking, cautious and slow attempt at tracing meanings as they are experienced by people. This is about making up for the failing of philosophers to take account of the reality of people and gradually coming to know how human beings, in different circumstances, do in fact live in the world and make sense of their own existence and the situations they find themselves in. They do this by entering into an existential dialogue with their research participants, using Socratic principles to draw out what the other feels, believes and knows. And though it is not possible to check things empirically, because their descriptions are personal, this idiosyncratic element is actually the most valuable aspect of the research. It teaches us something about human existence that is unique and remarkable. But we should never assume we are collecting a universal truth, in the sense of being 100 per cent accurate about all human existence. The value is precisely in not seeking to be accurate in terms of all human beings, but totally truthful to the special experience and observations of reality of specific individuals in terms of their particular experiences. It is necessary to study quite a few such experiences in order to get a rounded view of different philosophical perspectives on human experience.

Kierkegaard's description of human despair in his book *Sickness unto Death* (1980) is not the same as Sartre's description of despair in his novel *Nausea* (1962 [1938]). Kierkegaard sees despair as a worthy cause, an inevitability for anyone who wishes to question themselves, whereas Sartre is more preoccupied with providing us a description of the specific emptiness of human existence, which makes people want to pretend that they are something when they are actually nothing. Yet, their views are compatible and help us understand something more about the role of human despair. Studying their ideas is a useful starting point for doing an existential study of young people's despair during the COVID pandemic, or for interviewing recently released prisoners of war about how they dealt with their despair during incarceration.

Heidegger's description of anxiety in his magnum opus *Being and Time* (1962) is not the same as Kierkegaard's explanation of it in his book *The Concept of Dread* (1944). Heidegger sees anxiety as an expression of our fundamental homelessness, '*Unheimlichkeit*', whereas Kierkegaard highlights the role that anxiety or '*Angst*' plays in our capacity to become energised and capable of taking responsibility. Yet, because these authors have thought so deeply about these human issues, they make us pause for thought and they make us observe our own despair or anxiety with more attentiveness and care. Each of their descriptions adds something new and different. We should never just assume that they are right, but we can learn an enormous amount from their struggles in formulating something about the human condition that can only be captured by a person willing to meticulously describe their inner experience. Their insights into anxiety will often inspire existential researchers who set out to interview students about exam anxieties, or researchers who are investigating how people with agoraphobia have managed to tame their anxiety. This is exactly why it matters to turn to the descriptions of existential philosophers in preparing us for research into existential matters. By informing yourself of the philosophical writing that exists in your area of investigation, you prime your brain to becoming inspired and activated. Alongside a search for recent studies in your area of investigation, you will be getting ready to ask yourself what has not yet been fully elucidated. When you engage with your participants in SEA research, you will be much more observant if you have previously deepened your own understanding of the subject and can come to a dialogue with your participants that is based in flexibility and a stance of reflection and exploration and deep understanding than if you had simply advised yourself of current data in the field. Reading Sartre's phenomenological descriptions of Flaubert (1971) or Genet (1963 [1952]) will show you how much detail you can enter into when observing a person's experiences in the world. It should prime you to do your own observations with much greater astuteness and perceptiveness.

It matters enormously to be familiar with the philosophical literature and to have thought about it clearly, in terms of the topic you are intending to research. It matters equally to do a proper trawl of available research studies on the topic too. You will always find a wide gap between the information that has been gathered by objective and empirical studies or by quantitative analyses and the much more granular and intensely subjective approach you find when you read the philosophers or indeed the novelists who have dealt with the same issues and ideas.

Many existential authors have written novels and plays to explore their themes more dramatically and more dynamically. Jean Paul Sartre (1962 [1938], 2002) and Simone de Beauvoir (1984 [1948], 1966, 1969), as well as Albert Camus (1948 [1947], 2003) and Iris Murdoch (1970) or Fyodor Dostoyevsky (2003 [1866]) and Leo Tolstoy (2000 [1873], 2008) are good examples of this. When you read these books, you get acquainted with the way in which existential issues are framed in people's lives in a very intimate and direct way. But there are also many novelists who explore existential themes without a philosophical background, and their contributions are worthy sources of human observations about the human condition, and we should never neglect them. In this respect it is interesting to note the themes that can be gathered from examining such literature.

The themes that philosophers of existence have listed as worthy of study are remarkably similar to the themes discussed and described by novelists. How could we ever feel we have investigated a person's life thoroughly unless we have had an opportunity to find out where this person is located in relation to these issues? This is not to say that everyone is necessarily concerned with that depth of reflection on human issues, but when we engage with our research participants, it makes much more sense to us if we have read widely around the topic of investigation in a literary sense as well as in a philosophical and psychological sense. Indeed, such readings develop your understanding and sensitise you to the different kinds of exploration that SEA enables and guides. It draws you to the heart of the matter, to the intensity and veracity of the experience of the things that preoccupy a person. Obviously for those researchers who are themselves psychotherapists or counsellors, there will be the additional bonus of having had many sessions with clients on similar matters, all of which will have forced you to expand your mind and your empathy and understanding of other people's take on things. This teaches you the necessary humility and care in approaching somebody's deepest feelings about the things that matter to them. It prepares you for an empathetic and open-minded approach to research. SEA is definitely a prime choice of research method for those who work in the psychology, psychotherapy, counselling or coaching fields. Even for those who haven't had the professional experience of sitting still with other people, listening to the narratives of their lives and their difficulties, there still is a lot of value in teaching themselves such sensitivity as part of the research process. They may have to draw more on personal life experiences and literary sources. We shall see that the latter can be truly eye opening.

Heuristic and Narrative Investigations

We have learnt in qualitative research that reflexivity is immensely important for the researcher. We engage closely with the people and the themes that we are listening to and therefore we must be extra aware and careful of the ways in which we come to these interactions and encounters and how they affect us.

Structural Existential Analysis invites every researcher to go down the heuristic path sufficiently to feel at ease with their own position in relation to what they are investigating. This means that you tell your story to somebody and become more aware of the experiences you have had yourself of the area under investigation. We must be able to differentiate between our own perspective on the situation and that of our participants. We also must extract from our experiences those things that are relevant and that may enable us to better understand what we are investigating. As co-authors of the book, we did a pilot study on freedom. We interviewed each other about our most intense experiences with freedom before we started on our pilot study. It was not only very revealing of past experiences we had all but forgotten; it also sharpened our minds to the challenges of exploring that topic and made us more curious in our reading around it. It profoundly engaged us with our own research.

We need to admit to ourselves what we think the theme that we are researching is about, so that we know what importance we attach to it and how we have our own narrative about it. Immersing ourselves in the depth of the narrative, on our own account, makes it easier to handle other people's narratives. Narratives are always existential in nature. So, we don't have to try very hard to get our research participants to speak about existential issues. Their stories will generate plenty of existential themes, all by themselves.

Just like the themes that novels deal with, these tend to be fairly predictable. They tend to include some of the following:

- Stories have heroes and villains and generally deal with a struggle between polarities.
- They often recount the battle between good and evil and the suffering of heroes as they fight for the light and against the dark.
- They consider the vagaries of love and close relationships, especially their making and breaking, speaking of attraction and rejection, connection and abandonment.

- They describe situations of war and the struggle for safety and peace and the effect this has on ordinary human beings who have to cope with insecurity, hardships and tragic losses.
- They describe the human desire for freedom and the various obstacles that prevent or obstruct it.
- They describe situations of despair, disappointment or loss, which ultimately lead to an experience of redemption or overcoming.
- They speak of exceptional dangers, deep suffering and the capacity for human endurance and survival.
- In this process we often learn much about courage, strength of character, dedication, commitment, fortitude and perseverance.
- There are often themes around wrongs that have been done, especially of people being deceived, robbed, swindled or short-changed by others. Such deeds can be either ignored, endured, forgiven or avenged. Human judgements on such situations are very important aspects of some of these stories.
- Time is often an important theme, either in terms of biographical changes, the circle of life and its transformations and crises, or in terms of the start of life, the coming of age or the ending of a human existence.
- There are many subthemes in stories that explore a person's loss or discovery of particular values or moral objectives and the emotions triggered by such ups and downs in terms of our spiritual existence.

Human narratives are always stories about experiences that educate people in some way or another. Christopher Booker, who researched recurring themes for his book *The Seven Basic Plots* (Booker, 2019), suggested the following basic plots:

1. Overcoming the Monster
2. Rags to Riches
3. The Quest
4. Voyage and Return
5. Rebirth
6. Comedy
7. Tragedy

You will often recognise these themes in your participants' stories about their lives. Stories are a search for understanding. People seek to make sense of a difficult experience and draw conclusions from it. The moral of a story is its point. When interviewing your research participants, you need to be aware of this tendency and make sure you throw light in the dark, by enquiring about another way of looking at things, or playing devils' advocate. Always explore the story you are told from multiple directions, to throw light in the round. Stories tend to teach us lessons about what it means to be a person, to be alive, to have to deal with the dangers of nature, the existence of other people and to be faced with continuous mental, emotional, relational and moral challenges. Make sure to collect the meanings attributed and the lessons learnt, even if these seem wrong to you. A story can be many different things at once and will throw light on many aspects of existence, if you look at it from different angles.

The stories told by your participants in the SEA research will speak of all these themes. They will be spiked through with feelings and sensory memories. Collect these. As researchers we make ourselves available to find out what people have encountered in their lives and how they have experienced these events and made sense of them, to find meaning. We can encourage people to think through some of these meanings, in an atmosphere of trust, proximity and intimacy. We must come to such conversations with a good sense of what life is about and what kinds of obstacles and difficulties it presents to people. We cannot be naïve about the themes we may expect to be confronted with in our dialogues. Being aware of these themes does not mean that researchers direct the research towards them or indeed away from them. Instead, it is about noting them and recognising them when they arise. When you simply remark that something has come up, for instance by saying 'and so you encountered opposition again', your participant will tend to deepen their understanding and their discussion of that issue. Be active in your listening and it will pay great dividends in terms of the material you harvest. Reading lots of novels, poetry, philosophy and psychology helps greatly in learning to be an SEA researcher. You have to gain enough distance from it all to come to a place where you can oversee someone's story, without imposing certain meanings on the themes, allowing research participants to freely roam around their own lives and minds, making sense of things and sharing their insights with you, knowing you will be respectful in the way you listen to them and collect their narratives.

We draw on philosophical understanding of the topic under consideration all the time. For our sample research project for this book, we chose the topic of the Paradoxes of Freedom, because both of us found this topic intriguing and interesting. But we also chose this topic because we had never come across any research that highlighted why freedom can be so problematic in its contradictory nature, despite discussions of this in the existential literature (Yalom, 1980). One of us had previously written about this and was also in the process of authoring a book on freedom (Deurzen, 2025). It was important to her to get some more direct information from a piece of qualitative research, especially since such research seemed hardly to have been done, despite the fact that there is a vast literature speculating about freedom.

We then went to the literature about it (e.g. Arendt, 2020, Camus, 1954 [1951], de Beauvoir, 2020, Dennett, 2001, Fromm, 1941, Sartre, 1956, etc.) and found that much had been said about freedom by philosophers, psychologists, anthropologists, educationalists, religious authors, sociologists and political scientists. None of what they have said seemed to have truly tackled people's personal experiences in facing the contradictions of a longing for freedom and a longing for safety at the same time. This was interesting.

Hermeneutic Explorations

SEA is always a search for meaning, and in this sense it will always have a hermeneutic aspect. Hermeneutics is the science of interpretation, where sense is made of something under consideration, not by interpreting it according to a standard set of theories or dogmas, but by seeing how the meaning is formed and evolved by the framework of meaning of the person experiencing it (Ricoeur, 1966, 1974). Ultimately a hermeneutic interpretation is usually arrived at, not by direct comprehension, but by a dialogue which explores the multiple connections that have been discussed and observed and that provide the parameters of the meanings that can be derived from the experience. When a person attributes meaning to an experience, it is almost always done with an eye to making sense of every element, whilst getting an intimate feeling of rightness about what it represents. This felt sense of truthfulness is checked by the person in terms of whether the meaning is coherent, complete and cohesive with their memory of the event. The meaning usually has a didactic element, in that the person wants to make sense of what has happened in order to draw some kind of lesson from it. This is not just about what they want to learn for themselves, but also in terms of what is true for other people, or even in terms of what might be universally true. Hermeneutic understanding therefore seeks to universalise ideas and grasp them as evidence of what human existence is truly about. It goes to the essence of the message and seeks to refer this to the transcendental aspects of phenomenological understanding. Hermes was the Greek messenger of the Gods, and his role was to mediate between humans and the divine. Therefore, hermeneutics is the science of checking how true any message or narrative is in divine, sacred or transcendental terms and how well it corresponds to the knowledge human beings already have of human existence. If a piece of insight fits with existing stories and myths this is usually very satisfying to a person. Hermeneutic coherence is always sought after in SEA and it is checked by verification with the participant. In our case we might for instance say to one of our participants, 'It sounds as if you have made sense of your freedom by seeing it as a special and privileged moment, outside of your normal obligations', and when the participant says: 'Yes, it's an occasional moment, that I have to prepare for and that I cannot hold onto forever', we can explore whether or not it would be desirable to the participant to hold onto such moments for longer, or whether the value of the freedom would be lessened as a result.

Phenomenological Explorations

At all times we proceed with phenomenological attentiveness and diligence. This is such a rich area that it will take a chapter all its own to elaborate and discuss.

Chapter 2
The Phenomenological Attitude in Structural Existential Analysis

Applying Phenomenology to Interiority

Phenomenology is every bit as important as hermeneutics or maieutics or heuristics, or narrative sensitivity when we do existential research, and it is a central part of SEA. Most qualitative researchers are aware of the importance of phenomenology and have some familiarity with its origins in the trailblazing work of mathematician, logician and philosopher Edmund Husserl (1859–1938) and his teacher Franz Brentano (1838–1917). Husserl endeavoured to create a new philosophical discipline that would go to the root of human knowledge, rather than remaining at the material surface of what can be observed, as is the case in empirical research in the natural sciences and often also in the social sciences. He believed that philosophy could provide a more sure-footed grounding for human understanding and that it was possible to create a philosophical science that was based on the intuition of essences and the understanding of consciousness. He wanted to go to the core of the human endeavour to know the world, which meant that subjectivity and objectivity had to be combined in equal measures if we were to get a full in the round understanding of the world. Most researchers have heard about Husserl's inspirational motto: 'to the things themselves!' which accompanies the key idea of the epochē (literally meaning 'suspension', which refers to the suspension of assumptions about the world), as Husserl named his method of the phenomenological reduction. It is a method that provides the discipline that allows us to break our natural tendency to interpret the world in a thoughtless way, following our usual assumptions and prejudice about things. It forces us to stop and to check and verify what it is we are really dealing with. It is never just about measurement of observations, but of probing what lies beneath our observations, revealing unseen and unknown aspects. It is about careful description of the phenomena we observe and getting to the bottom of how and why we observe the phenomena, but also being aware of our bias and of what we are leaving out. It is about returning to the raw experience of consciousness in all its manifestations.

Before we look at the way in which SEA uses the phenomenological method in research, it is important to recognise that there is quite a controversy between academic philosophers who specialise in phenomenology on the one hand and social scientists who use phenomenological methods in an applied form on the other hand. Academic philosophers who specialise in phenomenology have generally been cautious or critical of the application of phenomenology to the social sciences and we briefly referred to this in the previous chapter. Some contemporary academic philosophers like Shaun Gallagher (2020) and Dan Zahavi (2018) have been critical and dismissive of decades of phenomenological social science research, without seeming to value this research or appearing to understand its importance (Gallagher and Zahavi, 2012, Zahavi, 2018). While Jonathan Smith (Smith, Flowers and Larkin, 2009, 2022) and Max Van Manen (1990, 2014) have defended themselves vigorously, it has not been an intellectual debate that has helped our field. It seems a shame that philosophers and researchers have ended up divided instead of collaborating in a much needed interdisciplinary, critical conversation about phenomenological research (Smith, 2018, Van Manen, 2018). We have no interest in adding fuel to this turf-war and believe that collegial collaboration between academic philosophers and phenomenological researchers would pay great dividends. (Zahavi, 2018, 2021, Smith, 2018, Van Manen 2018, 2019).

Zahavi (2018) undoubtedly makes some valid points about the importance of providing more philosophical training for those who wish to use phenomenological methods. While learning about Husserl's work is indisputably important, if we are going to use his method of epochē and the reductions, we also need to learn about the many variants of applied phenomenology that have evolved since the early days of Husserl's work (Moran, 2002, 2005, 2023). While Zahavi (2018) seems to have devoted much of his career to investigating the finer points of what Husserl meant and intended, it is clear that phenomenology is no longer the monopoly of Husserlian philosophers. Via Heidegger, Sartre, de Beauvoir, Merleau-Ponty, Stein, Arendt, Ricoeur, Gadamer, Henry and many others, phenomenology has unfolded an entire landscape of practice. Authors such as Van Manen (2019) have argued that contemporary philosophers have adopted a more pragmatic phenomenological focus in an attempt to be more relevant to everyday life and more attuned to existential understandings. Van Manen's (2019) paper 'Rebuttal: Doing Phenomenology on the Things', is a well-argued refutation of Zahavi's repeatedly dismissive claims against phenomenological research methods in the social sciences. In this paper Van Manen reminds us that those of us who are used to doing clinical work are better placed to speak about phenomenological research in relation to subjective experiences than academic philosophers. Van Manen gives examples of how phenomenological inquiry has evolved whilst still remaining true to the phenomenological endeavour. Van Manen argues 'Phenomenology can be practiced as a human science (Geisteswissenschaft) that remains grounded in its original philosophic sources' (Van Manen, 2019: 912). Phenomenology is after all a method of thinking, an attitude one takes towards what one is experiencing.

In SEA we take the view that phenomenology is not owned by the philosophers who claim to be the true heirs of Husserl. It is a method that has travelled far and wide for well over a century. It has multiplied in its many uses, versions and applications and SEA is a very pragmatic example of that. It is a method that will continue to evolve as it yields more and more results and is shaped by each of the researchers who experiment with it. Our many decades of work with SEA have shown it to be an important and effective method in coming to a better understanding of human experience. It is true though that this is for a large part based in our structured existential approach alongside the phenomenological method of inquiry. SEA is a work in progress, along with many other phenomenological methods. This is well illustrated by the work of Wardle, Rapport and Piette (2023) who edited an impressive international handbook of existential science, demonstrating how existential phenomenological methods have globally evolved beyond anything that Husserl would have recognised. This evolutionary process has created essential new research resources in many disciplines, including sociology, anthropology, education and psychology (see Wardle et al., 2023). This ongoing process is very much alive and hugely exciting for those of us who have been part of it. We have worked in psychology and psychotherapy research with doctoral students for many decades and are acutely aware of the difficulty for practitioners of these disciplines to find methods that suit their investigation of human experience. There are some good books on the subject that we will talk about later in this volume.

SEA is a research method that has organically grown out of the marriage between philosophy and existential psychotherapy practice. It borrows from many sources to enable practitioner scientists to be more methodical, careful and insightful in their work. It is true however that social scientists have sometimes applied phenomenological methods without truly grasping the full extent of the power of the method and without having studied phenomenology in any kind of depth (Deurzen, 2010, 2014a and b, 2016) so we have some sympathy with the academic phenomenologists' objections to the plethora of phenomenological research projects that fail to do justice to their origin. It is also true that academic philosophers have sometimes criticised social scientists without understanding their objectives and methods and without appreciating that applied philosophy can be a vital resource in making academic philosophy relevant again. This is to us what existential-phenomenology is ultimately all about: it is an important philosophical method that can help us learn new things about human beings, which in turn can inform new philosophical thinking. It is therefore to be hoped that a closer collaboration between academic philosophers and social scientists can be developed, beyond a mere polemical and critical exchange (Van Manen, 2019).

Going Beyond Husserl

One of the challenges for psychotherapists has been to do phenomenological research that focuses clearly on the intimate experiences and worldviews of individuals, but to do so thoughtfully, combining a philosophical with a psychotherapeutic approach. This is something Emmy van Deurzen and her colleagues have been doing since 1996 (Deurzen et al., 2019, Deurzen and Arnold-Baker, 2018, Deurzen and Adams, 2016) at the New School of Psychotherapy and Counselling, which is an internationally acclaimed centre for existential research, in conjunction with the Existential Academy. Deurzen's interest in phenomenology stems from her early training as a philosopher, with Michel Henry between 1972–1976, at the University of Montpellier, France. She learnt phenomenology from him, initially in the lectures he was still giving to post-graduate students at that time, and subsequently when he agreed to work as supervisor ('directeur de recherche') of her two-year master's dissertation in existential phenomenology. Henry was deeply interested in her work in psychiatry and the fact that she was starting to train as a clinical psychologist and psychotherapist after the completion of her French philosophy degrees. He was developing his phenomenology of interiority at the time and was keen to discover everything he could about psychiatry and psychoanalysis. Much later, in the nineties, Henry was to support Deurzen in her doctoral research in philosophy at City University, London, with Alfons Grieder. This centred on Heidegger's ideas of authenticity and inauthenticity in relation to psychotherapy, something that made her aware of the importance of returning to Henry's phenomenology of interiority, which she had come to believe, with Henry, was as important as the phenomenology of the things, still championed by many phenomenologists. Deurzen's work with Henry on solitude and solipsism from a clinical, philosophical and literary perspective (Fabre van Deurzen, 1975) became the basis of her precise and specific existential therapeutic method, which in turn led to the formulation of Structural Existential Analysis. It is an applied form of Michel Henry's phenomenology of interiority (Henry, 1989, 1990). It is this form of phenomenology that creates the perfect philosophical foundation for SEA, not Husserl's, Heidegger's or Sartre's to name a few of the well-known phenomenologists. Henry's existential phenomenology of affectivity and pathos was a major though not yet widely recognised contribution to the field of phenomenology. Phenomenology had remained all too caught up in exteriority, belying Husserl's own desire to achieve a radical Copernican revolution where the study of human consciousness would be put in its right place amongst the sciences.

Michel Henry has done more than most phenomenological philosophers to place phenomenology on that new platform. In his article for the *Continental Philosophy Review* on phenomenology and language (1999), Henry put it like this:

> The implementation of a defining method requires phenomenology however, to thematize itself, and, more generally, to become radically self-conscious. The presuppositions upon which phenomenology is based then progressively come to light for it.
>
> (Henry, 1999: 343)

Henry took the view that his work was merely an elaboration of Husserl's phenomenology, but it was nevertheless an original contribution that is much needed in the field of psychotherapy and social sciences. Henry, in his 1999 article on his version of phenomenology, details the presuppositions of phenomenology as stated by Heidegger in *Being and Time* (Heidegger, 1962), where the latter emphasises that the true object of phenomenology is phenomenality. Henry points out that the phenomenological reduction has actually disappeared utterly from Heidegger's work. By applying a phenomenology of interiority, Henry seeks to bring back the epochē in all its glory and at all levels. This is precisely what SEA seeks to implement in an applied way: to bring the phenomenological, eidetic and transcendental reductions to bear on the experiences of individual human beings of important existential events. Zahavi's paper 'Applied Phenomenology: Why It Is Safe to Ignore the Epochē' (Zahavi, 2021) can be safely ignored, because it is utterly impossible to do proper existential and phenomenological applied research without the discipline of the epochē, which is central to the method and indeed central to existential psychotherapy practice. Zahavi in this paper seems to distance himself from the phenomenological method and indeed, rather more surprisingly, given his relatively early work on Michel Henry (Zahavi, 1999), appears to ignore the possibility of a phenomenology of interiority.

Henry focused his entire phenomenological philosophy on living subjectivity. Already in his book *The Essence of Manifestation* (Henry, 1973), he said:

> Affectivity is the essence of auto-affection . . . it is the manner in which the essence [i.e. immanent life] receives itself, feels itself, in such a way that this 'self-feeling' as 'self-feeling by self', presupposed by the essence and constituting it, discovers itself in it, in affectivity, as an effective self-feeling by self, namely, as feeling.
>
> (Henry, 1973: 462)

He was deeply interested in gleaning understandings from clinicians who listen to such affectivity every day of their lives, especially psychoanalysts and psychotherapists, and he continuously focused on extending the phenomenological method into the direction of interiority instead of staying focused on a phenomenology of the things in the world. His objective was to unify our understanding of ourselves and of the world and the way we make sense of it. He reminds us that Husserl intended the use of a triple reduction. He did not just speak about applying a phenomenological reduction to clear our minds for a transparent apprehension of the noemata, the objects of our intention. He also sought to bring us back to the *Wesenschau*, an intuitive grasp of the essence of things, and he spoke about an eidetic reduction to address these essences. Furthermore, he favoured the much less well known, often scorned and neglected but nevertheless imperative transcendental reduction in order to bring the whole process back full circle into the interior experience of the thinking subject (Husserl, 1973, 1977, Henry, 1973, 1975, 1993, 1999).

In his book on *Phenomenology in Practice*, Van Manen (2014) also considers many varied ways in which the epochē can be executed and he introduces the idea of having a heuristic, a hermeneutic, an experiential, a methodological, an ontological, an ethical and a radical reduction, in addition to the phenomenological, eidetic and transcendental ones. Perhaps this opens the phenomenological envelope a little bit too widely, but it certainly speaks of the creativity and playfulness of applied philosophy in the social sciences and illustrates the need for experimentation and the importance of going beyond Husserl's work. It is particularly the turn towards the investigation of human experience that is relevant to existential rather than purely phenomenological research. There are many other phenomenologists who have lit the way in that direction.

Phenomenology of the Life-World

So many philosophers have been inspired by Husserl's method of phenomenology to explore new avenues. Those who are most relevant are those who were interested in Husserl's later work on the life world and inter-subjectivity. Martin Heidegger's descriptions of Dasein's being-in-the-world have many strands of interiority, especially in terms of his descriptions of authenticity and inauthenticity (*Eigentlichkeit und Uneigentlichkeit*) and in his observations of the human struggle with the discomfort of not being at home (*Unheimlichkeit*) and living in anticipation of death (*Sein-Zum-Tode*) (Heidegger, 1962, 1994, 1995). But these tend to be theoretical descriptions, based on argumentation, rather than being derived from research and the actual observation of people's inner experience. As Husserl pointed out, Heidegger ended up with a theory based on his personal anthropological descriptions rather than on an in-depth exploration of interiority. It was as if he were considering the process of being human as he imagined it to be. Heidegger in his early work on *Being and Time* (1962) and the *Basic Questions of Phenomenology* (1994) or the *Fundamental Concepts of Metaphysics* (1995) was laying out his worldview. In his later work, he turned towards the consideration of the human experience of being in a more specific way, looking at language, providing examples and generally becoming a little bit more modest in his observations (Heidegger, 1968 [1954], 1966). But in many ways his philosophy becomes most relevant to SEA, where it was applied to psychotherapy, in his work with young psychiatrists in Zollikon, Switzerland, alongside his host, existential psychiatrist Medard Boss (Boss, 2001). There he aimed to respond to clinical observations and come to some new formulations about how human beings are in space and time, and how they may get lost. Merleau-Ponty's work in his *Phenomenology of Perception* (1962), but particularly in his later work (Merleau-Ponty, 1964, 1968), also showed this concern for a phenomenological analysis that was relevant to people's understanding of their mental and emotional experiences. Though still based in his own reflection and argumentation, rather than in qualitative research, he took a much broader and more carefully evidence-based and reflective approach to his observations. The same is true for Sartre's early work (1956, 1962 [1938], 1962 [1939]), though in his later work, especially his three volumes on Flaubert, he did a great deal of radical and painstaking applied phenomenology in relation to human experience (Sartre, 1971). De Beauvoir too introduced a much more subjective and personal element in her work (1953, 1970, 1984, 2004) in applied phenomenology by looking at the subjective experiences of concrete individuals in a physical and social situation. She came very close to doing a full existential analysis of certain topics, such as womanhood or old age, and she also applied this enquiry to her own life (de Beauvoir, 1953, 1966, 1984 [1948], 1984 [1972]).

It is often in their novels, autobiographic writing and plays that Sartre and de Beauvoir were most astute in their existential explorations. These are indeed essential reading for students of SEA as they remind us of the importance of the narrative strand of structural existential analysis. That biographic element is so much missing in Heidegger. Sartre and de Beauvoir were existential philosophers who focused on the interior world in a way Heidegger never did (Sartre, 1962 [1939], 1971). Their work foreshadowed the Existential Phenomenological Research in the psychotherapeutic field and indeed Sartre wrote the foreword to Laing's book *Self and Others* (Laing, 1961). Interestingly such a focus on interiority is very much in line with Husserl's own investigations. In the *Crisis* (Husserl, 1970), he noted that we already live in an existential world without realising it but find it hard to bring this to awareness. Existential research, most especially Structural Existential Analysis, does just that: it brings the existential world into awareness and makes it explicit instead of leaving it to be implicit and tacit.

Husserl wrote: 'Consciously we always live in the life-world; normally there is no reason to make it explicitly thematic for ourselves universally as world (Husserl, 1970 [1938], appendix VII, 379, Hua VI 459). In the *Cartesian Meditations*, Husserl (1973 [1929]) speaks about the community of monads that suffuses our everyday world.

In *Formal and Transcendental Logic* (Husserl, 1969) he speaks of the transcendental ego as being constituted internally, in openness to a plurality of egos. Somehow, Husserl argues, we recognise our kinship and the similarities of our existence and our thinking and feeling (Husserl, 1969). This sense of everyone in the transcendental ego's connection with the wider community flows out of actual existential experience and is not an ontological given. We discover our selfhood by staying true to what we experience and we discover others as part of our transcendental experience in the same way.

Phenomenology as Claude Romano (2015) has described it is based in the phenomenological thesis that what exists in the world is structured in a particular way and that our experiences become intelligible as we grasp these structures. We do so through language, but also through the givens of society and the implied concepts and rules we pick up by relating to each other. These structures are expressed in many other ways than by words. They can be made evident in the way we move, paint a picture, make a movie or sing a tune, but also in the way we think about the world, the way in which our worldview is constituted. It is a subtle and intricate business in psychotherapy work to get a true grasp of the way in which a person is connected to their world through all the complex but invisible tendrils of meaning and significance we take for granted. Structural Existential Analysis uses phenomenological methods to describe, recognise and articulate some of these unspoken assumptions and pathways that are so vital to the way people experience their world.

In SEA we seek to apply hermeneutic and phenomenological approaches in an evenly balanced manner, so that they keep each other in check. So, as we probe for meaning in a hermeneutic pursuit of in-depth understanding we also stay true to the phenomena we are observing. It is a toing and froing between interpretation, observation and verification all the time, whilst we use our heuristic stance to check things out with our own experience and knowledge, thus verifying whether what we are describing and formulating makes sense. We also return to the people we are in dialogue with to give them a chance to probe our work and respond to it, letting us know whether they can verify our understanding of their understanding of the world they have so emotionally described to us.

Phenomenology is the study of what is apparent about the phenomena offered to us. As Jean-Luc Marion (2004) puts it, it concerns itself with the study of 'what gives itself'. However, the gift of what is hidden in the intimacy of a person's life experience and inner world may need a little bit more than this to be unearthed and made sense of. The meanings that exist inside of people's hearts and minds are well worth mining, as they are derived from their unique life experiences and worthy of being grasped and understood. We need to find specific, careful and accurate ways to capture this richness. The way in which the phenomenological reduction works has to be adapted in order to get close to such understanding. We have to go into the person's most intimate experience to collect these meanings and cannot be passive in our observations nor remain on the outside. This is why Deurzen has argued that the phenomenological reduction needs to be extended with the eidetic and transcendental reductions, both described and prefigured by Husserl and further elaborated by Henry. Deurzen has described this in her published work for many years (Deurzen, 2012 [1988], 2010 [1997], 1998).

The objective is to explore how people are in the world, at many different levels, and how they make sense of life. We study the phenomena of personal emotional experience in order to grasp the deeper meanings of human existence. We are tuning into each person's world experience and aim to resonate with it to do justice to it and make sense of it. In this way we begin to inhabit the world as it is structured and experienced by the person we work with, be it as a client or as a participant in our SEA research. In doing this research we enable the other to articulate the depth of their experience. Rather than trusting a single philosopher on what it is like to be human, we investigate what ordinary human beings in many different walks of life, cultures and situations actually experience and we aim to make sense of the picture that emerges.

As Thompson and Zahavi (2007) have argued, when we do a phenomenological investigation, this: 'should focus on the way in which reality is given to us in experience. We should, in other words, not let pre-conceived theories form our experience, but let experience guide our theories' (Thompson and Zahavi, 2007: 5). This means that we make every effort to stop being merely immersed in our everyday assumptions and usual ways of comprehending and approaching the world, and we take pains to reconsider things cautiously and meticulously recording what is the case. We step outside of the natural attitude, which is full of prejudice and careless jumping to conclusions, and we cultivate an attitude of wonder and curiosity, but also one of care and philosophical clarity. This is what we call the phenomenological attitude. In attuning ourselves to this kind of philosophical observation we combine our ability to look at the world objectively with our capacity to look at the world subjectively. At the same time we take awareness of the process of our own observations.

Jean Luc Marion has also created a new take on Husserl's work, proposing a return to intuition as originally suggested by Husserl, in a radical new reduction taking us back to what is intuitively felt as the gift of consciousness (Marion, 2004, 2006, 2008). His objective is to go beyond Husserl's transcendental reduction and Heidegger's existential reduction, with a return to givenness. In many ways SEA is a way of formalising this search for what is existentially true and valid for individuals in a very deep and experiential fashion. Marion would argue that this takes us full circle back to Husserl's 'Principle of all Principles', which Husserl formulated in this way:

> every primordial dator intuition is a source of authority (Rechtsquelle) for knowledge, that whatever presents itself in 'intuition' . . . is simply to be accepted as it gives itself out to be, though only within the limits in which it then presents itself.
>
> (Husserl, 1969: 92)

SEA seeks precisely to connect with what presents itself to a person about their experience and to delve into it so as to collect all the existential elements of the person's experience.

Both Paul Ricoeur, who, much like Heidegger, combined phenomenology with a hermeneutic approach (Ricoeur, 1966, 1967, 1974) and his student, Jean Luc Nancy (1993, 1998), demonstrated very different ways of doing phenomenology of human experience. Their work could also be mined for new ways of doing SEA, and there are many other resources that could be brought to bear on SEA as it becomes more established. Deurzen has spent her entire 50-year career since she first trained in philosophy with Henry in applying such phenomenological ideas and methods to working with individuals. Her doctorate in philosophy examined the internal process of self-deception which stands in the way of making accurate philosophical observations and life decisions (Deurzen, 2003). She has evolved SEA as a consequence of this work, as it became clear that not only can existential phenomenology enable us to understand individuals, but it can also help us to research human experience in a very precise and acute manner. This is all about gaining a deeper understanding of human endeavours and disappointments, whilst establishing a disciplined method for doing so both in clinical and research terms. This has meant adapting Husserl's original ideas in various ways. The personal and finite lives of people are indeed a fascinating subject for phenomenology, especially when linked to the many variations of the human ways of interpreting the world and accommodating the things in the world or accommodating those things to themselves (Deurzen, 2014a and b, 2016).

It is crucial to be continuously aware of the tension between the visible world that is manifested in the world of the exact sciences and of the invisible world that is manifested in interiority or in transcendental ideas. The separation between those worlds can be overcome by disciplined research. Henry's objective was to enable people to see the invisible. This is a very similar objective in psychotherapy: to listen for what is unsaid and to speak what has been silenced. It is also what artists and novelists aim to do. Henry (2009) wrote movingly about the painter Wassily Kandinsky, who tried to express emotions, sensations and passions rather than just the things in the world. He was also deeply inspired by the work of Proust, through his wife Anne, who was a professor of literature and a Proust expert.

It is not that others have not investigated the inner experiences of existential awareness also. Many have, but none of them as systematically as Henry, Marion and Nancy.

Applied Existential Phenomenology

We shall look at the specific way in which SEA works in the second part of this book and there we shall show how our use of phenomenological principles, attitudes and methods is interwoven with our scrutiny through the existential lenses we use. In SEA we make sure to work closely with at least six to ten people on any particular research project, in order to create a broader field of investigation and have a chance to look at the same phenomenon of interiority from a number of different angles and perspectives.

Phenomenology as applied to existential concerns is first and foremost about revealing what goes on in a person's mode of being. This is not just about their internal world, but about the way they dwell in the world and are embedded in it. How does the person appropriate the world in a particular situation and how does this change their sense of who they are and what is or is not possible for them? What are a person's binding commitments and utmost values? We do not apply a simple Husserlian method but borrow from applied phenomenology as exemplified by the work of Merleau-Ponty, Sartre, de Beauvoir, Marcel, Heidegger, Henry, Levinas and others. We take an interest in a person's existence in the world as it is experienced by her, in all its totality, ipseity, alterity, identity, affectivity and directionality. We are dealing with narratives and experiences, not just physical phenomena. We are confronted with pathos, the way in which a person lives emotionally through their existence and suffers life in a dynamic and interpretative fashion. We are exploring life itself in the rough, in authenticity and inauthenticity. We are seeking the living spirit of the people we interview. We are interested in past, present and future as we study the person's experience in its onto-dynamic totality. We are interested in a person's internal dialogue about the issues at stake, their inter-subjectivity, their intentionality, their embodied being-in-the-world, as we seek to unite mind and body, experience and reality, understanding and interpretation. We have to penetrate through the concealments the person uses to hide the phenomena of their experience, for various reasons. This is where the therapeutic mode becomes vital and we forge a connection with the person in question that will allow trust and a joint exploration of what is hidden behind the usual phraseologies.

We search for genuine insights and for a profound communication of life as it is lived by this particular individual. We explore in a pre-theoretical and non-theoretical fashion, but we are systematic in our explorations. We want to make a map of the person's existential history, geology and geography, so that we can understand and record their evolution and trajectory, from origins to destination. We resist objectification and do not force the person's experience into a pre-set mould. Each personal map is different and each is modified continuously as new living experiences add new layers and dimensions to it. As we journey through the landscapes of being we come to know more about the overall territory and join up with that of others more and more. Our task in addressing these individual experiences is not to force them into a pattern, but rather to use each experience as a piece of the overall puzzle of life; the more different the experiences, the more of the territory is revealed. We share our perceptions with each other to help each other out in getting a wider angle on the total vision we can achieve of life.

There are many ways of doing phenomenology and over the decades we have seen a loosening of the grip of the philosophical dictatorship over the method. Heidegger's phenomenology is nothing like what Husserl described. He looks at human phenomena rather than at physical phenomena and, as we argued above, his existential anthropology is based in his observations of himself and his own beliefs about the world. The same is true for Sartre or Merleau-Ponty, who stretched the phenomenological modality well beyond Husserlian precepts and concepts. When we use the phenomenological method to investigate existential phenomena, even though we use heuristic devices, we cannot follow in Heidegger's footsteps and reduce our observations to Heideggerian or Sartrean concepts. If we did so we would have ceased to do phenomenology. The phenomena speak for themselves and are made sense of by reference to the person's own consciousness. When a person speaks for instance of a dream image of being afraid of being drowned in a river, we investigate carefully what the whole landscape was like, what the atmosphere, time of day, climate, weather and scenario was like. We find out how the physical environment affected the author of the dream and how they interacted with it, and we find out whether the protagonist of the experience was facing this alone, was in the company of a trusted person, or an enemy, or surrounded by people helping or hindering the process. We ask questions about where the person was headed and with what purpose and why the river was so swollen, and we find out more and more of the actual intricate meanings of that one image. As the person is setting aside their assumption of impending death, they discover that they were faced with a challenge, which they immersed themselves in, rather than avoiding it. Now they figure out how they were in fact able to drift on their backs until they reached a bend in the river, where they managed to swim towards an accumulation of trees and other flotsam and jetsam, so as to steady themselves in the wide stream and find a way out of the river. If we had plunged right in with our assumption of a dread of death or drowning, we might have missed the broader significance of the experience. We suspend our desire to jump to a conclusion about the meaning of the image. We investigate carefully and with circumspection what their being, experiential and existential landscapes are and we focus on what is pertinent to our particular investigation, but see it within the context of the person's life. It is a creative process. We seek to understand how a person validates their particular experience and invite them to account for it in a meticulous but personal manner. The people we speak with are immersed in their reality, and we need to come close enough to their perspective to do justice to their take on the world. We note what is significant to them and how their perspective is located, coloured and situated. How do they appropriate the topic under discussion? How did they arrive at this perception? What meanings did they derive from it? We apply Kierkegaard's dictum: to be subjective about objectivity and objective about subjectivity. How is this person explaining the world phenomena to him or herself and making sense of them? What is their purpose in doing so? What is their direction of travel? How do they memorise their experience and how do they use their imagination to attach purpose to it? The people we interact with are lenses of consciousness who are addressing issues that are important to them. They are involved in that human dynamic project of leading their life in a particular direction, because they understand and interpret their situation in a particular fashion. What is their accountability? How do they verify their experiences and their meanings? How do they account for their narrative about their experience to themselves? What would it take to change it?

Clearly, if we wish to do all of this, we need some structure to our investigation, lest it becomes a free for all. We cannot just launch ourselves into an emotional dialogue with our research participants without knowing how to go about extracting true, accurate, deeply felt and reliable information from them. We have to ensure that we cover the whole ground, rather than extracting certain samples from certain areas of the person's life whilst neglecting others. Deurzen has described the importance of tuning into the person's emotional experience, to make observations about the way participants in the SEA research study use space and time, and how they deal with paradox and purpose. If we are going to have a truly existential method, a phenomenology of interiority and human experience, then we have to address all the layers of a person's experience that are significant to them (Deurzen, 2014b).

As we have already stated above, central to this phenomenological work is the epochē. Husserl spoke of many different reductions that could be accomplished in order to overcome the natural attitude. Føllesdal's work in clarifying these reductions is perhaps one of the clearest formulations of the way in which Husserl conceived of the interaction between the phenomenological, eidetic and transcendental reductions (Føllesdal, 1969, 1990, 2006). The reason why we need several reductions, rather than just the phenomenological reduction, is that the world is manifold and has many different aspects. Husserl himself used to give the example of dice, which have six sides, meaning that when we play with them, we are always double guessing what is happening on each side and which one will come up top for us. Deurzen describes the story of the diamond on the mountain in her book *Paradox and Passion* (Deurzen, 2015) to illustrate the way in which the spectrum of colours is refracted differently by a diamond, that we approach from different sides of the mountain. It would be easy to jump to a conclusion about the colour of the diamond, by simply relying on our first impressions and judging the diamond by what it looks like from where we stand. That would be to go down the subjective observation path. The objective observation path would probably lead us up the mountain to inspect the diamond and analyse its internal composition. But there is still more to gain in our knowledge about the diamond and the way it affects the mountainy areas over which it refracts its light. If we suspend our natural attitude and take the trouble to go around the mountain to investigate the diamond from many different sides and angles, we shall find out about light and atmospheres and moods and beauty and learn about the whole spectrum of light. Rather than just stating that the diamond is a five-karat artefact, a mineral, composed of pure carbon, we now begin to examine the impact of the diamond on its environment. Rather than remaining subjective and arguing about which colour that diamond is, we accept it is white and by investigating carefully what various people have experienced around the mountain, we come to know the diamond as being capable of refracting all colours of the spectrum, whilst being essentially white (i.e. composed of all wavelengths). The phenomenological reduction in relation to that diamond would be to set aside our assumptions about its colour, taking awareness of the fact that we need to find out from scratch what is actually going on, allowing ourselves to describe our perceptions with clarity, intensity and accuracy and doing so in the round, all around the mountain, asking other people about their impressions and experiences too, so we can make sense of the diversity of views and information we gauge. The eidetic reduction would involve our investigation of the essence of each of the colours we perceived, but also of the essence of the diamond itself, especially of its capacity to refract all these colours. The eidetic reduction examines the actual features of something. This is why Husserl called these features essences, using the term eidos, which means form or essence in Greek (Føllesdal, 2006). We could also do an eidetic description of each of the experiences of the mountainfolk observing the diamond. To do a transcendental reduction would require us to reflect on the process of our own consciousness in relation to all these observations, and indeed of the process of reflection and self-reflection going on in each of the mountain people experiencing the diamond's magic properties.

The Reductions as We Apply Them in SEA

The three reductions correspond to the three aspects of the intentional arc.

Whenever we observe, perceive or do something, there is a subject, a process (a verb) and an object. When we apply the phenomenological reduction, we isolate our observation of the process. We commit to a systematic questioning of our prejudice and bias about the world and we proceed to make a careful investigation of the phenomena in front of us. It is a sharpening up of the process of observation, where our previous thoughts about something are set aside, in the margins, or in brackets, as Husserl liked to say, though we may still be influenced by our bias and will have to account for it.

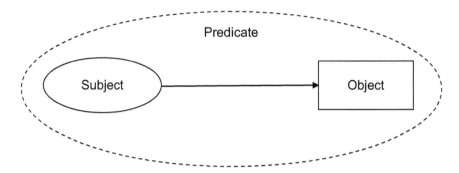

Figure 2.1 The intentional arc

When we apply the eidetic reduction, we isolate our understanding of the essence of the object. We systematically inspect the essence of what we have experienced or perceived and have now observed with care. When we apply the transcendental reduction, we isolate the cogito, the thinking subject. We restructure our consciousness to reflectively inspect what is going on in our own consciousness as we occupy our minds with these processes. The transcendental reduction is consciousness reflecting on itself. Even when we are relating to objects in the world, we can still examine how these affect our own consciousness. When we do consider our own consciousness, we become aware that it always functions with intentionality: like a beam of light, our consciousness always relates or directs itself to something specific. This directionality or intentionality creates the way in which we structure our lifeworld. And it is this that Structural Existential Analysis is particularly interested in: how individual human beings structure their world experience in such a way that it changes their interiority and affectivity, their very consciousness, and in doing so also changes the way they experience the world. As psychotherapists this is one of our principal preoccupations and the transcendental reduction helps us to be more disciplined in our observations.

SEA seeks to apply the phenomenological method to the inner workings of people's minds in relation to their life experiences. It is not so much interested in mental phenomena as in the whole atmosphere and mood that is created as a person composes their life experience and computes the world and their part in it in a certain way. The way we direct our consciousness, or, as Husserl likes to speak about it, our ego cogito, to the cogitata in the world, i.e. the objects in the world as we see them and live them, is what makes a person's experience, their cogitatio, what it is. In Greek rather than Latin words (and Husserl likes to use both), our mind or 'nous' directs itself through its 'noetic' action, referred to as the 'noesis', towards the noema or noemata in the world, which are the expectations we have of the objects in the world. We filter our perceptions through what Husserl calls the 'hyle', a kind of distorting filter, named after Aristotle's word for the original matter of the world, out of which Aristotle claimed the four elements of earth, air, water and fire arose.

When we do Structural Existential Analysis, we try to capture as much as we can of the way in which a person structures their life world in relation to a specific idea or issue or experience they have had in the world. So, for instance, one of our research students did a doctoral research project on discovering how Iranian refugees perceive, experience, process and understand their situation in their host country (Danesh, 2019). He wanted to find out what had happened to them, how their experience had affected them and changed their physical, social, emotional and spiritual world experience. He was interested in finding out how they had processed these very challenging experiences to make meaning out of them (note that a hermeneutic aspect almost always has to come into the phenomenological analysis for it to make any real sense). In order to capture such experiences with care we need to collect data in an ultra-sensitive way, creating a very safe and trusting environment, in which our participants feel at ease enough to have an open dialogue about what has happened for them and how this has impacted on their life. When we sift the data, we need to do so very carefully and as gently as we can, staying closely connected to the actual experiences of our participants, without distorting them to fit in with any of our own theories or observations. This is the phenomenological commitment: to be receptive to what is actually the case for the person we are in dialogue with and to verify continuously that we are aligned with this and are not attributing meanings to things that are not actually there. After we have engaged in a deeply probing and intimate dialogue, recording all of their observations and remarks, we approach the data with the greatest of respect but nevertheless in a systematic and thorough manner, in order to grasp the way in which their world has been restructured and how this affects them. In the example we gave, we figure out what the situation and their understanding of it means not just for them and other Iranian refugees, but also for any human being in a similar situation. And this is where we reach towards the transcendental reduction, which is the way in which we go beyond subjective observations towards the shared human meanings that surpass each of our personal experiences. We need to have a set of finely attuned existential sieves to take our data through all these instruments, in order to make sense of what we have been told, extracting all the depth of the experiential reality of the person. We will seek to do so whilst suspending our own prejudice about what such people may experience (phenomenological reduction), looking at the essence of what they have experienced with great care (eidetic reduction) and encouraging them to explore how their own consciousness has been affected and their life world altered in the process and how this goes beyond their experience towards a universal phenomenon (transcendental reduction). Here is a schematic summary of the three reductions:

I. **Phenomenological reduction** In relation to the Noesis or cogitatio: the process of consciousness
II. **Eidetic reduction** In relation to the Noemata or cogitata: the objects of consciousness
III. **Transcendental reduction** In relation to the Cogito or Nous: the subject of consciousness

Meanwhile we keep track of our own bias, throughout the process, applying a phenomenological reduction to our responses and taking the time to examine the essence of the experiences that this evokes in us, studying the way in which all this affects and alters our internal consciousness as well (transcendental reduction). So, we apply a double helix of reductions to both our participants and ourselves as their research partner.

In order to be thorough in the process we will apply various existential lenses to the material that we gather and we may already be prepared for this material by ensuring that our dialogue will harvest some material from all of the dimensions of a person's experience. We shall go into the detail of the existential lenses in the next section of the book.

For a full phenomenological analysis, in the round, we need to ensure that we ask ourselves what is happening to the person at a physical level, in their own body, in relation to the other bodies in the world and to the natural world as well. We need to ask ourselves what is happening on the social level for this person, in relation to the other people in their world, both at a public and private level, in their way of relating. We need to wonder what is happening in the intimacy of their internal, private world too and how this has been affected and changed by the situation we are investigating. Finally, we have to probe into the meanings in this person's life world and how these have been transformed by the experiences we are interested in. How has their very worldview, their spiritual belief system, their framework of meaning and values been affected by this experience?

While all four dimensions of the person's world will be connected and intertwined, it will help us to understand exactly what is changing in their world when we are structured and systematic in our examination of how this comes across in the words they have conveyed to us. This is particularly obvious in a piece of research that investigates shattered lives, as for instance with Iacovou's research on Falkland service survivors (Iacovou, 2015). This research recorded intimate interviews with service men who had survived the sinking of HMS Sheffield and who had witnessed the violent death of many of their mates, only to come back into the civilian world, alive, but unable to truly connect to anybody. Looking at the words and experiences of these very isolated and deeply hurt and often damaged people, Iacovou concluded that the traumatic realities they were living were not just symptoms of PTSD.

> ... active service confronted the participants with the existential givens of existence, including death, freedom and finitude, and meaninglessness and absurdity. This confrontation shattered their worldview, changing them and their priorities, and creating overwhelming emotions that they struggled to understand.
> (Iacovou, quoted in Deurzen, 2021: 121)

Iacovou's work in distilling the essence of these men's lives and memories brought out something much more potent and meaningful to them than the notion that they suffered with PTSD. They already knew that they could not adjust to civvy life, that their relationships had broken down and that they struggled with substance addictions. Understanding that their framework of meaning had been shattered was more surprising to them and much more accurate and poignant in helping them in making sense of their experience. The fact that they had been through an internal revolution in their worldview had never occurred to them previously. It made sense of their intense experience of isolation and being out of synch with the social world that they had re-entered.

To arrive at such findings, Iacovou had to set aside all her previous assumptions about PTSD and other forms of mental health diagnosis. She had to keep her mind trained on what these men were actually going through, without letting their words be overshadowed by her bias and professional knowledge, listening as deeply and accurately as possible to the expressions of their distress and carefully collecting their words, to sieve them through the many sieves of the phenomenological framework of SEA.

In the paper Deurzen was invited to write for the British Psychological Society on the use of phenomenology in Structural Existential Analysis, she listed some of the elements necessary for each of the reductions to be applied, reminding readers that:

> Bias can never be eliminated, but it can be accounted for and altered as truth emerges. You cannot un-think or un-know anything once you know it, but you can become more aware of what you believe and what may not be true. Our bias is our cutting edge on the world, the lens through which we regard it. It is of some value in making sense of things.
>
> (Deurzen, 2014b)

Having remembered this, we move on with the consideration of how we engage with the three reductions.

The Phenomenological Reduction (Epochē)

1. Suspend your assumptions and track, observe, and bracket your bias, watching your own intentionality and intentional arc.
2. Describe what you observe and experience. Don't analyse or interpret.
3. Horizontalise your observations, by seeing their context and situation: note the limit of your observations.
4. Equalise your experience and pay attention to every aspect of it, instead of allowing certain things to stand out or be given more weight.
5. Verify your observations, by checking from different angles, or later on, or by asking others to confirm your observations.

The Eidetic Reduction

1. Pay attention to the noemata: the objects of your intentional arc.
2. Be aware of their many facets and different aspects, seeing as many adumbrations (*Abschattungen*) as is possible.

3. Look for essences behind the appearances (*Wesenschau*).
4. Pay attention to the genetic (or historical) constitution of the entities you observe, as everything is dynamic and in flux over time.
5. Aim to grasp the universal qualities in what you observe, taking the view from the infinite.

The Transcendental Reduction

1. Focus on the process of your awareness, on the ego cogito itself, the subject of your intentional arc.
2. Through self-reflection find the transcendental ego, the thinking subject that is outside of this specific experience, seeking your connection with consciousness itself.
3. Overcome solipsism in a movement towards inter-subjectivity.
4. Find the horizon and limit of your own encompassing understanding around the point zero of your intentionality.
5. Check and verify your own perspective against that of multiple others, checking for truth value.

Clearly there is a lot to learn if you are going to be truly applying yourself to being in a phenomenological frame of mind and if you are to be systematic and artful in applying these phenomenological skills. Sometimes it is easier for new researchers to start with a simpler set of ideas around bias. Deurzen has referred to this as SOAR, which is an acronym. Bear in mind that doing phenomenology in practice is not an easy thing to do. Your bias will continuously get in the way, but you can learn to challenge yourself and remember SOAR, the four aspects of bias that you can check for.

S stands for **State of Mind**,
O for **Orientation**,
A for **Attitude** and
R for **Reaction**

So let's look at how you may apply this.

SOAR

Remember that bias is not a sin, but a natural part of our consciousness. It is not something you can ever fully eliminate. Your bias is the particular angle of your vision and it is often your leading edge. In order to not just approach the world through that one leading edge, you can learn to systematically vary your perspective on an issue. This was illustrated above by the example of the person giving the dream image of drowning in a river. As a therapist, the immediate response to this, with usual therapeutic bias, might be that of empathy, and resonance with the dreamer's plight and distress. But after setting aside that response and starting a thorough investigation of the physical scene, the social arrangements on the scene, the dynamic and evolution of the scene, and the intrapersonal experiences involved in this, as well as the meaning of the experience, a very different picture emerges. Empathy alone could never have brought out this whole world experience of struggle and desire to flow with the river, moving towards others standing on the side, not helping, but nevertheless encouraging efforts from the floating/swimming/overwhelmed/drowning protagonist. What stands out immediately is that things shift. They are not one thing and cannot be interpreted in a one-dimensional way. There is a hidden existential meaning that deserves to be retrieved and that yields much more meaning than commiseration with such a difficult and horrific dream would have provided.

You just need to learn to raise yourself far enough above your position in relation to the image in question, to start seeing your own point of view with some perspective, and indeed that of your participants. Don't try to overcome or turn away from your bias. Turn to your own bias continuously and learn to probe yourself for a number of aspects of your input to the situation.

S: What is your **state of mind** and how does this affect your observations? What is your mood or disposition at this time?
O: What is your basic **orientation** to the world and in relation to what you are observing? How does your worldview get in the way? What are your cultural and historical biases?
A: What is your **attitude** and your intentionality towards what you are observing? How do your values impact on what you are concerned with here?
R: How is your **reaction** and emotional response to what you are observing?

How does your encounter with what you are immersed with affect you? What does this disclose about yourself that may get in the way?

This provides you with the beginning of the unravelling process that phenomenology requires of you. You will learn much more about it in the following chapters.

Chapter 3
Designing Structural Existential Analysis Research

Passion: The Beginning of the Research Process

As we showed in the previous chapters, SEA research is a passionate enterprise and one that is borne out of the desire to understand the experiences of other people, their lives and the context in which they live. Quite often this passion stems from the existential researcher's own experiences, or the experiences of those they live or work with. But the most fundamental part of this passion is a basic thirst for better knowledge and understanding about the human condition, making this kind of existential research a truly philosophical pursuit. It is through research, as well as through clinical practice, that we explore questions about ourselves, our lives and experiences. In adding a research strand to our clinical work, we may be directed to broader questions such as: 'How can we develop our knowledge about the world and other people?' We liberate ourselves from the narrow focus on one particular individual's life experiences and centre our explorations on seeking knowledge that sets our clinical work into a wider perspective. Research can also be directed to broader questions such as: 'How can we understand our struggles and challenges as human beings?' In this way we widen our philosophical understanding of human existence by drawing on our therapeutic skills as well as on our capacity for self-reflection.

Indeed, Socrates (469–399 BCE) famously referred the human quest for knowledge to its most profound source in self-knowledge, in line with the oracle of Delphi's exhortation to: 'know thy self'. SEA joins this rallying call for people to reflect and search within themselves to find answers but perhaps more importantly to ask themselves questions. Socrates believed that 'wisdom begins in wonder' and it is this sentiment that lies at the heart of SEA and in many ways at the heart of the phenomenological enterprise. The origins of the word *research* can be found in the French word 'recherche', meaning *to search again*, prompting us to look anew at what can be seen around us and to not take for granted our everyday experiences. As we saw in the previous chapter, this is directly linked to Husserl's phenomenology and his dictum to return 'to the thing's themselves' (Husserl, 1985). Our day-to-day living can easily become mundane and trivial and our awareness and self-awareness can all too swiftly seep into the background of our lives. When we inject passion and curiosity into our experiences, they come alive once more and stand out to be seen, noticed, described, questioned and understood.

This quest for knowledge and understanding is the primary focus of philosophy. Philosophy differs from the exact sciences in that it is *a priori*, i.e. it concerns aspects that come before, or prior to, experience, and the results are derived through thought and argumentation, often in inductive ways, though logic also uses deductive methods. The exact sciences on the other hand always involve testing theories against evidence in a deductive manner; they use pragmatic measurements, based on hypotheses that are clearly formulated and tested, to arrive at data that confirm or deny the hypothesis. Hypotheses are however often arrived at by inductive thinking, and philosophy is helpful to science in this way as well as in making sense of findings. Social science is positioned in between these two endeavours and concentrates on investigating human phenomena. This requires a different type of research as we enquire into people's experiences of the world. Some forms of social science research approach human experience from a more or less objective stance, seeking to quantify human experience as we would do in the physical sciences, and this will usually involve statistical observations. Qualitative approaches always involve some aspect of subjectivity. As we have shown, SEA, as a qualitative and phenomenologically based method, sits between philosophy and the social sciences. SEA investigates the individual's subjective experiences of a particular aspect of their human existence and therefore the means and method of analysis will be philosophical and specifically existential in nature. As a phenomenological approach it brings objective structure to this subjective investigation.

Starting on Your Research Journey

Anyone who is contemplating undertaking a piece of qualitative research will begin with their inner sense of curiosity, pondering on a particular topic or a question that they wish to answer. Existential researchers will almost always conduct research on an aspect of human experience that matters to them in a deeply personal way. They will tend to choose a topic that they are concerned about, or something that has happened to them or to people close to them. Because the topic of their research matters to them they are also often passionate about it. Existential researchers have a desire to find out, to investigate, or explore, to think about the subject matter deeply as they immerse themselves in reading and writing. Van Manen highlights the importance of this when he states that the:

> starting point of phenomenological research is largely a matter of identifying what it is that deeply interests you or me and of identifying this interest as a true phenomenon, i.e. as some experience that human beings live through.
>
> (Van Manen, 1990: 40)

As previously mentioned, this personal connection to a research topic can be both positive and potentially negative. It is positive because the motivation to complete the research and to discover meaningful findings is strong and will push the researcher onwards. The drawback, however, is that our personal connection to the topic means that our research judgement and decisions can become clouded or biased due to our own experiences, knowledge or thoughts about the topic. This is particularly so when the experience that puzzles us has been a negative or destructive experience in our life. This is why it is vital to pay attention to the bias with which we approach the question, by working reflexively with the SOAR rules (as described in Chapter 2).

Designing a Piece of Research

In the initial stages a research question will usually be ill defined, and not quite fully formulated. Existential researchers may have an area or an experience that interests them which has not quite settled into a formal research question. For novice existential researchers this area might be quite broad, and it may be difficult for them to give up part of their topic in order to refine and narrow the research area into a question that is realistic and can be usefully explored in one SEA study. Having too broad a research question will mean that it is difficult to gain something meaningful from the research. An undefined research question will mean that the vista to be explored will be too vast to gain a rich understanding of a subjective experience, as it becomes too diluted. If a researcher states that they want to research human freedom and really want to come to grips with its true reality, we immediately know that though this is a fascinating existential topic, it is far too broad for one piece of SEA research. The researcher needs to pinpoint one aspect of freedom, for instance freedom of religion or physical freedom, and focus on this. A research supervisor or research partner will then ask what about that topic is problematic to them. So, for instance, what is it about physical freedom that troubles you? The researcher may then reply that they experienced a sense of panic and claustrophobia when they had broken their leg and had to be in a cast for many weeks, unable to walk. Now it becomes clear that what could be investigated usefully is how people respond to the deprivation of their physical freedom in that particular way after an injury. Novice existential researchers often feel that narrowing down their research area means that they have to give something up that is important to them or that a focused research question will not produce enough or not the right kind of knowledge that they were seeking. Some want to be able to make bold claims about existence in general! In our example, the researcher might have preferred to investigate the whole landscape of human freedom, but by focusing on the experience of loss of physical freedom after an injury, they end up being able to extract some real existential information, based in experience, that actually pinpoints new information and knowledge worth having. Ultimately this is what SEA research is about: to learn something new about existential issues, that is based in human experience rather than in thought or argumentation.

Here we can learn from existential therapy as it shows us that when clients bring a broad overview of their lives or experiences to the therapy space, what is often most useful for them is to identify and then focus in on a specific area of difficulty or challenge. Therapists help their clients to home in on what they are struggling with, pinpointing each problem and unravelling all its inner threads. They help clients see how each problem connects to the way in which they understand themselves, their lives, their values and beliefs, thoughts and feelings. This focusing process is about getting to the heart of the matter, of uncovering the many layers that can obscure the real issues and distract a person from gaining a deep understanding of themselves. It is about helping them see why this particular experience, feeling, relationship etc. matters to them and what is making it so challenging or difficult at the present time. The therapeutic process involves moving from broad and general experiences to centring in on a particular issue for deeper exploration and understanding, before expanding out to see how this new understanding impacts the broader context of the client's life. The same process occurs in SEA research. We take an area of interest and focus in on an aspect of this topic to gain rich and detailed descriptions and understandings before zooming out and applying this understanding in a broader way. Of course, as with any piece of qualitative research the findings of a piece of research with only a few participants can never be generalised to the whole population. We don't seek to make universal statements. We investigate particular and specific human experiences in a fine-grained way. We have to remain cautious and remain aware of the limits of our scrutiny. But nevertheless, in undertaking an existential analysis as part of SEA, the aim is to discover something distinct and noteworthy that applies to all the members of that group of participants who are taking part in the research, who have had similar life problems to contend with. So, we find out if all ten of our participants in our SEA study on the experience of restricted physical freedom after an injury had similar or different feelings and sensations about that experience and whether they derived similar kinds of learning. This may disclose some aspects of the restriction of physical freedom that throws new light on our existential understanding of freedom and even of the ontological structures of human existence more generally. This can give rise to further explorations and research.

Before they can engage with this process of seeking existential knowledge, existential researchers need to understand knowledge in a deeper philosophical sense and become familiar with some of the limitations they will need to contend with.

Understanding and the Clearing

Heidegger, in his book *Being and Time,* explored the ontological nature of understanding. It is important to be clear about how people understand their world when embarking on a piece of existential research. Heidegger stated that *understanding (Verstehen)* was a 'fundamental *existentiale*' (Heidegger, 1962: 182) of human existence, 'a basic mode of Dasein's *Being*', and one that derives from our earlier ways of making sense of the world, through affectivity (*Befindlichkeit*), i.e. by tuning into our feelings and discourse (*Rede*), i.e. by tuning into our words. Understanding then is not concerned with uncovering an aspect of something external to ourselves but it is the basic way in which we exist as meaning-making human beings, the way we exist *as* understanding. Heidegger describes how the world is disclosed to us through understanding. He speaks about this as human beings existing in the world as a place where things come to light, a channel for understanding. He uses the term '*the clearing*', like a clearing in a forest, where the light can suddenly shine and disclose the things that live on the forest ground, which were previously hidden from sight. In the same way human beings are like an opening in consciousness, a place where the light of understanding can manifest and be seen. This is a metaphor for the manner in which elements of our existence and the world become unconcealed and accessible to ourselves by them being disclosed in our consciousness. In this way human beings (*Dasein*) disclose the world and they also disclose themselves and most importantly they disclose Being itself. This is how we come to an understanding of the nature of our being. What is interesting about Heidegger's conception is that this understanding does not 'first arise from an immanent self-perception, but belongs to the Being of the "there"' (Heidegger, 1962: 184). What he means by this is that understanding emerges from our context, our situation and our interconnectedness to the world, as being-in-the-world, rather than through introspection and turning in on ourselves. He states: 'understanding always pertains to the whole of Being-in-the-world' (p. 194). Much of qualitative research focuses on this introspection and is an attempt at describing and understanding the individual's perceptions and experiences, by asking that person to turn inwards into themselves and delve more deeply into their awareness of their world. They always come to this understanding via their feelings and their way of structuring their worlds as in a language. However, Heidegger highlights how understanding comes into its own through looking outwards at how our Being emerges from the interconnections and experiences that we have. He declares:

> We choose this term ['transparency'] to designate 'knowledge of the Self' in a sense which is well understood so as to indicate that here it is not a matter of perceptually tracking down and inspecting a point called the 'Self'; but rather of seizing upon the full disclosedness of Being-in-the-world *throughout all* the constitutive items which are essential to it, and doing so with understanding.
> (Heidegger, 1962: 186–187)

Yet we are only able to grasp what has already become transparent to us. Heidegger talks about 'seeing', which not only refers to what we can see but is connected to his concept of clearing; it is the process by which entities become unconcealed and accessible to us. We are only able to understand that which we have grasped in our awareness and which has been opened up and made available to us to look at because we have allowed things to come to light. This is also the process that occurs in existential therapy, where we enable a client to turn their attention inwardly to see for the first time what they have only felt and guessed at previously. This is how they become aware of their way of being-in-the-world. By focusing on what is there and exploring all the interconnections, we create a map of a person's being-in-the-world, where they gain a true understanding of how everything coheres together and links them to the world. We ask clients to turn their attention and awareness to some element of their existence, asking them to uncover something that is there, to be looked at and then understood. It is that moment of 'seeing' what is really 'there' and which emerges out of our experiences of the world and other people that allows the person to become aware and get a feel for how they are situated within this sphere. Similarly in SEA research we ask our participants to talk about their *understanding* of a phenomenon or experience, not in an abstract, objectified way but rather as how it constitutes their understanding of their *Being*. This always means inviting them to recount their own experience of something that has happened to them and to explore how this occurrence has created a certain mode of being and of understanding their world.

Understanding does not exist in isolation and is always connected to interpretation and meaning. We may grasp an understanding of something in terms of our whole being but then two further processes take place, interpretation and meaning. Heidegger clearly states that he sees interpretation as a development of understanding, a deepening of our understanding rather than a transformation into something else. He states:

> In interpretation, understanding does not become something different. It becomes itself. Such interpretation is grounded existentially in understanding; the latter does not arise from the former. Nor is interpretation the acquiring of information about what is understood; it is rather the working-out of possibilities projected in understanding.
>
> (Heidegger, 1962: 188–189)

Therefore interpretation, according to Heidegger is not about analysing understanding and transforming it into something else, it is a process of working out the possibilities that understanding has brought forward. In other words, there is no separation between phenomenology and hermeneutics. The two are always intertwined. This is not only true for Heidegger but also for other phenomenological authors like Sartre (1956, 1982), de Beauvoir (2004) and Ricoeur (1974). Understanding is always a projection, as it concerns understanding Being and when Being has been understood in a particular way it allows Dasein to be projected forward in a new more purposeful way. Interpretation, therefore, involves seeing what new possibilities have been uncovered by understanding. Thus, when we talk of making sense of something what we are describing is the process of how a new understanding about our Being is interpreted for the new possibilities that it has revealed and how our sense of Being has been changed by this new understanding. It is connected to the fact that we are dynamic and constantly changing. We are continuously in a process of transformation. It is a genetic evolution, in Husserlian terms. Once we know something there is no way of going back to a time of unknowing and that new knowledge will project us forward in a new way towards fresh discoveries.

Similar to understanding, meaning is an *existentiale* of Dasein rather than being a 'property attaching to entities' (Heidegger, 1962: 193). Heidegger stated that 'only Dasein can be meaningful or meaningless' (p. 193), so meaning is attached to the being of Dasein rather than to objects, people or experiences. How is our being-in-the-world meaningful or meaningless? Our SEA research will seek to grasp how meaning has come about through participants' understanding something about their existence and how through the process of interpretation they have come to see how this understanding has opened up new possibilities. Quite often it is only in the process of recounting their experience that they discover what it is they have understood. The words translate the experience into something they can grasp, which they can then reflect on. Heidegger describes a circle of understanding, the so-called 'hermeneutic circle', which contains understanding, interpretation and meaning as fundamental ontological structures of human existence that follow from each other as our experience, understanding and interpretation of the world is reiterated constantly, changing meaning as new contexts and information are absorbed. Gadamer further developed this idea to show that we can develop new understanding out of exploring the details of existence and slightly shifting the circularity all the time, to tilt it into a spiral, where more and more information is included and greater understanding is arrived at.

Intuitive Knowledge

For Sartre 'There is only intuitive knowledge' (Sartre, 1956 [1943]: 172). He disputes Husserl's claim that knowledge is the presence of a thing in consciousness as consciousness must always be directed towards something. Instead, Sartre notes that the definition needs to be reversed: 'intuition is the presence of consciousness to the thing' (p. 172). Similar to Heidegger, Sartre believes that knowing is a certain mode of being:

> Knowing is neither a relation established after the event between two things, nor is it an activity of one of these two beings, nor is it a quality of a property or a virtue. It is the very being of the for-itself.
>
> (Sartre, 1956 [1943]: 174)

Therefore, knowledge is actively created through knowing rather than passively received. Sartre goes on to state 'Intuition has often been defined as the immediate presence of the known to the knower' (Sartre, 1956 [1943]: 178). He argues, however, that being immediate means there is no mediator between the thing and consciousness, suggesting a direct and automatic process. He suggests that the process between knowing and being involves realisation. One must realise something for it to appear in consciousness and become knowledge. This is the distinction between pre-reflective and reflective experience.

> I realize a project in so far as I give it being, but I also *realize my situation in so far as I live it and* make it be with my being . . . to know is to realize in

both senses of the term. It is to cause being 'to be there' while having to be the reflected negation of this being.

(Sartre, 1956 [1943]: 180)

Knowledge then is a dynamic process that has to be grounded both in temporality and spatiality. The thing which becomes reflected on in consciousness arises out of the world, as one thing among many. However, Sartre cautions against trying to measure knowledge in an ordered and systematic way. He notes that 'this is because the scientist is concerned only with establishing purely exterior relations' (Sartre, 1956 [1943]: 200). Sartre believes that to understand the reflected nature of the thing it has to be in the temporal realm of the past, as a *was*. As soon as we realise something it has already become a *was* and is available to consciousness as knowledge. Therefore, Sartre states that 'Knowledge is nothing other than the presence of being to the For-itself, and the For-itself is only the nothing which realizes that presence' (p. 216). Sartre sees knowledge as an 'absolute and primitive event' which is 'reabsorbed in being' (p. 216). 'Knowing has for its ideal being-what-one-knows and for its original structure not-being-what-is-known' (p. 218). Sartre presents a different view than Husserl, who was looking to capture the phenomenon as it presents itself to consciousness.

The Problem with Perception

Both Heidegger and Sartre note how knowledge and understanding are modes of *Being* rather than objectifiable truths that can be studied and measured. It is this objectifying aspect of science that Merleau-Ponty also argues against, when he speaks of his concern about the fact that 'science and philosophy have for centuries been sustained by unquestioning faith in perception' (Merleau-Ponty, 1962: 54). This faith has been based on the assumption that perception is both instantaneous and available to consciousness and also that perception occurs in a coordinated way so that it flows seamlessly from the previous instant to the next. However, perception does not act in this way and therefore the scientific process of 'fixing and objectifying phenomena' (p. 54) is doomed. Merleau-Ponty goes on to argue that we cannot approach the study of subjective experience in the same way that we can study an inanimate object. Using that scientific process would 'bring experience down to the level of physical nature [i.e. behaviour] and convert the living body into an interiorless thing' (p. 54). Merleau-Ponty highlights that human experience is too complex to be treated in a way that fixes and objectifies, where human experience is treated as if it were 'merely a machine', and it does not allow for the richness of experience, that involves perception, reflection, emotions, expressions, behaviour and the interactions with the world. It also does not allow for contradictions that are inherent in human being. 'Thus, while the living body became an exterior without interior, subjectivity became an interior without exterior, an impartial spectator' (p. 56). For Merleau-Ponty this requires a reconceptualisation of the phenomenon, that it is 'not a "state of consciousness", or a "mental fact", and the experience of phenomena is not an act of introspection' (p. 57). He argues that 'The return to the 'immediate data of consciousness' became therefore a hopeless enterprise since the philosophical scrutiny was trying to *be* what it could not, in principle, *see*' (p. 57).

Therefore, in order to study the subjective experience, one needs to start at the beginning of reflection, when individuals begin to reflect on themselves. Merleau-Ponty notes that 'As thinking subject we are never the unreflective subject that we seek to know; but neither can we become wholly consciousness or make ourselves into the transcendental consciousness' (Merleau-Ponty, 1962: 62). Therefore, our experience can only ever be understood from the point of view of reflection which always takes place after the fact.

Heidegger, Sartre and Merleau-Ponty provide arguments against Husserl's phenomenology (see Chapter 2) and the feasibility of its project to 'go back to the thing's themselves'. They have shown the impossibility of the task of capturing something in consciousness in an unreflective way as expounded by Husserl. Instead, knowledge and understanding are gained through a process of exteriority and interiority. It arises out of our being-in-the-world (exterior), through our experiences, interactions and relationships with everything around us. Through those experiences we learn something about ourselves (interior) and the world, but we also become aware of our negation, i.e. what we are not. This process cannot be attained through introspection alone and is also not automatically given as it occurs after the fact through a process of making sense and interpretation. As we saw earlier Michel Henry (2008) has drawn the conclusion that there needs to be a separate phenomenology of interiority in order to achieve true insights into the intimate process of human experience and existential awareness.

This aspect of inner knowing and understanding of one's world is also emphasised in existential therapy. Clients come to therapy knowing themselves in a certain way. They have difficulties that seem unresolvable, yet they have all the 'facts' at their disposal. The process of therapy allows clients to 'see' themselves and their situation in a new way, from a new angle, a new perspective, so that a new understanding and way of being with oneself is gained. Often clients will say at the end of therapy that they couldn't have achieved the same understanding on their own. That they couldn't think themselves out of the problem, that introspection on its own would not be the answer. They needed to be resituated into their context, to have all aspects of their being attended to and made sense of. This process needed to arise through a dialogical relationship with another, external to themselves, so as to gain a number of new perspectives and vital new experiences of their own position and situation in their world.

Knowledge and understanding are also not purely cognitive, as Merleau-Ponty highlighted, and involve all our senses, our expressions and emotions and our relationships. But importantly the subjective knowledge that we seek is not one truth that can be extracted in a scientific way. Human existence is paradoxical and contradictory, it is complex and onto-dynamic. If we approach the study of existence in the same way that we would approach the study of an objectifiable truth, then we would reduce human existence to the realms of cognition and behaviour and turn the human being into a machine. This was emphasised by Merleau-Ponty when he argued against Husserl's phenomenology and stated that 'The most important lesson of the reduction is the impossibility of the complete reduction' (1962: xxvii). As Zahavi explains 'this procedure is something that has to be performed repeatedly, rather than completed once and for all' (Zahavi, 2019: 69). The reduction is a never-ending process, a mode of being that allows us to disclose what is.

Capturing Existence

The problem posed by phenomenology and existential analysis as it relates to therapeutic research is how phenomena, which in the case of SEA research will involve elements of subjective experience, can be studied in a systematic yet philosophical way. As has been noted above it is impossible to capture a phenomenon or existence as it is occurring, there must always be a reflective aspect that occurs after the fact. Zahavi notes that 'an important part of the phenomenological work is precisely to understand the transition between our pre-reflective and pre-conceptual grasp of the world and our subsequent conceptualization of and judgement about it' (2019: 125). Husserl's phenomenology attempted to capture the former, whilst Heidegger, Sartre and Merleau-Ponty acknowledged the impossibility of this task as we are never able to be truly pre-reflective; there will always be some level of interpretation or lens through which we relate to our experience. Gadamer summed this up well when he stated, 'when we interpret the meaning of something we actually interpret an interpretation' (Gadamer, 1986: 68).

Therefore, it is not enough to focus purely on descriptive accounts of the phenomenon, as with Giorgi's Descriptive Phenomenology (2009), although obtaining rich descriptions of phenomena or experiences will always be part of the phenomenological and analytical process. There also needs to be a second stage, that of understanding or interpretation from a Heideggerian perspective, which arises through the process of relating. These two stages relate to Husserl's concept of *noesis* and *noema*. Through our focus on the descriptive element of the object or the event (i.e. what happened) under investigation, we address the noema (or noemata). Through our focus on how that object or event impacts the individual, i.e. the mental process involved in understanding the noema, we address the noesis. Both 'what' and 'how' need to be accounted for in existential research. The process of the transcendental reduction focuses on the thinking subject itself, and seeks to approach the inner process of intentionality that has brought the person to be in the world in the way they are being.

Another element that is important to consider is that phenomenology as described by Husserl, Heidegger, Sartre and Merleau-Ponty was conceptualised as to be undertaken by a philosopher. It was a process to enable them to access something fundamental about human existence. In a research situation the existential researcher may not be a qualified philosopher and the participant will usually be unfamiliar with the process of the phenomenological reductions. The task of the existential researcher then is to ensure that through the existential dialogue between the existential researcher and participant, the existential researcher guides the participant so that they are prompted to provide a full and rich description of the phenomena but also to begin to see how it uncovers an aspect of their being and discloses a lived existential understanding of their own existence in the world. The existential researcher has a dual role in this process: they need to attend to their own attitude and to complete the phenomenological processes (as described in Chapter 2) and at the same time guide their participant through describing and reflecting on their experience in a full and open way, helping them to undergo the first two phenomenological reductions. This process will be described more fully later in this chapter.

Existential Researchers' Orientation to the Topic

To begin with, existential researchers need to embark on their own journey with their topic. Before a piece of research can be designed the researcher needs to find their orientation towards the topic under investigation as previously mentioned when describing the process of SOAR (see Chapter 2). There are several reasons for this. The first is that through the process of thinking about and talking about the topic the researcher begins to clarify what it is that actually interests them. It is part of the focusing down process to help existential researchers to settle on the narrowly and precisely focused question they wish to explore. The other aspect of this is that this process helps the researcher to understand their own position in relation to the topic. As part of the phenomenological process the researcher needs to understand their values, beliefs and thoughts about the phenomenon and their own experiences of it and reactions to it. They need to take the opportunity to observe their bias and prejudice about any aspect of the study they are about to carry out. Sometimes the bias is too great for a person to tackle the topic. If they are determined to prove that something is a particular way, for instance that immobilisation makes the experience of freedom impossible, it will be hard for them to genuinely study how immobilisation affects the experience of freedom. It is therefore crucial to trace the beliefs and thoughts and assumptions that the researcher holds, often unknowingly, as these can lead to bias within the research process. As Van Manen states, 'The problem of phenomenological inquiry is not always that we know too little about the phenomenon we wish to investigate, but that we know too much' (Van Manen, 1990: 46). Before the researcher can understand the position of the other, they need to understand their own position first, so that they can stand aside from interfering with the process of revealing the participants' actual experiences.

The best way for the researcher to do this is for them to talk to another, normally their research supervisor, therapist or colleague, about the topic. To talk freely about what the topic, phenomenon or experience means to them, what makes it interesting to them and what they are hoping to find out about during the research process. This needs to be stated at the beginning of the research so that the researcher is aware of any potential areas where confirmation bias may creep in during the research design process. This initial step will help the researcher with the focusing process, enabling them to settle on what they really want to know.

> Questions to consider during this initial process are:
>
> - What makes this topic interesting to me?
> - What am I hoping to find out?
> - What has been my previous experience of this phenomenon/experience?
> - What are my beliefs about the phenomenon/experience?
> - What are my thoughts about the phenomenon/experience?
> - How has the phenomenon/experience affected how I think about myself, other people or the world?
> - How has the phenomenon/experience affected my values?
> - What do I think my participants will describe?
> - What am I hoping to find out during the research process?
> - What do I not want to find out during the research process?
> - What assumptions do I hold about this phenomenon/experience?
> - What are my blindspots or biases regarding this phenomenon/experience?

It is good practice for existential researchers to record their answers to these questions to help them become more aware of their relationship to the topic under consideration but also to challenge their biases and blind spots by making them explicit. This process will form part of the researcher's reflexivity. A further reflexivity process will take place before the existential dialogue with a participant. It is critical to bear in mind that the practice of reflexivity is not just limited to these two areas and existential researchers are encouraged to continually think about themselves in relation to their research and the impact that they bring to bear on it as a qualitative researcher. It is often helpful for a researcher to ask the question 'what aspects of this phenomenon have I left out of the picture so far? What other, thus far invisible, sides are there to this problem?' It can help enormously to think about opposites, conflicts and unwanted aspects of the research. For instance, the researcher who investigated the impact of injury on the experience of freedom learnt a lot by imagining the possibility that injury could be a liberating rather than just a constricting experience. A brainstorm about these unseen aspects can bring both mirth and new discovery to the research process.

Reviewing the Literature

Once the research area has been defined the existential researcher needs to undertake a wider look at the subject area. Existential researchers need to understand the ground that their research will build on. This involves undertaking a review of the previous literature and research in a structured and systematic way so that relevant literature is discovered and taken account of. As with any qualitative research, existential researchers need to think about the terms they are going to use in their search. These terms need to be varied and this process often involves several stages of searching, with each stage involving a change in terms. Searching continues using all relevant databases until a sense of saturation has been achieved, i.e. no new literature or research emerges. Researchers tend to use systems such as PRISMA (Preferred Reporting Items for Systematic reviews and Meta-Analyses) (Page et al., 2021) to ensure that all the relevant literature has been captured and reviewed. It is as important to be as unbiased in the review of literature as in the research design, interview and analysis. The use of these systems enables other researchers to assess the validity of the research which is important for qualitative research. Existential researchers will then review the literature, sorting it so that literature closest to their research area is also highlighted. This process of searching for and reviewing the existing literature will enable the existential researcher to demonstrate that their research question will potentially seek to find answers that fill a gap in the current understanding or knowledge in this area.

The process of reviewing the literature will also enable the existential researcher to start thinking about how they can refine and focus their research question in light of the previous research. This refining process will also help the existential researcher to determine the limits of the research so that the question becomes focused and narrowed to a particular experience. An example of such focusing is for a researcher to move from wanting to study the impact of war on people's lives, to deciding to study the impact of the experience of war on veterans, to interviewing several survivors of a specific battle about their current state of mind and life experiences, especially in terms of their relationships (Iacovou, 2015).

An important, if not essential, part of existential research is the researcher's ability to understand and have knowledge of existential philosophy. We have already touched on this in Chapter 1, but any review of the literature will inevitably include a review of existential literature and philosophy which is related to the area to be studied. This will be a different type of review as it will centre on existential themes which may be brought out in the experience the existential researcher wishes to investigate, such as freedom, choice, responsibility, mortality, natality, guilt, anxiety, self, authenticity and inauthenticity, temporality, intentionality and meaning to name a few. This is a particularly important part of existential research as it will guide the existential researcher in their analysis, enabling them to understand and make sense of the participants' experiences at an existential level. As already previously discussed the main existential philosophers that are often considered here are Søren Kierkegaard (1813–1855), Friedrich Nietzsche (1844–1900), Martin Heidegger (1889–1976), Jean-Paul Sartre (1905–1980), Simone de Beauvoir (1908–1986), Maurice Merleau-Ponty (1908–1961), Albert Camus (1913–1960) and Michel Henry (1922–2002). However, many other writers such as theologians or psychiatrists have also written on existential ideas which can also be relevant, such as Martin Buber (1878–1965), Ludwig Binswanger (1881–1966), Karl Jaspers (1883–1969), Paul Tillich (1886–1965), Medard Boss (1903–1990), Rollo May (1909–1994) and Irvin Yalom (1931–) for example. It is good for researchers to broaden this out by bringing in more culturally diverse and relevant sources for their topic, as was the case for us in our study on freedom where for instance Hannah Arendt (2018, 2020), Frantz Fanon (1963, 2021) and Nikolai Berdayev (2020), all turned out to be important sources for philosophical understanding. For further information on existential theorists see Deurzen (2010) and Deurzen et al. (2019). An existential literature review should not be limited to the field of philosophy as understanding human existence cuts across theoretical divides.

Formulating a Research Question

The research question is a fundamental aspect of any piece of research. It is the question that the piece of research seeks to answer. It provides the focus for the research and sets the limits and boundaries of the area to be investigated. For qualitative research in general research questions tend to ask what or how questions. 'What was the experience of X like?' Or 'How can X be understood?' for example. The former concentrates on a description of the phenomenon (event, experience, object) under investigation and the latter focuses on a process. Moustakas (1994) elucidates five characteristics of a phenomenological research question:

1. It seeks to reveal more fully the essences and meanings of human experience;
2. It seeks to uncover the qualitative rather than the quantitative factors in behaviour and experience;
3. It engages the total self of the research participant, and sustains personal and passionate involvement;
4. It does not seek to predict or to determine causal relationships;
5. It is illuminated through careful, comprehensive descriptions, vivid and accurate renderings of the experience, rather than measurements, ratings or scores.

(Moustakas, 1994: 105)

For Existential Phenomenological Research, Churchill argues that the research question should ideally follow Heidegger's 'threefold structure of "asking a question"' (Churchill, 2022: 22). Heidegger notes that 'Inquiry, as a kind of seeking, must be guided beforehand by what is sought' (Heidegger, 1962: 25). Heidegger's point here is that we always already have the answer available to us in some way and therefore an inquiry is a way of bringing that knowledge into awareness in a particular way, which is brought about by being asked. This element can be seen in the therapeutic relationship where a client who sees two therapists can have very different experiences because the client is asked about their experience in different ways. Therefore, the act of asking brings forth, or creates a new understanding of something that may already be known at some level.

The existential researcher, therefore, needs to have a sense of three aspects of what is asked, i.e. the:

a) *Erfragte* – what is being 'asked for' – i.e. the knowledge that the research wishes to produce, such as a clarification of a concept or an understanding of an experience. This relates to the outcome of the research – what the research hopes to 'find', or the findings of the research.

b) *Gefragte* – what is being 'asked about' – this relates to the phenomena that the researcher is interested in understanding. This is connected to the research question.

c) *Befragte* – the situation, event or experience that allows the phenomena to show themselves and to be understood. This relates to the 'data' of the study.

(Churchill, 2022: 22)

As already discussed above, phenomena cannot be investigated in isolation, they emerge out of a situation, event or experience and are a combination of internal and external relations.

The experience that SEA research seeks to investigate will bring to light the phenomena of the research question. It is also important that the research question remains just that, a question to answer, so that all possibilities remain open as Gadamer (1975) highlights. Existential research is therefore not about proving something the researcher already believes or has a hunch about. Existential research is about being naïve to the outcome of the research, to allow multiple possibilities to emerge.

Research questions for SEA research need to hold the tension between defining a phenomenon to investigate which is focused and specific but also allowing something to emerge which is unknown and surprising. Existential researchers need to allow themselves to be curious and to wonder, not in a way that pre-determines the outcome of the research but in a sense of being open to any possibilities that may arise.

For the purposes of this book the authors undertook a piece of research regarding freedom. Below you will find the research aims and research question formulated using Heidegger's threefold structure, as outlined by Churchill (2022), for asking a question as an example:

a) *Erfragte* – We wished to explore the experience of absolute freedom and to capture the paradoxical nature of freedom which can lead to people feeling lost and open to unexpected challenges or struggles with nothingness, at the very height of their freedom This piece of research aimed to fill the gap in the literature to get a better insight into how people actually describe their struggle with freedom.

b) *Gefragte* – The research question was 'To what extent and in what ways do people struggle with their freedom when they are in the midst of it?'

c) *Befragte* – We produced a description for participants of absolute freedom (see below) in order to orientate them to situations where they might have experienced what we were interested in exploring and asked participants to think of times in their lives when they might have experienced this.

We would define complete freedom as a state in which you recognise that your life can go in any direction and that many choices are available to you, because you are not tied down by everyday concerns, things, people, commitments or duties. You are in a position of facing the prospect of needing to make choices and act without necessarily having a clear understanding of the direction in which you want your life to go.

We were surprised by what we discovered in many ways, as people described some very happy and exceptionally open moments of freedom in their lives, often with some regret or melancholy memories of those moments, but also with an awareness of how their freedom was often carved out deliberately by suspending certain concerns or commitment temporarily. Freedom was almost like the phenomenological reduction: a parenthesis, a bracketing of various tensions and concerns, that would eventually have to be dealt with again. It wasn't so much that people felt lost in their freedom or panicky at the emptiness that it exposed them to. It was more that they were aware that freedom was a resource always available but rarely practical to practice. The paradox of freedom that we were expecting – i.e. the lack of a sense of safety and identity during a period of freedom – was not described by those we interviewed. They were rather elated at the idea that they had at least experimented with living freely at some point in their lives. Perhaps there was some idealisation of that moment, and for some these memories were so precious that they had become a reason for living with courage and hope through tough times. Good qualitative research usually throws up unexpected results, as we really listen to other people's varied and very personal experiences and learn something new through the stories of our participants.

In the box below there are some other examples of research questions used in previous SEA research. As can be seen the research questions can be varied and wide reaching. For SEA a research question is not limited to uncovering a fundamental aspect of human being, as for phenomenological research. SEA research is focused on understanding elements of human existence as they are experienced by others, and this may or may not include uncovering ontological structures.

- What are participants' experiences of chronic back pain, and what do these experiences tell us about recovery? (Christophy, 2017)
- From an existential perspective, what is the experience of coming out in the Orthodox Jewish community? (Feigin, 2021)
- What is the lifeworld of a female binge drinker on a night out in South Yorkshire? (Bennett, 2014)
- What are the 'lived experiences' of fathers living with new mothers diagnosed with PND? (Sadia, 2020)

When formulating a research question it is also important to distinguish between your potential findings and your question. Often researchers make assumptions about what they might find and want to include that in their research question. Taking one of the questions above for example, the researcher might have been tempted to investigate shame in the experience of coming out in the Orthodox Jewish community based on their experience of living in the community or working with clients who had come out. If the existential researcher had wanted to investigate shame specifically in this research question it would have meant presuming that all men who came out in that community would experience shame. The question presupposes a finding that such an experience involves shame and because the research is focused on that specific aspect of the experience it does not allow for the complexity of the experience to be revealed in full. Settling on a more open question allows a multitude of experiences to emerge and as the existential researcher found in this research the experience involved a complex interplay between the participant, their embodiment, their social and spiritual relationships and their relationship to themselves, which evolved over time (Feigin, 2021). The complexity of the findings would have been reduced if only one aspect of the experience had been explored. This makes SEA research different from other types of research in that it seeks to discover complexity and paradox and dynamic movement, rather than finding what might be described as neat cause and effect responses. This is because human life *is* paradoxical *and* contradictory *and* dynamic.

Another example of how assumptions can come into a research question can be seen in the existential research conducted by Iacovou (2015), already referred to above. Iacovou was interested in investigating the impact active service had on the intimate relationships of service personnel. Iacovou formulated her research question as 'What is the impact of active service on the intimate relationships of ex-servicemen?' When reflecting on her research Iacovou noted the following:

> During my project's data gathering stage I realised my participants weren't answering my research question directly but rather were describing the impact of active service *on them as individuals* and then stating how these changes in them impacted on their relationships. In retrospect, I can see that the question contained two assumptions or hypotheses (firstly that active service *does* impact on intimate relationships and also that this impact is experienced *directly*). As such, my question was arguably not open-ended.
>
> (Iacovou, 2015: 99)

The assumptions that Iacovou made were very subtle and had only become apparent after the research had been started but this serves as a good example of the importance of considering the words used in the research question, their position in the question and the meaning and purpose that they serve. Moustakas highlights the importance of this: 'The position of each key word, or focus, of the question determines what is primary in pursuing the topic and what data will be collected' (Moustakas, 1994: 104).

A final point about the research question, which is valid for any piece of research, is the value of the knowledge that the findings will produce. This is a point made by Willig who stresses the importance of needing 'to think about in whose interest it may be to ask the question in the first place, and how the answer to it may be used by individuals and organizations in society' (Willig, 2009: 21). This is an important element to consider as it has ethical and potentially political implications. If the research that we wish to undertake has no value or has been conducted in such a way that the findings are meaningless then it is unethical to ask individuals to give up their time to disclose their experiences for research that is flawed or compromised.

Participants

Once the existential researcher has conducted their review of the literature and has settled on their research question, they need to focus attention on who their participants will be. The narrowing down of the research area will automatically reveal who should be included in the research, i.e. which individuals have had the experiences that the existential researcher wishes to understand further. As with any piece of qualitative research the existential researcher may wish to limit their participant selection based on inclusion and exclusion criteria. Inclusion and exclusion criteria will be determined by the potential impact that such aspects as age, gender, culture, for example, may have on the experience. It could be argued that existential research does not necessarily need a homogeneous sample, where everyone needs to be similar, as the aim of existential research is to uncover the existential structures that are present in everyday experiences. However, existential research is not only concerned with understanding ontological aspects of human existence but the ontic experiences too. To uncover ontic experiences there will be a need for participants to have some background and experiential similarities. As Van Manen states: 'a phenomenological concern always has this twofold character: a preoccupation with both the concreteness (the ontic) as well as the essential nature (the ontological) of a lived experience' (Van Manen, 1990: 39–40).

Ontology 'is the metaphysics of Being'. Ontology is an investigation into the nature or essence of Being.

Ontic 'is concerned with particular beings or things (existents), as they are actually manifest in the world, beings whose existence is taken for granted'.
(Deurzen and Kenward, 2005: 146)

If we take one of the research questions above as an example, 'What are the "lived experiences" of fathers living with new mothers diagnosed with PND?' we can see that the key words were 'lived experiences', 'fathers', 'living', 'new mothers' and 'diagnosed with PND'. Therefore, the participants of this research needed to be a father, whose partner was a new mother who had been diagnosed with postnatal depression (PND) and with whom they were living. The research intended to investigate what their experiences were of being in relationship with a mother with PND. The existential researcher added further inclusion/exclusion criteria as follows:

1. Living with a partner/wife diagnosed with PND within the past three years
2. Being a first-time father aged between 30–40 years
3. Having only one child
4. Working full time
5. Not an adoptive father
6. Having no extra, familial support. (Sadia, 2020: 59)

These further inclusion/exclusion criteria ensured that the fathers being interviewed had similar life situations so that their context or situation would be comparable. If the father had extra support, his experience would be different from a father with no support, although there would also obviously be some similarities of experience. The task of thinking through who the participants will be for a piece of research comes down to asking what might make a difference in the experience. Will age make an experience different? Will gender change the experience? It is more important to try and capture similar experiences than to try to find similar individuals. With the case of Feigin's (2021) research, on the experience of coming out in the Orthodox Jewish community, for example, the age of the participants was important to control for, as living at different times in history would have a different impact on the experience of coming out. Each research question will automatically highlight who the participants should be.

In the next chapter we will consider how to go about capturing experiences through existential dialogue.

Chapter 4

Designing, Conducting and Recording an In-Depth Existential Research Dialogue

Introduction

Arguably the most important part of any piece of research is the collection of data. Yet, it is often the most overlooked aspect of research, while the focus is placed on the analysis of the data rather than on ensuring that the researcher has conducted a thorough and in-depth investigation of the issue under consideration. The success of a research project is determined by the quality of the data collected. All too often in our supervisory work we have seen novice researchers missing out on the opportunity to explore deeper into their participants' experience resulting in findings that only touch the surface of the experience and that miss out on an existential depth that can only be guessed at by reading between the lines. Two reasons for this have emerged in our work with hundreds of doctoral students. The first is the barrier created by the received assumptions about semi-structured interviews, which often tend to be treated as structured interviews, with students remaining aloof and anxious to jinx the results by engaging too much with their participants. The second, which is linked to the first, concerns the lack of understanding of phenomenology and in particular of the possibility of a phenomenology of interiority, as people often stick closely to the way in which they believe Husserl's method is meant to be applied. They stick with the surface of what appears to them, believing that this is the meaning of phenomenology: to stick with the things themselves as they are presented. They lose track of the difference between the social and natural sciences and the distinct ways in which an existential phenomenological method can create a clearing for understanding and for penetrating through to the essence of something. People are often missing out on applying their carefully honed therapeutic skills to get closer to the roots of an issue or an experience. This chapter will demonstrate how existential phenomenology can be applied in conducting Existential Research Dialogues, which is the data collection method for Structural Existential Analysis. We shall consider carefully what the discipline of existential therapy can teach us about conducting in-depth qualitative research interviews.

In qualitative research data collection is most frequently undertaken through interviews, where researchers will ask participants questions in order to elicit their responses. Most often in qualitative research this will comprise a semi-structured or structured interview. For structured interviews researchers will have developed

DOI: 10.4324/9781003148043-6

a set of prescribed questions which they will then ask each participant in turn, recording their answers. The interviews tend to follow the same format and order and remain in the realm of question and answer, although the questions are usually framed in an open way to encourage the participant to expand and be descriptive in their responses. This way of interviewing relies on the ability of the researcher to develop an interview schedule ahead of time which will set out to capture the phenomenon or experience under investigation. Novice researchers tend to prefer this type of interview structure as it feels a safe and predictable way to conduct the research when they might be feeling uncertain and unconfident in their research abilities and doubt their ability to engage their participants in a discussion about their experience which could provide deeper understanding and insight.

This chapter will highlight the importance of engaging with a dialogical process when conducting existential research. Existential researchers need to understand the foundations of dialogue from both a philosophical and therapeutic perspective, which will give them a grounding in how to conduct this type of unstructured interview.

Dialogue as the Basis of Philosophy

Dialogue, Socrates believed, was the art of speaking and thus thinking through something. This is what the word dia (through) logos (word) literally means. Dialogue and argumentation are central tenets of philosophy, and existential philosophy in particular. They are a key element of existential therapy as well. Socrates' contention was that dialogue was far superior to the written word. He believed that when something gets written down it becomes fixed, frozen, unmovable and circular. No further understanding or knowledge can be gained in the process of engagement with the written text, he contended. Words once written down were dead thoughts. Ideas became carved in stone by writing them down. Dialogue on the contrary was a way of bringing ideas to life in a fluid, expansive and dialectical way. Socrates had a very particular way of dialoguing, in which he positioned himself as not knowing and seeking to find out what was true about a particular issue by finding definitions of the things under discussion that both interlocutors could agree on. In Socratic dialogue, a process of discussion and questioning would take place which Socrates believed could enable new understandings to be discovered and illuminated, so that a greater depth of insight and knowledge about human issues could be obtained. Socrates developed these ideas to demonstrate how dialogue and dialectics were essential tools in philosophical investigation and this method over time became known as the Socratic method. Socrates used dialogue and dialectics to investigate statements of fact, by looking at direct and indirect evidence that witnesses may provide before analysing the probability or likelihood that the fact may be true and then examining any proof or supplementary proof there may be (Plato, 2005). Through this type of questioning and resulting discussion Socrates believed one was able to get closer to truth. The Socratic dialogues reported by Plato are an impressive demonstration of his capacity to show up prejudice in the people he conversed with and to guide their thinking towards a more rational and clear way. Socrates believed that the questions he asked were more important than the answers that were produced. His objective was to challenge prejudice and bring people to more careful thought (Vlastos, 1991). He kept an open mind at all times, because he believed he continued to be ignorant and that the ongoing search for truth was far more valuable than the assertion of truths that turn out to be false.

The dialectical process always involved bringing together different aspects, or parts, of a concept or experience in order to come up with a definition. The truth or accuracy of such a definition is not important in the initial stages as a further investigation through dialogue is undertaken using the Socratic method. In Plato's Laches (Plato, 1997) for instance Socrates is in dialogue with Laches about what courage is, as he tricks him into giving ever more precise definitions. Their dialogue is initially a process of elimination of false definitions. Socrates challenges Laches' contention that courage is endurance of the soul. Socrates shows Laches that not all endurance is courageous, and that courage is not a foolish endurance. As they look at the issue from many different sides, they eventually come to formulate courage as a kind of wisdom, which clearly deepens the initial idea of courage. It is not just the endurance shown by a soldier in battle but is based in something more profound. Socrates is sometimes provocative and sometimes obstructive and maddening, but he always makes his opponents think more precisely and carefully about their assertions and beliefs. Although it is tempting to see the Socratic method as a technique, this was not Socrates' intention. He did not want strict adherence to a particular way of doing things as this in turn would lead to a reductionist view of the type of conversations involved. Socrates wanted people to think for themselves, to practise philosophy in order to deepen their knowledge of themselves and of human existence. He showed them that they had the capacity for deep reflection inside of them and saw his role as that of the midwife helping to give birth to ideas. His kind of dialogue was therefore called a maieutic method, a birthing method. This practical application of philosophy is echoed later in the work of the existential philosophers Sartre and de Beauvoir (Sartre, 1968; de Beauvoir, 2020) and was adopted as the method of choice by existential therapists who defined philosophical dialogue as an essential and ongoing process of finding truth (Deurzen, 2012, Arnold-Baker, 2023). It was only after Socrates' death that his way of questioning became known as a method. What was important for Socrates was to highlight the contradictions in what people believed and spoke. The objective was to bring to light the paradoxes and limitations inherent in their descriptions and definitions and to clarify thought. It is only through dismissing certain elements and challenging assumptions that it is possible to get closer to the truth of the matter.

Wharne (2021a) cautions that Socratic questioning in a therapeutic relationship, or indeed as part of qualitative research, may be experienced as bullying and might introduce a power dynamic if the questioner presents as being more 'knowing' than those who are being questioned. The dialogue can then be taken over, leading the conversation to what the questioner believes. It is important therefore, as Wharne cautions, to ensure a 'more faithful following of what Socrates was doing, [where] the therapist allows truths to be revealed in the understandings that their client is moving towards' (Wharne, 2021a: 2). It is vital to remember that Socrates' stance was always that of ignorance and not knowing, never that of trying to impose his views on an ignorant debater. This cautionary note is vitally relevant for the existential researcher who needs to adopt a position of not knowing, wonder, curiosity and search for truth, whilst at the same time holding the research question in mind. The dialogue is centred on uncovering the participants' truth about the meaning of their existential experience, rather than on confirming the researcher's truth. For this the researcher needs to follow SOAR (Deurzen, 2015), which is described in Chapter 2.

Dialogue as Relation

Martin Buber (1878–1965) was a theologian and philosopher who took a slightly different view of dialogue to Socrates, exploring it in terms of its relationality. In his famous book *I and Thou*, Buber stated that: 'all real living is meeting' (Buber, 2000: 26). He argued that human beings are born with an inbuilt relational connection and capacity for intimacy, which is demonstrated in the way babies are drawn to connecting with others. Buber distinguished two ways in which human beings related to each other, either as *I-It*, where the other is seen in an objectified way, or as *I-Thou*, where mutual relating or meeting occurs in the present moment. In *I-Thou* relating a person will be meeting the other in a direct, embodied way in the present moment. This meeting is without agenda or purpose, it is the meeting of two people who are reaching out to each other in mutual understanding. As Buber explains: 'the primary word *I-Thou* can only be spoken with the whole being' (2000: 19). We cannot be whole unless we relate wholly to another. We become whole by being in relation in that immediate, direct and complete way, willing to see and hear the other fully. We can only discover ourselves and another by meeting another in mutual relating and understanding. As soon as the meeting or the relating is reflected upon, examined or made sense of, it moves into the realm of the *I-It* and becomes objectified.

Buber describes these moments of pure meeting as follows:

> On the other hand, man meets what exists and becomes as what is over against him, always simply a single being and each thing simply as being. What exists is opened to him in happenings and what happens affects him as what is.
>
> (2000: 42)

For Buber (2000), *I-Thou* relating is a natural combination and *I-It* a natural separation. He notes three ways in which *I-Thou* relating can take place, the first through nature, the second through our relating with other people and the third through spirituality. It is the second mode of relating that is particularly pertinent to existential research as it occurs through speech. *I-Thou* relating involves a particular way of entering into dialogue with the other so that understanding can be gained and shared. Being able to share yourself with another is a central element of this type of relating. Not fearing the other, or trying to convince the other, or dominating the other, but risking yourself in a truly reciprocal encounter in which both parties listen to what passes between them, is what an *I-Thou* dialogue looks like.

Dialogue as Understanding

Gadamer was influenced by the work of both Buber and Socrates and applied their ideas to his conceptualisation of hermeneutics. It was the conversational aspect of dialogue, and how language is used to convey understanding, that Gadamer (1975) was particularly interested in. He believed that 'Understanding each other (*sich verstehen*) is always understanding each other with respect to something' (Gadamer, 1975: 180). Intentionality, therefore, is an essential aspect of understanding. But he also showed that mutual understanding materialises as a result of communication. He believed that 'every problem of interpretation is, in fact, a problem of understanding' (Gadamer, 1975: 185). Gadamer draws on Buber's ideas when he proclaims that understanding cannot be gained through question and answer alone as it needs to involve an awareness of the individuality of the other and this involves an inner dialogue which enables understanding to be uncovered. Therefore, understanding takes effort and action, even if this is something one undertakes internally. Understanding is not passively received but actively created during the dialogue. What limits understanding is a person's *horizon*, according to Gadamer. This is inspired by Husserl's idea of the horizon of intentionality and an application of that idea. If a person has a limited horizon, they are not able to see anything other than that which is right in front of them. For those with a wider *horizon*, however, they are able to see beyond what is nearest to them and it is this aspect that is essential for existential researchers. Existential researchers need to be able to see beyond their own sphere of existence and experience and be able to enter into the world of the other. They need to enlarge their horizon in order to fully understand the other's experience and worldview, but additionally they also need to help their participants in expanding their horizons as well in order to see beyond their initial limitations. This is what we do in existential therapy, but it also applies to existential research. We cannot discover anything new until we are willing to look for it beyond our ken. Existential therapy is in essence a form of research. And existential research by the same token is also a prototype of therapy, in that it enables a person to reflect on their experience and gain new understanding.

Gadamer, taken by the ideas of Socrates and Plato, states: 'only a person who has questions can have knowledge' (1975: 359). For Gadamer, knowledge can only be obtained through questioning and a question can only 'occur', 'arise' or 'present itself' through dialogue with another (p. 359). But Gadamer warns that the art of questioning is not a technique that can be taught but rather it is the art of going beyond the question which he terms 'the art of thinking' (p. 360).

Setting up a dialogue requires a question-and-answer structure to avoid misunderstanding or talking over each other. It is not about trying to get the other to see your opinions, beliefs or values but rather to draw out the strength of the other person's opinions, beliefs and values. Gadamer describes the attitude of those asking the questions as cultivating 'the art of using words as a midwife' (1975: 361). This is a direct reference to the Socratic method of *elenchus*, literally meaning 'refutation', where Socrates used syllogistic challenges to show the contradictory or wrong-footed nature of his dialogue partner's argument. This too was part of his maieutic method, his midwifery of the soul, as described in Plato's Theaetetus (Plato, 1997). Dialogue is never about favouring one person's thoughts over the other, but it is about getting to a joint truth which is found through working out a meaning through dialogue, that process of 'question and answer, giving and taking, talking at cross purposes and seeing each other's point' (Gadamer, 1975: 361) and this meaning is only possible through language. Gadamer describes how dialogue is a 'constant going beyond oneself and a return to oneself, one's own opinions and one's own points of view' (Gadamer, 1975: 547). Therefore, existential researchers are in a constant process of reaching beyond themselves and going back to themselves to take in their own point of view and that of the other, in a dialectical process. It involves continuous reflection and questioning, a thinking through. Dialogue, as we saw, literally means to talk through something, and if we do this with full presence, we shall find new meanings together.

Other phenomenological approaches such as Interpretative Phenomenological Analysis (IPA) (Smith, Flowers and Larkin, 2022) and Van Manen's (1990) lived experience approach make use of Gadamer's double hermeneutic approach, in that the researcher is making sense of the other, who is making sense of themselves. This is an essential part of phenomenological analysis, but it is also an essential part of the existential dialogue that produces the text on which a double hermeneutic can be performed. Therefore, the existential researcher is not passive in the existential dialogue but actively clarifying and asking questions as they arise during the dialogical process.

Dialogue and Existential Therapy

Dialogue is also an essential aspect of existential therapy, as it is through dialogue that the client comes to understand their inner world in a deeper way and is challenged to consider not only how they are living their lives but also what they believe, what they value and hold true. Deurzen describes the way in which the therapist needs to become flexible and expansive in the way they see themselves, the client and the world around:

> We should train ourselves to become more and more flexible so as to extend ourselves beyond the scope of our usual worldview. We should, in other words, bracket our prejudice about the world of our client and actively relate to it in order to learn to make sense of it. This is a collaborative venture.
>
> (Deurzen, 2010: 281)

The same is needed for existential research; while the focus and outcome of therapy and research is different the means of connecting and creating understanding is the same. Deurzen notes that 'each bit of phenomenological research represents the outcome of a dynamic dyadic interaction, whereby two parties are co-creating a picture of reality' (Deurzen, 2014b: 74). What we are doing is using the understanding of several people to come to a better understanding of the world in some particular respect.

The process of setting up a therapeutic dialogue involves creating a safe and trusting environment for the relationship between the therapist and the client. This is important if the client is to open up to another, for they need to feel held and safe and protected before they will venture out of their shell. The therapist is there to support and guide them in their journey of self-exploration. They need to be available, open, warm hearted and fair minded, but never weak, nonchalant or laissez faire in the way they relate to the search for truth. Similar elements are needed for existential research; often the type of research that is undertaken involves participants divulging personal experiences which they have long kept hidden. These need to be exposed and explored in greater detail and that can be quite a feat to achieve. The contract that the researcher holds with their participants is different from the one therapists hold with their clients and yet there are similar expectations in terms of disclosure for the participant/client. For research the participant is sharing their experiences in order to further general knowledge and research. For the client they share their experiences in order to gain understanding and help for themselves in relation to the aspects that are troubling them in their daily lives. Both need to contend with their initial reluctance to reveal painful experiences. Both need to feel assured that their disclosure will be treated with the greatest respect and utmost care.

Developing Trust and Rapport in Research

Trust, therefore, and rapport are important aspects of existential research. Much can be borrowed from the therapeutic field in this respect in gaining an understanding of the importance of boundaries and frame.

Information Sheet

In order to facilitate trust the existential researcher needs to be clear and transparent with participants about the nature of the research. A clear Information Sheet (IS) is essential to provide potential participants with the information they require in order to make an informed decision about whether to take part in the research. The IS will set out the nature of the research in general terms, briefly describing the topic and scope of the research. It will include any definitions of terms that might be needed. For instance, in the previous chapter (Chapter 3) we mentioned the authors' research project on freedom for which we provided participants with a definition of absolute freedom to enable potential participants to assess whether they had experienced the events under investigation. The definition will also orientate the participant towards the aspect of their experience that will be most important to relate during the existential dialogue. This is the equivalent of Socrates entering into a dialogue about something specific and very clearly delimited such as courage or justice or virtue, and always starting by trying to agree a definition. The IS will also describe who are being sought as participants of the research and what inclusion or exclusion criteria have been decided on. Again, this is an important part of the IS as it will help participants make a decision as to whether they are eligible to take part in the research. Finally, the IS needs to give details of what is required of the participant, whether they are taking part in an interview or focus group, the length of time it will take up, if there are any follow-up activities and what the benefits or potential drawbacks of taking part might be. A final section stating that ethics approval has been given will enable participants to feel that the researcher is bone fide, trustworthy, responsible and accountable for their work.

Consent Form

In addition to the IS a consent form will give information to participants which will set out how their data will be used and stored and the measures that will be taken to protect the participants' confidentiality and anonymity. These measures give the participants faith in the research process and give participants all the information they need to have about what will take place and what they can expect. The researcher needs to also bear in mind when designing their research whether the participants they are seeking are able to give informed consent or whether there are any obstacles to this. Do participants fully understand the implications of what is being asked of them, or may they be too young or have other difficulties which will prevent this? If this is the case, measures could be taken to make the dialogue more appropriate for this particular individual or group. Adjustments for hearing impaired people may for instance be necessary.

Debrief

After the interview is over it is essential to give the participant a full debrief. This is not just a case of giving participants a list of places of support they can go to if they need to talk about anything that came up for them with someone else. It is also important for the researcher to talk about what it was like for the participant to disclose and discuss their intimate experiences in this way, what impact this dialogue has had on them and how they are now feeling. This part of the dialogue is important as it means that participants are given time to process their experience of the existential dialogue they have entered into and to leave the experience feeling supported and held by the researcher. It is also an important aspect for the researcher too who may be left holding some painful and difficult experiences that the participant has disclosed with no way of working through them with the participant, as would be the case in a therapeutic relationship. For these reasons the debrief should not be rushed. It needs to be given a fair amount of time and attention. Twenty minutes to half an hour is a good ballpark figure, after an interview of one to one and a half hours.

Rapport

Rapport focuses on the relationship that is developed between the researcher and the participant. That relationship starts from before the first contact is made through the way that the advertisement is designed and through the information provided on the IS. The first contact between researcher and participant is an important opportunity to connect with the participant, to develop empathy and understanding and demonstrate a real interest in the participant and their experience. Being accommodating and flexible through the process of making arrangements for the existential dialogue and ensuring that the setting of the existential dialogue has also been thought through carefully will help create a sense of safety and security for the participant.

An aspect of existential therapeutic practice that can be helpful in the research setting is for the existential researcher to consider what it is like for the participant to be taking part in the research. We recommend that the researcher takes some time to think about what it would be like for them to be in the same position as their participants, talking about often sensitive and delicate personal experiences. If possible, the researcher should go through the heuristic experience of being interviewed on their own topic of research by a supervisor or colleague. We began our joint research on the limits of freedom by interviewing each other about our own paradoxical experiences with freedom and discovered just how exposing and humbling it was to rediscover the fears and doubts we had once experienced around this existential event. Reflecting on this aspect will help the researcher to connect with the experience of the participant and will help the researcher to acknowledge aspects that the participant may be feeling uncomfortable with. Directly acknowledging what the participant might be feeling will help put the participant at ease. The existential researchers' orientation to the topic has been discussed further in Chapters 2 and 3.

It is also important for the existential researcher to consider the impact they will have on the participant and how that might influence how the participant responds in the existential dialogue. Careful thought needs to be given when considering how the researcher is going to introduce themselves, especially if they are a psychologist or psychotherapist, or how they describe their connection with the topic as both areas may influence and direct the pathway that the participant will take in tackling the questions put to them. There is a balance to be found between challenging and reassuring and between closeness and distance that the existential researcher needs to attend to and learn to play with. This needs to be practised to achieve a certain ease in the situation. Pilot projects are a good way of doing this.

Dialogue as Empathy

Emotional attunement is an essential part of the dialogues that take place in therapeutic work. In existential therapy we often refer to this as the experience of creating 'resonance'. Resonance is the process of being in synch with another and being in tune with their feelings. It starts to happen when we are able to attune ourselves to the other's wavelength. This attunement allows us to directly relate to what the other is experiencing. The existential therapist learns how to tune into the client's emotional experience whether the client is expressing emotions explicitly or implicitly. Emotional attunement enables the therapist to reflect back to the client what emotions they are feeling, fine tuning these in such a way that the client can begin to move from being affected by something to beginning to understand the meaning of their experience. Deurzen has clearly illustrated this in her chapter for Schulenberg's book on *Clarifying and Furthering Existential Psychotherapy* (Deurzen, 2016). This also shows how the therapist tunes into her own emotional experiences during the work and considers whether they were evoked by the client, by her own past experience, or by something more in the domain of the transcendental ego, shared by all human beings. In the process of our interviews on the limits of freedom there were numerous moments of resonance with participants. These were often marked by a pause in the dialogue, or by joint laughter, or joint tearfulness, or by a shared 'Aha' experience of recognition of the importance of a certain element of the experience of freedom. Each time this occurred the dialogue deepened after this shared moment of understanding.

Historically social research has not investigated emotion or feeling despite the amount of research undertaken by psychologists. Cromby (2012) believes that psychology research has taken an 'affective turn' more recently but highlights the difficulty researchers face in how to capture emotional content which relies on language as the form of expression. This is in contrast with the existential approach which positions working with emotions and the emotional compass (Deurzen, 2010) at the core of all existential work and which will be discussed in some detail in Chapter 8. For the purposes of this section, however, reflection will be centred on how emotional attunement and empathy can facilitate greater understanding during a piece of research.

Wharne (2021b) suggests that Edith Stein's conceptualisation of empathy can provide a framework for researchers conducting qualitative research. Stein (1964 [1921]) believed that when we encounter another person, we gain knowledge of their emotional experience, and that by attuning to this emotional expression we can gain an understanding of the emotions or feelings the other is experiencing. This requires the person to try and put themselves in the other person's position. As Atticus Finch notes in *To Kill a Mockingbird*, 'you never really understand a person until you consider things from his point of view . . . until you climb into his skin and walk around in it' (Lee, 2015 [1960]: 33). This is very similar to Karl Jaspers' definition of empathy or *Einfühlung* (Jaspers, 1963), which was to allow yourself to *participate* in another person's experience. Stein was influenced by Husserl's work, and she built on his ideas around intentionality and inter-subjectivity. Husserl believed there were three ways in which we encounter others. Either we encounter others as we would an object in the world, or we experience others as subjects and through that gain an experience of how another might experience us (this idea was further expanded by Sartre (1956 [1943]) in his concept of 'The Look' or 'The Gaze'). Individuals can also encounter the world as inter-subjective, which is a position we can only arrive at by a transcendental reduction, allowing us to take a wider view and broader horizon to the community of monads we live in. At that moment our relationships with others do not remain in the realm of a separate subject and object but we become aware of the way in which our lives are intertwined by similar experiences and feelings. We feel ourselves as part of a human community that we both belong to. We also become more aware of the way in which we interrelate with others through conversation and dialogue. Husserl (1991) describes this aspect as empathic intentionality which he believes is made up of two processes, 'analogical apperception' and 'pairing'. Husserl noted that often our perceptions involve a combination of what we can see or sense but also what we infer from what we see. Human perception has a tendency to fill in the gaps as it were and helps us to make sense of what we are experiencing. Husserl's three reductions were an attempt to overcome this tendency so that the focus is on what we experience not on what we have inferred or assumed. As part of apperception there is also an inclination to treat things as if they are alike if we perceive them to be similar, transposing qualities onto what we believe is its pair. In Husserl's phenomenology empathetic intentionality is a discipline, something to be guarded against by using the three reductions. However, for Stein it is used as a way of gaining a deeper understanding of a person's emotional experience. In existential therapy and existential research both are used. It is important to tune into a person's emotional experience and we need to allow ourselves to resonate, but at the same time we need to be mindful of the assumptions or inferences that we make and to be aware of the process that we go through. Drawing from the concept of the reflective practitioner espoused by counselling psychology the existential researcher needs to undergo a process of double reflection. The first is reflecting *in action*, i.e. reflecting on what is happening in the dialogue and how the researcher is responding and thinking about what is driving those responses. The second is reflection *on action* which refers to how the existential researcher reflects on the dialogue as a whole afterwards in a more analytical way (Douglas et al., 2016).

Wharne provides an example of how Stein's ideas can be applied to research. Speaking about research participants, he suggests that:

> to start with you need to notice that this is a meaningful event for them. You then need to sit beside them, to see what they see, but then to turn again to see them in how they are seeing. If you are viewing these things only from the remote position of an objective scientist, you will not see with the illumination of that moment.
>
> (Wharne, 2021b: 5)

Attunement in this way is not only focused on the emotional content of a participant's experience but also their being-in-the-world which is brought into that very moment. Wharne offers questions for researchers to reflect on to help them to turn towards the other in attunement, such as:

> What bodily response am I having while being with this person as they describe their experience, how does it feel? How is this feeling opening my awareness of what it would be like if the experience that this person describes happened to me, or for someone who is emotionally close to me? How is this person different from me in the circumstances of their life and how might the experience they describe make sense within the context of that life? Am I fully present with this person, unfolding different aspects of their experience in a way that acknowledges our similar and different responses?
>
> (Wharne, 2021b: 5)

Wharne makes an important point about presence, that during research the existential researcher must be fully present with the other and connected to them.

Empathy as has been demonstrated above is an important element of both existential therapy and existential research. However, Vanhooren (2022) makes a distinction between what he terms *ontic* empathy, the empathy one might experience in relation to another person's daily struggles, and *existential* empathy, which he describes as being focused on existential or ontological concerns. The difficulty, he believes, that arises in therapy with existential empathy is that for daily struggles the experience of the *self-other difference* is easier to maintain, whereas it is harder to preserve when discussing existential concerns that are ontological in nature and therefore shared by all. The difference between ontic empathy and existential empathy in therapy, Vanhooren goes on to suggest, is that the former is orientated towards understanding in order to find a solution or resolution, and the latter is concerned with being with the client with their concerns without any attempt to find solutions. He states that existential empathy helps the client 'to *experience* her human condition in a different way, although the human condition as such has not changed' (Vanhooren, 2022: 7).

When considering this in relation to existential research it is clear that the existential researcher has to engage in both ontic empathy and existential empathy, as part of the aim of SEA is to draw out the existential conditions that are present in the phenomenon under consideration. Vanhooren's suggestions of how to attend to existential concerns in therapy are also relevant to research. He offers the following guidance that: 'the therapist helps the client to stay with this concern, to fully sense it, and to find words or other symbols that express how the client experiences their existential struggles in the here-and-now' (2022: 5). This involves the existential researcher not steering away from or overlooking existential concerns but directly engaging with or drawing them out in the existential dialogue. In this process there is a constant deepening of understanding of the issues being investigated.

Conducting Dialogues in Existential Research

A limitation of social research is that its positioning is still seen in relation to empirical research which has an impact on how research is conceived. This is most notable when considering data collection. Churchill (2022) argues that the use of the word data derives from a theory of knowledge that assumes that information can be given by, or collected from, the world in a clinical manner which supposes that the collection procedure will not have an impact on the knowledge uncovered. Churchill prefers Laing's ideas of *capta* rather than *data* as it refers to knowledge being taken which assumes an active element to the creation of knowledge. He states that 'Technically speaking, we should (as phenomenologists) drop the term *data* from our vocabulary because what we are really doing is actively gathering meanings' (Churchill, 2022: 37).

Capturing Meaning

Capturing meaning is an essential part of Churchill's (2022) Existential Phenomenological Research, Van Manen's (1990) lived experience approach as well as Smith et al.'s (2022) IPA methodology. This raises questions about how the existential researcher can best capture meaning during the existential dialogue.

The first step is to keep the phenomenon under exploration in mind and central to the process. The aim of the existential dialogue is to look at the phenomenon in a 360-degree way, so that it is examined from every angle, and in doing so every possible aspect of the phenomenon is brought to light for that person. Like in existential therapy the existential researcher will be looking to clarify assumptions and meanings. They will draw out and make explicit implicit meanings, values or beliefs. They will do this as well as bringing to light the emotions, feelings and sensations that are connected to the experience the participant has brought. We shall see in the second part of the book how all these different elements can be gathered together by using a number of different existential lenses for our observations. What we aim for is for the participant to not just disclose what they already know about the topic, but to dig a little deeper and discover new elements to their experience in the research process. These could be elements they had not previously allowed themselves to see or feel because it didn't seem safe or possible to face this alone. It could also be elements that emerge from the research dialogue.

Whilst the existential dialogues for SEA research are conducted in a fairly open-ended and unstructured way existential researchers do need to think about possible areas to prompt for during the dialogue to ensure a thorough exploration of the experience. Prompt areas or questions can be developed in advance but held lightly during the dialogue as the purpose of the dialogue is to remain firmly with the participants' experience and seeking further clarification. They are the broad existential structure of reality that we use to ensure that all avenues have been explored. We know we must find out about a person's physical embodied experience, about their relational and social reality, about their internal processing and relating to themselves and also about their beliefs and values, for instance. We also know that we need to pay attention to their sensations, feelings, emotions and intuitions. We need to get a sense of the dynamics of their experience and their historical trajectory. We need to engage with the layers of meaning they have woven out of what has happened to them.

Van Manen describes it as follows:

> I must recall the experience in such a way that the essential aspects, the meaning structures of this experience as lived through, are brought back, as it were, and in such a way that we recognize this description *as a possible experience*, which means *as a possible interpretation* of that experience.
>
> (Van Manen, 1990: 41)

In the box below you will see the prompt questions developed for the piece of research that the authors undertook on the concept of freedom. During the existential dialogue the prompt questions act as a guide or a map of the terrain that might be covered by the phenomenon; a framework to structure the dialogue. It helps as a way to open up the horizon both for the existential researcher and for the participant. It is not to be used dogmatically or prescriptively, however, but more as an image of the world that will allow us to enter into the dance of the dialogue with the participant and to let ourselves improvise to cover all the angles. We need to be light on our feet and make sure we visit all of the person's existential territory. For this we need a reminder of what that involves. We visit all the poles of a person's encounter with the particular reality under investigation. We allow for lots of leeway and freedom of exploration, but make sure we probe the depths and the heights as well as the four corners of their world. The more multi-dimensional the dialogue, the more depth the capta will have. The prompts also help the existential researcher in remaining connected to the research question and the purpose and aim of the research. They guide the dialogue and keep it focused on the salient aspects of the experience that are under investigation. This stops the exploration veering off onto a different track.

Freedom Research – Interview Questions

1. Was there a time in your life when you were totally free? [time and temporality]

    a. Where did it come from?
    b. How did you encounter it?
    c. How did you experience it?
    d. How did you transcend it?
    e. How did you make sense of it?

2. What was the physical experience of this freedom? [physical]

    a. How did it feel?
    b. What sensations did it evoke?
    c. How did it affect your sense of security/insecurity?

3. Did your experience of freedom affect your relationships with other people? [social]
   a. If so in what ways?
   b. What was your lifestyle during this period? Were you well connected up with people around you or were you living in an isolated way?

4. How did your experience of freedom affect your relationship to yourself? [personal]
   a. Did you come to this period from a position of confidence having opted for your freedom deliberately or were you thrown into freedom from unforeseeable losses?
   b. How did the experience impact on your identity?
   c. What did you learn about yourself?

5. How did you make sense of this experience at the time? [spiritual]
   a. How did your worldview change during this experience of freedom?
   b. What sense do you make of that experience now?
   c. Did it teach you anything new about life?

6. How did this experience of freedom make you feel? [emotions]
   a. What emotions did you go through during this period?
   b. Were there any particular moments of drama or depth of experience during this time?
   c. How did you process your emotions, or did you suppress them?

7. What were the challenges that you faced during that experience of freedom? [paradox]
   a. Did you have any surprise experiences? Was your freedom what you expected it would be or did it expose you to experiences that were more challenging than you bargained for?
   b. How did you deal with these tensions or contradictions?
   c. Did they make you change direction?
   d. Did you derive a new sense of purpose and commitment at the end of it? If so, what did you commit to as a result?

8. What was your general sense of direction in your life at that time? [intentionality]
   a. What were you aiming for during your experience of freedom?
   b. Did the experience re-orientate you and if so, in which direction?
   c. Did you derive a new sense of purpose and commitment at the end of it? If so, what did you commit to as a result?

> 9. What was the sequence of your experience of freedom? [time]
>   a. What did it derive from and where did it lead you?
>   b. What were the significant moments in the experience?
>   c. Were you different before and after?
>
> 10. Were there times during this experience that you felt confronted with nothingness or death? Did you feel alone, insignificant, or did you have a sense of connection to Being or to the universe or to anything else?

The prompt questions are usually developed in discussion with a supervisor or colleague, through the existential researcher's examination of the literature as well as their experience of being interviewed about the phenomenon themselves. All of these aspects ensure that the existential researcher is aware of the possible horizon of the phenomenon, borrowing Gadamer's term. However, during the existential dialogue, the existential researcher must be open to new horizons that present themselves and also be aware of their own assumptions that they are bringing to the dialogue and how these are being challenged. Never forget that changing your perspective and gaining new insights and understanding is always the objective of existential research.

The most important question for any piece of research is the opening question, which for the research on freedom was:

> I would like you to let me know whether there have been times in your life when you felt particularly free and whether that gave you a total sense of freedom or not. I'd love to hear about your experience in every detail.

The opening question is the question of the research and forms the focus of the dialogue. Each participant will choose to begin their answer to that question in their own way and based on their own experience. It is worth remembering that 'Big questions do not always produce detailed answers' (Fujii, 2018: 63). Existential researchers need to consider the language they use in the information they send to their participants as well as the language they use for their questions. The use of everyday language will help here. Just because the researcher may understand particular terms in particular ways, doesn't mean the participant understands them in the same way. Find out. Ask people to define words for you. Enquire about meanings, feelings, experiences. Stay curious and aware that you do not yet know what your participant experiences, feels and believes.

The art of the existential researcher is to keep the dialogue orientated to the phenomenon under exploration but at the same time immersing themselves into the experience that the participant is talking about. This is always about holding a tension and being fleet of feet in adjusting and accommodating to the way in which the participant begins to develop their story and gets deeply engrossed in their experience. Existential research is much easier to do if you have trained as an existential therapist. The existential researcher needs to gain a feel for what their participant is really describing, using empathy and attunement and resonance with this experience at the same time as reflecting on it and making sense of it, whilst staying true to what it was like for the participant. The following questions might be helpful to consider in getting deeper into the nitty gritty of that raw experience:

What was that like for you?
How did it feel?
What did it mean?
What were the elements that stood out for you?
What were the emotions involved?
How did you make sense of it?
Did you recognise this experience?
What values and beliefs did this experience touch off in you?
What did you learn from it?
What were the most important moments?
What were the most powerful learning points?
Did this change over time?

As part of this exploration the existential researcher will also home in on parts of the dialogue to gain further clarification and insight. The following excerpts from one of the existential dialogues that were conducted as part of the freedom research will highlight how this can be done.

Participant: When I've felt free however, the time I was reminded of the most was 20 years ago when I used my hard-won financial freedom, which is always the most difficult aspect for me, to do things that I couldn't have done otherwise . . .
Researcher: So what does that mean, being financially free, what did it mean for you?

Here the researcher was clarifying what the participant meant by financial freedom, as it may not have been the same meaning as it had for the researcher. Clarification of words, assumptions, values and beliefs are important ways of opening up the dialogue and ensuring that neither the participant nor the existential researcher is making assumptions about the phenomenon or the experience.

Later on in the transcript, the participant began describing an experience of lying down in a desert at night and how they felt connected to the planet and the galaxy. The researcher asked the following questions to open up the exploration of that experience:

Researcher: Can you go back to that moment, when you lie in the desert and you see the stars going all the way round you, what is that like?
Participant: Rather I am going round them!

Researcher: What is that like? What does that feel like? What did that do to you in the moment? What were your emotions? Your sensations?

Here the researcher is not directly referring to the prompt questions but using elements that the participant has brought to the dialogue. This is done to draw something out about the obviously very powerful experience that the participant was describing but was hesitant to elaborate on. After this intervention the participant felt freed to open up about this experience in much more lyrical and deeply felt ways. It is important that the researcher allows herself to open the dialogue out, expanding it, delving into the experience in a deeper way. Staying at the surface level of the story never yields the same detailed understanding. Sometimes the intervention might be challenging, as in a Socratic dialogue.

An example of this is highlighted in this excerpt:

Participant: I almost found it a little bit comforting.
Researcher: Comforting? How was that comforting? As that is almost the opposite of what people experience when they feel free isn't it? Freedom tends to go with insecurity?
Participant: I don't know, I think for me, all my life I wanted to be free, this is one of my motivators in life . . . comforting because all the troubles on this planet, that are so limiting and which impacted me . . . and if we could just get rid of [the troubles] we could enjoy that comforting presence of the cosmos so much more.

Here you can see how the researcher tentatively challenges, poses an opposite position to the participant but in such a way that the participant feels able to engage with it, think about and then reject it. This allowed the participant to go on to delve deeper into what they actually meant by the word 'comforting'.

Later the participant ended their description with the following words:

Participant: . . .it was like sort of a metaphysical kind of experience really.
Researcher: Like you were in direct touch with the universe in some way.
Participant: Yes! Literally! By seeing it
Researcher: and feeling part of it
Participant: yeah I mean the galaxy goes all the way round so you can see, you know, this place where we live, that's the place where we live.

In this excerpt from the interview, you can see that the researcher is not a detached observer, a collector of data or capta, but an active member of the dialogue, always focused on the participant's experience. Through the dialogue meaning is created both for the participant to understand their experience in a deeper way but also for the researcher to gain a deeper understanding of what that experience was like for the participant. They are literally on a journey of exploration together. This excerpt also provides an example of how the existential researcher engaged with the participant's existential concerns to enable a fuller exploration of the experience the participant was trying to describe, by checking out the horizons and limits of the experience and what it contains.

Another example of how the researcher questioned the participant to expand her horizon to consider what she was really saying and what she meant by those words and experiences:

Participant: I realised that if more people lived their freedom as much as they could the world would indeed be a much better place. I think there is absolutely no question about it.
Researcher: Because? Why would it be a better place? What would happen if people lived with more freedom?

The participant now launched into a philosophical consideration of her fantasy of utopia, and she really began to describe what she would like freedom to be. This was set in contrast with her actual experiences of freedom, which were discussed in a different part of the interview. This tension between a fantasised freedom and the reality of freedom was very poignant and helped clarify the paradox of freedom, which the research was investigating.

Textualising Experiences

Ultimately, the purpose of the existential dialogue, as Van Manen states, is:

> to transform lived experience into a textual expression of its essence – in such a way that the effect of the text is at once a reflexive re-living and a reflective appropriation of something meaningful.
> (Van Manen, 1990: 36)

Once the existential dialogue has been completed and a thorough debrief has occurred, the existential researcher will transcribe the dialogue, adding in contextual notes such as the participant's embodiment and responses during the dialogue. This transcript then becomes the textual expression of the experience and of the capta from which to work in the Structural Existential Analysis.

It is worth keeping in mind this aspect of the research process whilst conducting the existential dialogue to help the researcher to ensure that they are sufficiently capturing the experience. Thinking about whether what the participant has said has been sufficiently encapsulated in the words used to describe their experience is an important part of the reviewing of the transcripts. We make notes about this which can later be used in the analysis. This process is very demanding, because the existential researcher has to really focus not just on what has been said, but what has been conveyed and implied by the participant. There is some reading between the lines that is required. Not everything is said in words. There is a need to pay attention to contradictions and tensions in the dialogue. There is a need to pay attention to what has not been said and to grasp what has been left out. This is a process of bringing to awareness what was significant in the interview. Pauses and silences are as significant as text at this point. Going over the text helps the existential researcher to adhere to the three phenomenological reductions to ensure they are fully exploring the phenomena or experience in depth. What is the process of examining the issue at stake and how is this proceeding? What is the description of the experience conveying? What is the internal state of the participant and what is the internal state of the researcher? Is there resonance, understanding, confluence, or misunderstanding or even conflict?

Transcription is a lengthy process but as seen in other phenomenological approaches (Van Manen, 1990, Willig, 2009, Churchill, 2022) it is the first step of analysis as it helps the existential researcher to move from a position of capturing meaning to being immersed in analysing meaning. Once a complete transcript has been produced the existential researcher can decide whether they wish to engage in member checking. This is the process of sending the transcript to the participant to ensure that the transcript has captured the experiences or phenomena accurately. Member checking can either be conducted at this stage of the analytic process or at the findings stage. For example, for this book we sent the extracts of the findings and analysis which appear in these pages to our participants for checking and approval. One of our participants, Olga, made clarification comments where she felt we might not have fully grasped her meaning and we amended our analysis in light of these comments. It is important to fully capture our participants' meanings and experiences during the analysis. Both Olga and Luke expressed how much they enjoyed reading the analysis and how it led to them being able to reflect again on their experiences from the new perspective of the analysis. Other methodologies approach this aspect differently; Churchill (2022) for example starts with asking participants to produce a written description of the experience under exploration which is then elaborated on and explored further in the research. We favour sharing the write-up of the interview with the participant in order to apply the important phenomenological process of verification, ensuring that we remain true to the participant's words, meanings and experiences. But we believe that there are many different ways of doing this verification and that it is helpful for there to be some freedom in how the researcher verifies their conclusions.

As we begin to pass a person's words and expressions through the sieve of SEA, so many new aspects of their experience will become evident that it may be tempting to bend their experiences in new directions. Verification is therefore of the essence.

In the following chapters we shall turn to the work of filtering the capta and sieving out the most relevant and interesting findings. We shall do this by using the existential heuristics that SEA takes into account. This provides us with a number of existential lenses that have been well established, developed and refined over the decades, both through therapeutic work and through existential research. We shall look at the lenses in turn to demonstrate their importance as filters through which to examine life experiences, understanding and analysing the extremely rich capta produced by the existential dialogues.

Part Two

Application

Chapter 5

The Filter of TIME

Introduction

As we begin to filter our participants' contributions through the various lenses of SEA, we are in effect using existential categories as heuristic devices to get clear angles and greater understanding of the issues they may bring into focus. By zooming in on specific aspects of participants' remarks about the issue under investigation, we are potentially distorting their words. Nevertheless, by amplifying certain aspects of what they meant, we are able to extract more information from their statements. This is exactly what happens when you use a magnifying glass or a microscope to look more carefully at something you are studying. Using the lenses makes us specific and minute in our investigation. It takes us to the opposite end of the spectrum of the general and comprehensive exploration of phenomenology. This produces a creative tension in our work. On the one hand we maintain our phenomenological stance and keep alert to the whole picture, its context and its horizon. On the other hand, we shine a spotlight on everything that is relevant to our research, element by element, and we apply the epochē, as we look for the essence of a person's existential experiences. We remain aware of our bias, and of the bias of the research participants too. We keep our perspective even as we bear down on our investigation and grind the data through the fine sieves of our five filters: Time, Space, Paradox, Purpose and Passion (see Figure 5.1). These capture the dynamic reality of the participant's experience in a more specific manner and provide us with new insights. The more we refine our understanding of the issue under investigation, the more important it becomes that we keep in mind how we are operating and how we may be distorting our findings. This is where it becomes crucial to stay in dialogue with a colleague or supervisor about how we are processing the participant's words through the mesh of our filters. We also favour going back to the participant after we have captured their words, to verify whether we are doing justice to their experience by the way we are processing it.

Why We Need a Filter of Time

The filter of time is a very significant one. Human existence always takes place in time and our experience and understanding of any phenomenon is always

DOI: 10.4324/9781003148043-8

82 Structural Existential Analysis

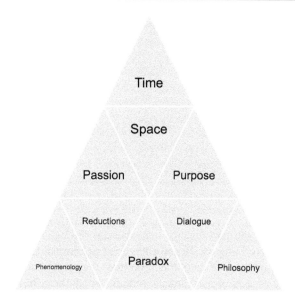

Figure 5.1 Structural Existential Analysis diagram

historically located, defined and determined. While many researchers in the past have limited their SEA research to considering the four dimensions of space, perhaps also bringing into view the tensions and paradoxes at each level, a Structural Existential Analysis can never be complete unless there is an analysis of the impact of time on what we are observing. We like to begin with the dynamic of a genetic understanding of a person's evolution in time in relation to the issue we are considering. In our pilot study on freedom, we interviewed people not just about various times in their lives when they felt most free, but we also made sure to encourage our participants to remember the sequence of their discoveries about the experience of freedom, tracing the dynamic change of it throughout their lives. Husserl attached great importance to the historical aspects of the phenomena we observe. He spoke about the way in which phenomena have a temporal character and are seen against a background of genetic development and historical progression (Husserl, 1991). This is quite different to the natural scientific theories of time, which are based in the notion of time as a series of points of experience that come in succession. Husserl distinguishes between worldly or objective time, personal or subjective time and the consciousness of internal time. As usual phenomenology seeks to transcend the division between objective and subjective apprehensions of the world. As Brough said:

> Husserl argues, that the 'flow' (*PCIT* § 37) of conscious life enjoys two modes of simultaneously operative intentionality. One mode of intentionality, which he terms *Langsintentionalität*, or horizontal intentionality, runs along protention

and retention in the flow of the living-present. The other mode of intentionality, which Husserl terms the *Querintentionalität*, or transverse intentionality, runs from the living-present to the object of which consciousness is aware.

(Brough, 1991: 54)

Heidegger's magnum opus *Being and Time* (Heidegger, 1962) was very much inspired by Husserl's thinking about time, and it was an effort to explore human time in exhaustive detail.

The passage of time changes phenomena and it also gives them a dynamic aspect that is easily forgotten, but that is the *sine qua none* of an experience feeling live and real. Because of this the lens of time is at the top of the diagram we designed to help you remember to use all aspects of a Structural Existential Analysis. It is the first point of meaning-making, which pierces into the experience in question.

Time as the Great Mover in Husserl's Work

As part of the eidetic reduction, i.e. the finding of the essence of what we are observing, it is important to remember that things come to us under different adumbrations (Husserl's word was *Abschattungen*, which literally means different shades, different nuances, different shadings or aspects of something). As you speak in dialogue with your research participants, their descriptions of the phenomena under investigation will be evolving over time. In other words, the process of the Existential Research Dialogue (ERD) encourages them to re-live an experience and bring it back into awareness. They will be recollecting this experience in time and if you provide enough attention and space for that process, they will take themselves through the historical and subsequent experiences that have come to mind. They will become more precise and specific in their recollections, as they travel back to a previous time in their mind. The story they tell you is probably more and more heavily laden with memories and feelings as they develop the narrative, especially if you are supportive of them taking the necessary time to ponder and re-experience. But they will also naturally begin to consider how they have viewed their past experiences over time, since the initial event they are speaking about. So, our participants on the freedom research would typically begin by saying something about a moment when they had felt terribly or wonderfully free, then would naturally move forward to consider whether or not what they experienced had turned out to be freedom, or just an illusion of freedom. They would gradually remember other moments and times of different kinds of freedom and would begin to reflect on drawbacks of certain freedoms. Sometimes, they would become very focused on moments when they sensed that they were more in possession of their own lives than they have been ever since. They were often not aware of this historical aspect of their accounts of freedom but would see it immediately if prompted with a statement like 'it sounds as if your experience of freedom was different at different times'. This would typically trigger very rich materials and observations about their own learning process around freedom.

When we made room in the research dialogue for this self-observation and for this awareness of participants' emotional, experiential, mental and personal evolution in terms of their understanding of their own freedom, we got a much more substantial narrative from our research participants. It is easy to flatten their account and even to kill any idea about their experience moving on dimensions of time. But it is important to invite participants into the experience of time in terms of their own developing understanding and experimentation with the issue in question, in our case with freedom. Similarly, it will be a good thing to probe in the dialogue for the multiple lenses through which the participant has viewed their own experiences over time, because such growth in their understanding will have brought them to a range of new and different meanings, over their lifetime. We don't want to capture a static or one-dimensional description of the topic under scrutiny. We want to capture the live, evolving, continuing, existential experience. We go around the houses of time as much as we go around the houses of space. We visit different moments and places in the person's life. We remain available for that journey. This takes time, attention and often requires a clear sense of permission for further exploration. When Husserl spoke of the genetic constitution of experiences, he meant exactly this: that anything to do with human experience and meaning is in movement and constantly changing. Objective observations alone can easily strangle the data we capture. What you do when you do SEA is to spend enough time to capture the live material instead. We make a movie, or a recording in depth of the process the person is trying to convey to us. We have found it helpful to do Zoom interviews with participants, recording the whole proceeding, so we get a very sharp record of the participant's experience in the ERD (and also of the researcher's prompts and responses). This makes it obvious that a participant gets to grip with an issue by mulling it over, remembering different instances of it and tasting these in their mouth, one by one. We only truly know something if we can describe its changing nature and the way it looks and evolves over time. When we do Existential Phenomenological Research, we need to be prepared to capture some of the emergent properties of the phenomena we are investigating. Time is of the essence in this respect. The idea that the participant's grasp of the topic under investigation is an emerging phenomenon is vital. Quite often the research dialogue turns into an almost therapeutic moment of discovery and new understanding of something that has long been kept in a mental box and that has now been allowed to roam free and breathe the oxygen of free dialogue, therefore changing in that process.

Time as Viewed by Heidegger

Time is an aspect of existential philosophy that has been most deeply belaboured by Martin Heidegger (1962). His insights can be helpful in the way we filter participants' experiences through the lens of time.

When we speak about the different aspects of time in a casual way, we immediately remember that time can be divided up into past, present and future. Heidegger's work has made us aware that there are other aspects we also need to take into account, i.e. eternity and timelessness. Heidegger linked the human experience of the passage of time to the fact of our birth and death. He said:

> as soon as man comes to life he is at once old enough to die.
>
> (Heidegger, 1962: 240)

This is something the SEA researcher may want to remember when starting to build the particular time lens to be applied to their capta.

You will want to examine carefully whether your participant was considering their experience in a past, present, future, eternal or timeless way. You may wish to be guided by the language used here and the tenses employed. You may want to remember that Heidegger showed how the human being lives in the ec-stases of time and what it means to stand out in life in past, present, future or any other tense and whether the person is continuing to experience this event in some way, or whether it has been relinquished.

We are always *in* time in some way. It is not possible to be completely time-less as a human being. In some ways lives are measured in time. And there are more dimensions to time than we ever imagine:

- Past
- Present
- Future
- Eternity
- Timelessness

We might even consider whether the theory that some physicists hold out as a possibility, i.e. that of the existence of parallel universes, may also be relevant to contemplate. For instance, in our freedom research, we discovered that many people dream about freedom and have a whole range of practices for re-experiencing or exploring freedom, either in daydreams or through their nocturnal dream life. These are like multiple universes in which they experiment alongside a well-regulated and clearly defined daily present.

People therefore may situate themselves in their stories in all the temporal ways that Heidegger described, as:

1. **In the past**: as having been: forgetting or regretting. These are all forms of *Gewesenheit*, i.e. of having been, and they can be recalled by repetition or recollection.
2. **In the present**: as being in waiting or rushing: These are forms of *Gegenwart*, *presence*, the way we actually are as Dasein, human being, as Being-with-in-the-world, abiding time or experiencing it as urgent.
3. **In the future**: as going toward, longing or dreading: These are forms of *Zukunft*, future, which we can also experience with anticipation, as a Being-towards Death.

4. **In temporality**: as being part of eternal Being or the infinite: *Zeit und Sein*, time and being as intertwined realities.
5. **As coming to time in a new way**, in the *Ereignis*, the event, which is a particular way to experience the event as a coming to life and to take a renewed ownership of one's world instead of just experiencing it, as out of time and without full awareness and responsibility.

These differentiated ways of experiencing time can be recognised, located, mapped and filtered for their meanings.

In a much more down to earth way, you might plot a person's experiences on a timeline, either a specific timeline, that records certain historical dates, or a timeline related to particular events and its various phases, or a timeline that simply records the years or months of a person's life, alongside the changes that are happening.

Minkowski's Contribution

Eugene Minkowski's work on time is also significant and can help us make more sense of a person's experience in time of a particular existential phenomenon. Minkowski showed how the present is really constituted of different aspects of the present. He showed how rich the present is, as it is composed of the different threads of past and future that we are weaving together. It is possible for a person to live in the present in many different ways. For instance, by becoming absorbed by the remote past, the mediate past or the immediate past. Though some existentialists take the view that people ought to live in the here and now, it can easily be shown that we constantly move in thought through different layers of past memories and future imaginings and that the present is the fleeting moment of constantly changing imagery that accompanies us in our inner life.

Minkowski (1970) demonstrated how different zones twist our experience of life in different ways:

- Present: here we are in the zone of activity, which requires us to focus on the task at hand. But when we begin to pay attention specifically to the present moment, we become aware that in the present moment we can visit all the other zones of time and that moments are constantly fleeting.

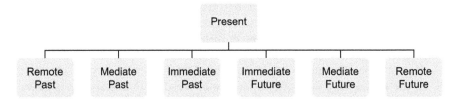

Figure 5.2 Eugène Minkowski: All time exists in the present

- Remote past: this is the zone of the obsolete and of history, including your own life myths. Talking about this is almost always an aspect of existential research as we ask our participants to recall experiences from the distant past.
- Mediate past: this is the zone of loss and regret, the time that has not yet become so far removed from us that we have mythologised it, but not so near that it is still in our short-term memory. It is the period of our life in which we do the work to lay down long-term memories about our own experiences and this may be altered in the research dialogue, in the same way in which it would be altered in therapeutic work.
- Immediate past: this is the zone of remorse or of live grief or joy about events that are still sharply in our short-term memory and that disturb or delight us. We may not have quite thought it all through, so that we are perturbed by these memories and experience them as feelings rather than as thoughts.
- Immediate future: this is the zone of expectation and of the things that are immediately ahead of us: the things we plan to do and ought to do next, though we may be in the process of procrastinating them. Procrastination is a category that is sometimes relevant for recording phenomena in time. It is a way of postponing the future, either because we dread it and dislike it or because we want to keep it in mind for longer, or because we want to sharpen our readiness for it, when it can no longer be avoided. Daydreaming may be a way to postpone or relate to the immediate future, but it tends to be more related to the mediate or remote future.
- Mediate future: this is the zone of wish and hope or of dread and anxiety. Whether a person is willing to entertain possibilities in the mediate future or is censoring such thoughts from their present or past experience can be very relevant. The process of worrying is often related to the mediate future. It can be argued that there are many forms of worrying, some that are fearful and burdensome, creating a sense of anxiety and apprehension in the person or perhaps even a sense of reluctance. This is what we might call fretting and perseverating or agonising and being troubled about things. But there is also a kind of worry that does the work of considering different possible futures and that is more like anticipation and planning. Sometimes it helps to distinguish between active and passive worry, and between constructive and destructive worry.
- Remote future: this is the zone of prayer and ethical action and also of ultimate meaning of life. Whether people are occupying this territory and laying claim to having a possible influence over the direction their actions and their life will take or whether they simply turn to prescriptive and dogmatic stances makes a big difference.

Deurzen developed her thinking about working with time in therapeutic practice by thinking of the movement of time as that of a continuous movement in the shape of a double figure eight, with the two figures sharing one of the loops. A person lives in the present moment, which is the middle loop of their experience, and yet their mind circles constantly back to the past, and forward to the future.

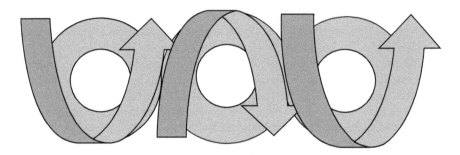

Figure 5.3 Double figure eight

We roam around the circle of the now, then loop into a circle of past memories, feelings and recollections, but come back around to the present moment, which is the middle loop of the two figures of eight. From there we then loop towards the future and go around our fantasies and imagination of what visions of the future we might realise, only to return to the events of the here and now, dwelling on this for a bit and rushing off to the past once more. Sometimes we circle around more in the present, or more in the past or the future, but there is always a looping forward and backwards, never a stagnant pausing in present time only. The double figure eight is a way of representing a person's continuous movement in time between a focus on the present, a memorising of something in the past, a return to the present and a reaching out to something in the future. This circulating and looping movement around time was also described by van Deurzen and Arnold-Baker in our co-authored book on existential therapy (Deurzen and Arnold-Baker, 2018). The conjunction of two figures of eight, where the first figure is that of going between present and past, and the second is that of going between present and future, can be merged as in Figure 5.4 below. This figure eight movement ultimately relates to the lazy, lying down figure eight of the symbol for eternity and infinity, the lemniscate. ∞

In the illustration that we did in *Existential Therapy: Distinctive Features* (Deurzen and Arnold-Baker, 2018), we showed furthermore how the movement of the mind in time, when it reaches out beyond the past and future towards infinity, can give the internal experience a spiritual direction by connecting to timelessness and eternity.

We called this figure the dialectics of time diagram (Figure 5.5 below), as it shows the renewal of the mind in time as it deals with contradictions and absorbs memories, projecting new ideas into the long-term future. It is an illustration of what Sartre, in his 1969 interview with the *New Left Review*, was referring to as the limit of freedom:

> the small movement which makes of a totally conditioned social being someone who does not render back completely what his conditioning has given him.
>
> (Sartre, 1969: 59)

The human capacity for thinking in time leads to the human capacity for evolution of thought. Learning to get better at roaming around the double figure eight and the lemniscate are the path towards dialectical change. The lemniscate, incidentally, resembles the double helix of DNA in its twisted figure eight shape.

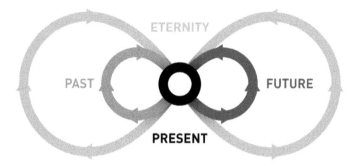

Figure 5.4 Movement around time (Deurzen, 2025)

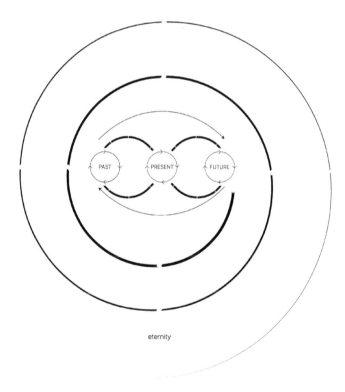

Figure 5.5 The dialectics of time (Deurzen and Arnold-Baker, 2018)

Application of the Lens of Time

So, how do we take all this information and use it as part of our Structural Existential Analysis?

1. Make a clear record of the sequence of events your participants are recounting and notice what percentage of these are in the past, present, future or eternity.
2. Systematically record how the participant is circling between comments about the present, the past, the future and eternity (or universality) and is engaging with time.
3. Find a way to plot the participant's dynamic movement in time, and where it may be blocked or stagnating in a pattern that no longer allows for full exploration of all time-zones.
4. Make a timeline of the progress a person has made or is making in terms of the particular topic of investigation. Include ups and downs and combine with The Four Worlds for more specific information to show up.
5. Make a formulation of how the person is shaping their ec-static movement in time.
6. To what extent are they aware of their playful exploration of the dimension of time in their lives and to what extent do they experience themselves as being in charge of their time experience, or at the mercy of it. Are they active or passive, steady or volatile in their movement?

Illustration from Our Pilot Project on Freedom

One of our participants, who we named Olga, described how she had moved on a lot in the way she regarded freedom, thus immediately introducing the dynamic theme of progress and improvement in her experience and understanding.

Right at the start of her interview she said:

> I can't imagine anyone being totally free, I don't think that is possible [**eternity**], but I do remember [**past**] quite a number of times in my life when I've felt free. However, the time [**past/specific**] I was reminded of the most was like 20 years ago when I used my hard-won financial freedom [**future planning**] which is always the most difficult aspect for me [**eternity**], to do things that I couldn't have done otherwise . . . It was a time when my life could have taken many different directions . . . [**past/future**].

Olga is looking back over her past life and wondering whether and when she may have been most free. Even as part of that statement she is looping back into the present ('always the most difficult aspect for me'), with a statement that establishes a universal stability about herself, despite the fact she is speaking about the freedom to go in many different directions.

She is also remembering how for a long time, she planned this time of freedom, as she goes on to describe how she had to work in an unpleasant job for a long time to accumulate enough money to buy her freedom. Her freedom then was poised at the end of a period of great unfreedom. In her memory this dynamic reality returns as evidence of her capacity for playing with freedom and with time. She positions herself very clearly as a mistress of time, musing over her capacity of planning for freedom, in her past.

She goes on to describe how she deliberately planned for this period of total freedom, dealing with financial obligations very firmly to be able to allow herself a space of complete openness of decision making. What she describes is like an experiment in living, an experiment to see whether she can capture and own her own life for a while and have the time to herself to do with as she wished.

The dialogue with the researcher then proceeds as follows:

Researcher: A lot of people would say that is frightening as it would expose them to a lot of things, wouldn't it?
Olga: Yeah, but I wanted that. I wanted to encounter life in ways that I hadn't encountered it before or only a little bit.
Researcher: Right – [pause]
Olga: That is really what I wanted and, um, for some time I did that in a very different way when I was young, but I never travelled a lot, so I wanted to see this planet.
Researcher: [nodding] But you are saying more than that: you're saying you wanted to do that on your own and yes, you wanted to explore the planet, but you also wanted to open yourself to life.
Olga: Yes, very much
Researcher: In a way you welcomed whatever was coming with that and you felt obviously able and capable and even excited to welcome all of that, is that correct?
Olga: I was very excited about all of that but also scared of course, um . . .

Olga was describing a position of total openness to whatever the future might bring. She notes that this was exciting and scary at the same time. Then she proceeds to remember how unnecessary it turned out to have been for her to be so scared, because in her travels she ended up feeling safer than in her town of residence, London. So, she is remembering (past loop), how she felt before her freedom, because she was projecting a certain image of that freedom onto the imagined future. She is then placing herself back in the present and making a judgement about how safe her freedom actually turned out to be (in the past). This is almost like looping into the past to remind herself that past fears were unnecessary and to remind herself of this ahead of future freedoms.

From there she goes on to consider the whole aspect of insecurity that tends to come with freedom and she is able to see that there was not much freedom in living a stable life in which she didn't own her own space. She could also see that spending several weeks in the first new place she went to, which was in the United States, provided her with temporary safety. She is beginning to explore how freedom becomes structured into different phases of time, with that structure providing the necessary security, but the knowledge of being able to skip from one phase to the other at will still providing the liberty.

Her round the world ticket was valid for a certain period of time only and allowed for a certain number of stops. In this way she was unintentionally bringing new shape to the otherwise boundless sense of freedom to go wherever she wanted and do whatever she chose. It is clear she found this reassuring.

She then proceeds to recount a series of events and random meetings that led her, totally out of the blue, to committing to directing an opera in the Far East, which could be said to be a very demanding and constraining experience, but which flowed out of her willingness to have an open mind about how she would spend her available time and energy. It is only in thinking about the sequence of events that it is becoming clear to her that she was in fact making new commitments and restraining her freedom in this way, at that time. And yet, in those days, when this was happening, it felt like exhilarating freedom, because it was all a spontaneous adventure and an experiment.

Olga goes on to describe that out of this random event she ended up returning to the Far East to live for ten years. She is clearly enchanted with the way in which her life evolved, by allowing herself this freedom. Freedom led to a huge and enduring change for her. She laughs a lot about this and begins to tell a number of stories of the amazing adventures she had in this process. She is delighted with herself, relishing her remembrance of the freedom she had created in her life. The researcher remarks that it sounds as if she became more confident about herself. This leads to Olga recounting examples of her sexual freedom and experimentation. This fed into her exploring how by travelling around the planet she got to know so many different people and how that changed her. It is as if it is dawning on her that allowing change in life is what defines that freedom.

The sequence then is of her remembering how opening space and time and travelling and allowing herself new explorations exposed her to a greater variety of experiences, opening up new options, so that change began to happen in her and for her. It became obvious that she felt that the fluidity of this change was characteristic of the experience of freedom and led to her increased confidence that she was able to deal with any change on her path.

This leads to Olga exploring other changes she made in her life, in the more remote past, when she first moved to London from her home country. She contrasts the magnitude of that change with the sort of experiences she had in the Southern Hemisphere, when she suddenly realised with a shock that the sun was travelling in the opposite direction. This is a very interesting observation in terms of time and relativity and says something about how a person's perspective gets widened when they realise that the way they normally see the passage of time in a day can be completely altered, when realising time is relative and even the earth's position in relation to the sun is relative to where we are. All of these, Olga realised, were markers of open change and freedom. All these memories plunged her into obvious joy and pleasure at recalling her adventures. Olga relishes the thought of all her discoveries during this phase of freedom. She says: 'it's a very different way of experiencing life'.

Difference is the marker of change and of dynamic movement from one thing or one state to another. Olga is highly aware of how this experience of difference affected her and made her freer. Olga notes that it was the experience itself that affected her. She says:

> It was the actual moment to moment experience – sensory and also emotional experience – of being in a different place. So for example, when you went to the desert right, if you were in it, it's very flat and when you sleep outside and you open your eyes the stars go all the way down to the ground. Which again for me was a very important experience and I didn't know that either. I didn't expect it, I didn't see anything like it before and it made me feel connected to beyond this planet, to the world that we live in, the real world, which is the world of the galaxy and that's, you can't get more real.

Olga's awareness of living a different moment to moment reality had put her in touch with a feeling of timelessness and belonging to something beyond space and time. It is as if she had opened up her capacity for observing, sensing, feeling and making meaning and in doing so brought herself back into the eternal flow of time.

She describes this experience as one of awe, but also mentions how it made her fear she might fall off the planet, as if she were no longer securely attached to it. This became like a metaphysical experience for her that affected her deeply. She contrasts it to her previous, past experiences of living in a small space, surrounded by walls, in a city and losing track of the vastness of the universe. She describes this sense of endless freedom as a very physical experience, which she recognised from reading science fiction books. Science fiction books are a very interesting category of reading, in that they project the reader into an unknown future, where very specific events and experiences take place. It is a kind of fantasy world which allows a person to travel in time and experiment with different ways of living and different ideas about the world. It is a world of imagination, outside of time, and Olga was able to really allow herself to merge into this experience of existing outside of time in a more endless way.

At this point the dialogue goes like this:

Researcher: Hmm, that sounds to me like you were travelling into the infinite as if you were . . .
Olga: Yes!
Researcher: going beyond human temporality into a sort of pre-death, post-death ultimate, infinite kind of perception of what is.
Olga: Yes that is extremely well put [laughter]. I say yes that is a really good description of it, yeah. Yeah, and I will say that I had, um, similar experiences in a smaller way.
Researcher: Yeah?
Olga: All along the way.

Olga now takes full flight into recounting how these experiences led to her writing and publishing about her new understanding of time and space. It is obvious that the years of freedom she gave herself transformed her life completely. The progression is vertiginous, as she talks the researcher through the many things she came to realise in doing all this. During this phase of the interview, Olga keeps skipping forwards and backwards, introducing different time zones and moments of her personal history, linking them together in various ways. It is almost as if she is weaving a tapestry of time.

As the interview is coming to its end, the researcher asks a specific question, which has thus far not yet been answered:

Researcher: You have shown us so much about the importance of freedom and how you lived it in so many different ways, but what was the dark side of freedom? What is the limit of freedom?

Olga: I think these are two different things. Like the limit of freedom, well the financial limits, the limits of the lifespan, I've always thought I've wanted to live several hundred years to see what happens. I've always wanted to travel to another galaxy, I probably won't be able to do that so I suppose what I would call real limits which is where the outside world limits my freedom and of course there are many, many, others. The dark side of freedom? I would say that for me personally for my own life I can't see any but . . .

Researcher: Hmmm.

Olga: because it may sound funny to you, but I've never had enough freedom.

Looking at this through the lens of time is again very interesting. Olga actually speaks about time travel, wanting to travel in space to a different galaxy. It is as if her real freedom would consist of travelling outside of time for real. She resents the limits of the human reality that stop her achieving that kind of freedom. So, she hasn't come to see any dark side of freedom because she has not yet been fully plunged into freedom or explored the limits of freedom.

With a bit of challenge, she comes to remember that she has been able to observe a dark side of freedom in other people, for instance in people who were given unlimited financial resources and opportunities from early on in life and who had ended up not being able to make anything of it. She saw that they ended up squandering that freedom, unlike her who had to work hard to buy herself a time of unlimited freedom and who therefore knew how precious it was and should be used carefully. This is an interesting observation in terms of time. It is as if she came to realise that the limit of the amount of time of freedom we are given helps us in appreciating the freedom. When it is dispersed in time and becomes uncontained and endless, it is boundless and becomes unusable.

To demonstrate that there are different ways to approach the SEA analysis we did a more formal analysis of the use of time of each participant. When the temporal

Table 5.1 Summary of Olga's temporal themes

Temporal Dimension	Theme	Descriptor
Past	Always needing but not achieving complete freedom	Have always wanted freedom for a long time
	Smaller jumps into freedom	Feeling free a number of times, where life could have taken different directions but it wasn't possible to have freedom in a more complete way
Present	Now is the time	Recognising the moment that freedom becomes a realistic possibility
	Freedom is fleeting	Freedom didn't last very long, travelling for a year, freedom is very, very, temporary but then the earth is very temporary too
Future	Limit of age	Does age limit the experience of freedom that is wanted?
Eternity	Total freedom can only be experienced outside of mortal limits	Wanting to live several hundred years, or to travel to another galaxy, the outside world always limits experience of total freedom

dimensions were tracked throughout the transcript and meaning statements were highlighted and grouped together under each temporal dimension, overall themes for each dimension were identified. In the analysis the aim is to bring out the underlying theme for that temporal dimension, to try to capture the essence, or the main meaning that the participant was describing, both implicit and explicit. It is important for the researcher to stay close to the participants' words and the sense of the meaning the participants are attributing to their experiences to ensure that researcher bias is not introduced. Theme titles should also include elements of the participant's expression so as to capture that individual experience. It is only when the analyses of various participants are brought together that researchers will need to craft theme titles that encompass different elements of an experience. This will be described later in Chapter 10.

The themes that were identified from Olga's experience of freedom over time, in the various temporal dimensions, are summarised in Table 5.1.

In terms of tracking the temporal aspects within the transcript we can see that for Olga there is more emphasis on the past and how it had been difficult for her to experience total freedom, either through a lack of financial security or it not being the right time for her to embark on experiencing freedom in the way that she wanted, i.e. through travelling. The present is also well represented for Olga

Table 5.2 Olga's experience of freedom over time

Total Freedom		Travelling the world			
Free	Migrating to London		Living in the Far East		Possibility of freedom in the future
Unfree Childhood			Brexit		Returning to home country
PAST →		**PRESENT**		→	**FUTURE**

when she describes her experience of freedom and how it came about and how it was experienced. There was less emphasis for Olga on the future, where freedom seemed to be blocked again by age or financial limitations and for the eternity dimension there is a real sense of how the physical dimension of existence, being unable to live for hundreds of years or travel through space, were the real existential limits on her experience of freedom.

If we wanted to represent Olga's experience of freedom over time in the various experiences she recounted it may look like that shown in Table 5.2.

Filtering the freedom interviews through the lens of time was extremely productive, but it brought out different aspects of the time limits of freedom for different participants. It made a big difference whether participants allowed themselves to re-experience the past (as if re-living it in the present) and whether they were prepared to speculate about the remote future, how expressive they were about the element of time and its impact on their freedom.

Chapter 6

The Filter of SPACE

Introduction

The filter of space is every bit as important as the filter of time. When we talk about space it conjures up the realm of the cosmos, of our planet, the universe and something beyond us. But space can also relate to our terrestrial space and the way we are situated in the material and physical world. We relate to this world through our body and we are always immersed in a natural or human made environment around us. This involves many layered relationships, as we remain stationary or move horizontally (left and right), sagitally (forwards or backwards), or vertically (up and down) in the world. Aspects of our relationship to space that are not often considered are the amount of space we take up in the world, our relationship to space and our internal representations of space. Spatial awareness will imply awareness of movement and of the type and direction of travel; it makes a big difference whether we move alongside, against, over, under, around, between or away from something. All these rather overlooked aspects of our existence offer up rich elements for exploration and understanding in existential research as we will demonstrate in this chapter.

Being-in-the-World and the Four Dimensions

The concept of space as it relates to our relationship with the world we live in was a key aspect of Heidegger's (1962 [1927]) philosophical work. Heidegger noted that human beings never exist in isolation; he stated that we are interconnected beings and therefore should never be considered as entities that exist in isolation. Heidegger coined the term 'being-in-the-world' (*In-der-Welt-sein*), which he used to denote and emphasise this interconnection. There is never a person without a world. He emphasised this essential connectivity by using hyphens to link the words together, mirroring that intertwining of human beings and their world. Heidegger believed that we were not just in relationship with other beings but also with the world at large and everything it contains. Heidegger stated that human beings existed essentially as being-with (*Mitsein*), and that an ontological aspect of our existence was that it was utterly relational. This means that humans are also *being-with* whatever and whomever they are in contact with, whether that is other people, animals, physical objects, ideas or the environment.

Heidegger's philosophy had a big impact on Ludwig Binswanger (1881–1966), a Swiss psychiatrist who was looking for alternative perspectives to understand his patients. Binswanger observed that when people came to him for treatment, they were not just bringing their symptoms but their whole world into his consulting room. Binswanger took a similar view to Heidegger and saw that different elements of a person's life cannot be examined in isolation, yet this was the way in which the medical model was designed; to only look at symptoms and diagnosis and ignore other unrelated aspects of a person's life. Binswanger was the first person to apply Heidegger's philosophy to therapy and his existential analysis, or *Daseinsanalyse*, consisted of trying to describe the structure of human existence.

Binswanger (1946) was particularly taken by Heidegger's concepts of *Mitsein*, or being-with, and *In-der-Welt-sein*, or being-in-the-world. He combined these concepts with the ideas of von Uexküll (1921), a German biologist who was interested in animal behaviour and had also observed that different species of animals related to their environment (*Umwelt*) in different ways, focusing on those aspects that were most important for their survival. Although Binswanger was later criticised for misinterpreting Heidegger's philosophy (Holzhey-Kunz, 2019), his combination of these two ways of looking at human existence was very productive. Von Uexküll is most famous for elaborating the notion of *Umwelt*, which refers to the specific environment each animal relates to. He showed that every animal species had its own specific way of relating to its surrounding world, depending on its needs and perceptions. The *Umwelt* comprises a perception world (*Merkwelt*) and an action world (*Aktionwelt*). These two worlds interact constantly so that the animal can make sense of its environment and meet its needs. Binswanger believed that von Uexküll's *Umwelt* could be made relevant for human beings too. However, he noted that human beings didn't just perceive and act on their environment, but they also related to this world and to others in their world. Binswanger stated:

> 'World', however, signifies not only world-formation and predesign of world, but – on the basis of the predesign and model-image – also the *how* of *being-in-the-world* and the attitude *toward* world.
>
> (Binswanger, 1946: 195)

In the same way von Uexküll believed each animal had its own *Umwelt* or environment, Binswanger believed every human being was connected to a world-project, which was unique to that individual. He further elaborated the world project into three dimensions as highlighted below, that of the *Umwelt*, the *Mitwelt* and the *Eigenwelt*:

> This *materialité* of the world-design, originating from the 'key' (*Gestimmtheit*) of existence, is by no means confined to the environment, to the world of things, or to the universe in general, but refers equally to the world of one's fellow men (*Mitwelt*) and to the self-world (*Eigenwelt*).
>
> (Binswanger, 1946: 212)

Interestingly, Alice Holzhey-Kunz (2019) notes that Binswanger's Daseinsanalysis was developed originally as a type of psychiatric research method before it became a therapeutic approach. In essence his world-project has returned full circle back into one of the lenses of SEA.

Rollo May (1983), an American existential psychologist, also applied Binswanger's structure to his therapeutic work. But it was Emmy van Deurzen, a psychologist, existential therapist and philosopher, who developed and integrated Binswanger's work into a framework to structure existential-phenomenological therapeutic practice and research. Deurzen (2012 [1988]) added a further world or dimension, that of spirituality or the *Uberwelt*, to Binswanger's formulation. This four-dimensional approach has become the cornerstone of the British School of Existential Psychotherapy's way of working.

The Four Dimensions of Existence

The four dimensions of existence as elucidated by Deurzen (2012 [1988], 2010 [1997]) and written about extensively by both of the authors of this present volume (Deurzen and Arnold-Baker, 2005, 2018, 2019) have been used as a framework for therapeutic practice by Emmy van Deurzen since the mid-seventies. This framework, used in conjunction with phenomenological methods, provides a structure to facilitate in-depth exploration of the client's ways of being-in-the-world. This application of Binswanger's world-project stays close to his initial desire to move away from a medical model which focuses on symptom reduction. It encourages a descriptive and expansive method which helps the client to understand for themselves how they relate in the different dimensions of their lives, thus gaining a deeper insight into themselves and the way they live their lives. This framework has been taught and used by therapists in the British School of Existential Psychotherapy for 40 years and therefore is a well-established method. For those interested in seeing how the framework is used in clinical practice please refer to the authors' joint chapter 'The Case of Rahim' (Deurzen and Arnold-Baker, 2019) for a more detailed demonstration.

Umwelt – *The Physical Dimension*

Human beings begin life as bodies that are *thrown* (*geworfen*) (Heidegger, 1962) into a physical world that pre-existed them and over which they have no control. *Umwelt* means the world around us, or the environment. Merleau-Ponty (2013 [1945]) emphasised how our experience is always an embodied one as it is through our bodies that we encounter the world and other people, as well as ourselves. The *Umwelt* therefore relates to our relationships to different aspects of our embodied existence. It includes our relationship with our:

- Embodiment
- Physical autonomy
- Bodily function – health and illness, strength and weakness

- Physical contact with others
- Senses and sensations
- Consumption of food and drink and other substances
- Comfort and discomfort in response to the physical qualities of the world around
- Wealth and poverty
- Wider physical environment, climate, light and dark and time
- Relationships with animals, nature and other creatures
- Sexuality and sexual drives
- Procreation – life and death.

(Deurzen and Arnold-Baker, 2005: 27–30)

Each of the above highlights or reveals something of an individual's relationship to the environment that they live in and their relationship to, or their experience of, their body.

Mitwelt – *The Social Dimension*

Heidegger's concept of Thrownness (*Geworfenheit*) into a pre-existing world extends to the social dimension too. Individuals are born into societies and cultures that are pre-determined and affect them. *Mitwelt* literally means with-world, and Heidegger's concept of *Mitsein*, or Being-with, is also relevant as we are always in relationship with others and indeed our relationships with others help us to get a sense of who we are. Developmentally, therefore, the social dimension comes after the physical dimension. Relationships with others also impact emotions and feelings. The social dimension therefore concerns:

- How we relate to others
- How we confront the peculiarity of love
- Family dynamics
- Relationships and emotions
- Belonging and isolation
- Competition and submission
- Different types of relationships
- Social structures and discourses
- Communication and language.

(Deurzen and Arnold-Baker, 2005: 89–91)

Each of these aspects will position, or situate, an individual in their relational sphere, and will emphasise the complexity of human relationships which are multi-faceted.

Eigenwelt – *The Personal Dimension*

Eigenwelt means own world and is usually translated as personal or inner world. The emotions and feelings that are evoked by our relationships with others and our experiences of the world allow us to create an internal sense of ourselves. As human relationships are dynamic it follows that people are also dynamic creations. We are more like a dynamic process than a solid entity, or an essential self, as has been elaborated amply by existential philosophers such as Kierkegaard, Heidegger and Sartre. The personal dimension regards the discovery of:

- The fact that we exist and that we are something rather than nothing
- That we are 'me' rather than anyone else
- Who we are
- The fact that experience will always be personal and private to the individual
- That reflection brings acceptance of oneself
- Personal characteristics that are brought to light through other people's observations
- The boundaries of personal freedom
- The anxiety that comes with being an individual
- Strengths and weaknesses
- Dependency and independence
- Loneliness and isolation
- The flexible nature of self.

(Deurzen and Arnold-Baker, 2005: 157–159)

The personal dimension concerns a personal discovery of who we are, how we identify and how we make sense of ourselves as individuals. It is also the realm of authenticity and inauthenticity and relates to our choices, freedom and responsibility, all existential themes and structures of human existence.

Uberwelt – *The Spiritual Dimension*

Uberwelt literally means 'over world', or world above, and refers to the world of ideas and transcendence. This final stage of development focuses on how individuals create meaning and purpose in their lives. There is often a misunderstanding that the spiritual dimension focuses solely on religion and whilst a person's relationship to religion would fall under this dimension, the spiritual dimension is much broader than this. It is about how people make sense of the world that they live in and of the relationships they have with others and themselves. It is about their worldview, and the ideas that determine what they value. Meaning is created through values and beliefs and what is important to a person. It is also created through intention and purpose and all these elements make up the spiritual dimension. It is in essence a philosophical dimension but also concerns our relationship with the metaphysical realm of existence, and our relationship to that which is beyond us. The spiritual dimension concerns a reflection of:

- How *thrownness* evolves into a person's worldview based on our culture, society and place in history
- Our relationship to differing and contrasting views and perspectives which can challenge our worldview

- Our experience of what is beneficial or harmful, good or evil
- The beliefs, assumptions and principles that we are aware of and the realisation that others are out of current awareness
- How intuition can be used to sense something that is invisible, intangible and beyond our experience
- How beliefs are connected to expectations
- How values shape what is important in life
- How events can lead to a re-evaluation of life.

(Deurzen and Arnold-Baker, 2005: 217–219)

The spiritual dimension centres on how people understand their lives and themselves, how they make sense of what happens to them and how that links to their meaning and purpose in life.

Taken together the four dimensions can chart out a person's developmental process and provide a map of their life. Table 6.1 provides an illustrative summary of the four dimensions and their main concerns. It would be foolish to suggest that a complete map can ever be charted, as human relationships are too complex and too interrelated and changeable to capture and fixate. Therefore, the four dimensions are best used as a framework or structure, to provide a snapshot of where a person is at that point in their life. In terms of research the four dimensions are useful in capturing and elucidating how a particular event or situation is experienced in a 360 degree view. Already you will see that if you start to apply the different aspects detailed above to a research topic a lot more detail can be elicited.

Space and Spatiality

The focus of the chapter so far has been on the differing aspects of relationships people have with things and people in the world and the relationship they have with themselves. The world in this context can be understood as the space in which a person dwells and interacts. *Being* relational is one way of existing in space but spatiality also involves our perceptions of space both internal and external. As this aspect of spatiality is connected to perception, Merleau-Ponty's (2013 [1945]) philosophy is pertinent here. He states: 'Space is not the setting (real or logical) in which things are arranged, but the means whereby the position of things becomes possible' (Merleau-Ponty, 2013 [1945]: 243).

In the same way that we are always connected to the world, we are also always orientated in the world in some way. Our senses give us an indication of where objects and others are in relation to us, and we get a feel of the things that are near and things that are in the distance. This also involves a dynamic element as we can assess how things move in space, towards or away from us for instance. Binswanger (quoted in a chapter by Ellenberger, 1958) was also interested in spatiality and proposed different ways in which we encounter space, such as Oriented Space and Attuned Space. Adams (1998) reformulated the dimensions to make Liminal Space a category of its own; Binswanger had situated it within Attuned

Table 6.1 Summary of the four dimensions and their main concerns

World	Umwelt	Mitwelt	Eigenwelt	Uberwelt
Physical survival	**Nature:** Earth, climate, weather, seasons, animals, plants, shelter, hygiene, sleep, competence in facing a range of dangers, materiality, birth and death, sensory experience	**Things:** Care for objects, crafts, technology, arts, bodily skills in handling instruments, objects, creativity, productivity	**Body:** Self-care, movement, comfort seeking, toughening, strength, appearance, sexuality, health, food, drink, elimination, hygiene, sleep, body sculpting	**Cosmos:** Connectivity, patterns, solar system, universe, death and birth, creation myth, afterlife myth. Understanding place in universe; deal with what is the case, in the present. Now
Social affiliation	**Society:** Human world. Public demands of individual, laws, rules, regulations, administration, order, duties, responsibility, abilities of communication and language	**Others:** Respect, care of others, love and hate, dominance/submission, competition, rivalry, collaboration, mutuality, generosity. Emotion. Space	**Ego:** Strength of self-presentation and representation, having a voice, achieving something for self and others, assertion	**Culture:** Past traditions established by others, personal contribution to culture, memes, things valued by the group, belonging. Deal with what humanity has established in the past. History

(Continued)

Table 6.1 (Continued)

World	Umwelt	Mitwelt	Eigenwelt	Uberwelt
Personal identity	**Person:** Private world, personal sphere or hiding, place of safety, intimate reality, sanctuary. Home. Managing aloneness and autonomy	**Me:** Feeling of mineness and authentic right to exist, a sense of inner reality, individuality and anxiety	**Self:** Authentic being, personality, character, selfhood, mastering strengths and weakness. Thought, memory, imagination	**Consciousness:** Awareness, intentionality, mindfulness, capacity for contemplation and understanding and knowing. Sciences. Deal with what it is possible to image and create. Future
Spiritual meaning	**Infinite:** Ultimate reality, the principles defining reality, ideology, the divine, the unsayable. Making sense of the world. Greatest Object of Devotion (GOD)	**Ideas:** The meanings and values we attribute to life and the world, concepts, beliefs, principles to live by. Capacity for doubt	**Spirit:** The spark of vitality of life energy, the core where we breathe: connection with all that is. Our essence or soul, that what matters	**Conscience:** Capacity of deciding, making meaning, by distinguishing between good and bad, right and wrong, transcending ourselves, transformation. Contemplation. Creativity, options, freedom. Time

Space. Adams also added a fourth category of the Natural Space, so that each spatial dimension corresponded to the Four Dimensions.

Oriented Space is as just described, our ordinary experience of space. As we use our senses to determine the space around us and the objects and people it contains, the central focus is the body. The body represents the point from which the space is perceived – Binswanger refers to the vertical axis and the horizontal axis of the experience of space. Merleau-Ponty also saw the body as central to our experience when he said: 'I cannot understand the function of the living body except by enacting it myself, and except in so far as I am a body which rises towards the world' (Merleau-Ponty, 2013 [1945]: 75). He believed that as part of our body image we intuitively know where our body begins and ends and have a sense of where our body, or parts of our body, are in relation to other objects for example. Likewise in relation to movement our body moves intuitively in response to stimuli in the world. This led Merleau-Ponty to conclude that the 'body is a meaningful core' (p. 147). It could be argued that it also encapsulates the space taken up by individuals in the world, some trying to take up little space, attempting to become invisible, whereas others may be 'larger than life' and are experienced as a big presence. This dimension would equate to the *Mitwelt* as it relates to the social dimension of existence. Most of this work has been further elucidated by scientific research on proprioception and interoception. This has proven especially useful in working with people with autism, or those recovering from strokes (Goodall and Brownlow, 2022). Binswanger's second spatial dimension is Attuned Space, which refers to a person's mood or emotion. He argued that how a person feels impacts their sense of space, or their experience of space affects their moods and emotions. Someone suffering from depression may describe feeling down, another person, who was having a good day, may say that their spirits had been lifted. This dimension relates to an internal representation of space, one that may feel constricted or expansive, depending on their context. Attuned Space links to the *Eigenwelt* with the focus on a person's thoughts and feelings.

The Liminal Space, which Adams (1998) suggests is the third dimension as it connects to the *Überwelt* (Deurzen, 2010), and has been developed by Minkowski's ideas around '"clear" and "dark" space', where *clear space* is a free space, connected to the horizon, perspective and distance. *Dark space* on the other hand refers to being in 'obscurity or in a fog'; it is a narrowed space, devoid of people. *Luminous space* is connected to more 'mystical and ecstatic experiences' and relates to the cosmos, an expansive space. Adams does not elucidate the fourth dimension, the Natural Space, further except to note that it refers 'to the solid reliability of the world which is there' (Adams, 1998: 8).

Spatiality and Phenomenological Research

Spatiality has been an aspect of previous phenomenological research methods, such as Van Manen's Hermeneutic Phenomenology and Ashworth's Lifeworld method. Van Manen states 'All phenomenological human science research efforts are really explorations into the structure of the human lifeworld, the lived world as experienced in everyday situations and relations' (Van Manen, 1990: 101). Van Manen highlights what he calls four existentials which he believes are the underlying aspects of the lifeworld. These are '*lived space* (spatiality), *lived body* (corporeality), *lived time* (temporality) and *lived human relation* (relationality or communality)' (p. 101). Van Manen suggests that these themes are useful to reflect upon during the process of composing interview questions and during the process of analysis.

Van Manen describes *lived space* as felt space and our relationship and orientation to space reveals meaning for an individual and therefore is important to investigate during research. *Lived body* refers to our embodied existence and the fact that we are always meeting others and the world as a body and our body simultaneously reveals and conceals something about ourselves in that meeting. For Van Manen *lived time* refers to temporality and an individual's experience of time (this has already been explored in Chapter 5). *Lived human relation* is similar to the social dimension and concerns how individuals relate to each other in an embodied way. Van Manen's Hermeneutic Phenomenology is concerned with uncovering meaning themes which form a description of the phenomenon under consideration. For Van Manen the writing of the findings is an important aspect of the research and one way in which this can be done 'is to weave one's phenomenological description against the existentials' (1990: 172).

Similarly, the Lifeworld method proposed by Ashworth (2003, 2017) shares similarities with Van Manen and SEA with its focus on the situatedness of an individual and how that situatedness impacts their experience. Ashworth (2003), influenced by Merleau-Ponty's philosophy, suggests seven Fractions of the Lifeworld which include Selfhood, Sociality, Embodiment, Temporality, Spatiality, Project and Discourse. The Fractions of the Lifeworld act as heuristics to guide the analysis in a similar way as the SEA heuristics do. Ashworth (2016) stresses that the fractions are not categories of a phenomenon and whilst they may be present in all phenomena some will carry more weight or significance than others. *Self-hood*, an element that is missing in Van Manen's four existentials (Arnold-Baker, 2015), refers to a person's sense of self as well as their identity or the relationship they have with themselves. It is also about a person's agency and aspects that matter to an individual. It is a lot like the *Eigenwelt*, the personal dimension, in SEA. Ashworth's *Sociality* fraction maps well onto the social dimension as it concerns interpersonal relations. *Embodiment* relates to an individual's experience of their body, and Ashworth considers emotions as well as gender in this fraction as well as the actual bodily experience. *Temporality* concerns the 'flow of events' similarly to Van Manen's *existentials* and the lens of Time in SEA. *Spatiality* for Ashworth links place with embodiment but it would also concern social norms as well as spatial meanings. It is covered by the lens of Space in SEA. The sixth fraction is *Project* which Ashworth draws from Sartre's notion of project. He describes this fraction as 'how does the situation relate to the person's ability to carry out the activities they are committed to and which they regard as central?' (Ashworth, 2003: 28). It links with the lens of Purpose or Intentionality in SEA. The final fraction *Discourse* concerns 'what sort of terms are employed to describe the experience in which we are interested?' This is a meaning fractal, similar to the *Uberwelt* in SEA. Also, he looks at the cultural forms that surround the experience (Ashworth, 2003: 29), which links with the social dimension in SEA. Ashworth (2016) later added an eighth fraction as he believed it was important to consider *Mood-as-Atmosphere*, drawing on the work of Henry and Heidegger, who both observed that there is always a mood attached to any experience. In SEA we focus very centrally on passion, mood and emotions through the application of the lens of Passion for the same reason.

Application of the Lens of Space

Space and the Four Dimensions are the most popular of the heuristics that doctoral students apply to their SEA research. This is mainly because students are interested in gaining a more holistic perspective of the phenomena under investigation and believe that this heuristic will enable them to explore the lifeworld or world-project in deeper ways. The use of this lens has formed part of the reproach Vos (2021) levels at SEA, critiquing the use of a structure, and in this case the use of the four dimensions as he believes it artificially leads researchers to try to fit their findings into these pre-determined categories. This criticism appears to be based on a misunderstanding on the part of Vos, who does not appreciate that the four dimensions are used in a flexible way rather than in such a rigid fashion. Phenomena are not uniquely allocated in one category. They are interwoven and have multiple touch points. The four dimensions as applied in SEA are based on philosophical thought and years of clinical practice entailing observations of thousands of hours of talking to people about their lives. The four dimensions in a clinical setting have been used as an organising principle to help practitioners deepen their exploration and understanding of the multiple aspects of phenomena rather than as a means of classifying things once and for all. This same framework can be used for existential research too. As Ashworth (2016) states, the structures, whether they are SEA heuristics or Lifeworld fractions, are a means of structuring data obtained, rather than distorting data by trying to fit data or capta into categories that do not appear or apply. In fact, dimensions that are not represented also tell us something about the experience or phenomena and that can be important to reflect on as part of the analysis. Fitting data into heuristics or fractions that do not belong to it goes against the practice of epochē in phenomenological research. Remember to keep an open mind and not to let your structures take over and close down your observations but keep returning to your phenomenological openness. This relates to the danger of researchers falling into researchers' fallacy which Brooks et al. warn is where 'a researcher can unintentionally impose their own meanings onto research participants' accounts or actions' (Brooks et al., 2015: 6). Epochē and the phenomenological method of SOAR (see Chapter 2) are essential in ensuring that researchers continually question themselves on *how* they are elucidating meaning statements but also *how* they are categorising them further. Going back to the phenomena themselves in a non-judgemental way will keep your lens as clear as is possible.

Because of this there are many variations of the four-world model that can be applied to SEA research. One of the most useful ones is to combine the *Umwelt*, *Mitwelt*, *Eigenwelt*, *Uberwelt* descriptors with the more down to earth physical, social, personal and spiritual ones, to arrive at a square of 16 existential locations, which can orientate the discourse of participants in more specific ways and which is also more conducive to recording flow and overlap.

Conducting Spatial Analysis

1. Orientation

Once the researcher has a transcript to work with, the task becomes to interrogate the participants' words and to organise and categorise them so that the meaning and experience of the phenomena under investigation is brought out. The most important part of this process has been highlighted by Van Manen's (1990) work and that is for the researcher to remain orientated to the research question at all stages of the analysis. Participants sometimes go off track in their descriptions of their experiences and researchers often get caught up in the story of what the participant is saying rather than focusing on what they are looking for as determined by the research question. Keeping the research question at the forefront of the analysis from the start will help. It will also help to connect the researcher to the epochē so as to prevent bias and researcher fallacy creeping in.

2. Highlighting Meaning Units

The second aspect for the researcher to keep in mind is what they are attempting to draw out. This objective is linked to the first but when the researcher looks at the transcript, they need to start identifying what other researchers have called meaning units. These are words, sentences or small paragraphs which capture something of the experience being studied. The researcher will initially read through the transcript several times to get fully immersed into the participant's experience before the procedure of highlighting meaning units. To start with the researcher may feel like they have highlighted most of the transcript text but during the process of analysis the text will be reduced and focused into main themes. The different stages of analysis represent a funnelling process, taking a large amount of data or *capta* and reducing it to a small number of major themes, usually fewer than ten.

A recommended format for dealing with the capta at this stage is to put all of the individual highlighted meaning units into a table, where each meaning unit takes up one row. A blank column can be added to the right for the researcher to add notes, tentative theme titles and coding of the heuristics. An example of this kind of table can be found in Table 6.2 as part of the analysis of Bonnie's transcript for the research on freedom.

Doctoral students at NSPC who have used SEA in their research often struggle with the coding of the dimensions as some aspects may cross different dimensions. This is understandable as life is not neat and structured, it is messy and complicated.

Table 6.2 Example of working with meaning units in SEA research

And that's about all I can remember, a bit like a dream but it really, really, happened but I did want . . . But I never told anyone. I didn't tell my parents I didn't go hey guess what? No, it was private.	Experience of freedom: Bit like a dream [spiritual] Private experience [personal]
I think it was real um and I have to say that . . . yeah . . . how can you put it? I've, I've, never, I've always, from a young age, wake up in the morning, often, and think ooo, I wonder what is going to happen today?	Experience of freedom: A real experience Wonder what is going to happen today [spiritual] What will happen today [temporal]

We recommend that researchers consider what and how the participant refers to a particular element and that will guide the researcher. As Sadia stated in her research:

> SEA provides us with this framework of the four worlds' model to enable us to grasp all the dimensions of the lived experience and not to inadvertently ignore, for example, the spiritual or the social aspect whilst considering the experience. An important aspect here is to understand that the four worlds' model does not in any way imply any separation between the various domains of experience. The challenges faced by the individuals cannot be neatly allocated to any one particular dimension; rather any challenge will involve facets spread over multiple dimensions of existence.
>
> (Sadia, 2020: 75)

Garland (2019) also applied this format in her analysis of the lived experiences of new mothers' transition to motherhood building on the research of one of the current authors (Arnold-Baker, 2015). Arnold-Baker demonstrated in her research on the experience of first-time mothers how the heuristic of space can be used with other research methodologies. Arnold-Baker analysed her data using Van Manen's hermeneutic phenomenological approach and then applied the spatial heuristic to the themes that had been identified. This process enabled Arnold-Baker to discover that becoming a mother impacted women on all four dimensions of existence. This was an important finding which went some way to explaining why mothers often experience motherhood to be challenging, and she went on to elucidate how motherhood constitutes an existential crisis for women (Arnold-Baker, 2020). It also strengthens the case of the importance of a four-dimensional approach to analysis.

3. Grouping of Meaning Units

Once all the highlighted statements have been coded the table is rearranged by the individual heuristics used. Below you can see the example of the meaning units for the Physical Dimension for the participant we are calling Bonnie. As can be seen the statements are then grouped by meanings so all statements regarding the same aspect are gathered together. In this way each element of the experience is drawn out. Some of the meaning units may duplicate others but at this stage it is important for all highlighted meaning units to be grouped according to the element or aspect that they relate to.

Physical Dimension

heart beating faster
suddenly had the feeling
knelt down and kissed the grass
response to nature
sun was shining
different from other girls physically
forever having the wrong body image
no connection to the feeling of being in my body
I think hey, I'll be gone [dead]
the thought [of death] is horrible
feeling over the line or feeling over the hill

Once there are some rough groups the researcher looks at each group in turn to assimilate all the meaning units into one sentence or small paragraph. At this stage a tentative title will be given to the group. It is important at this point to keep the research question in mind to ensure that the groups the researcher is creating are elements of the phenomena under investigation. As can be seen in the box above the participant described her experience of her body. These meaning statements were not included in the final themes as when analysed it was decided that the statements were not related to the participants' experience of freedom and so were left out of the final stage of the analysis. At the end of this stage the researcher may well have identified more than ten groups as some may represent different elements of the same theme.

Group Meaning Units

Freedom arises suddenly and involves connection

- The feeling that freedom can suddenly appear
- Response to nature, kissing the grass, feeling connected

Death limits freedom

- I'll be gone, death is a horrible feeling, approaching death, feeling over the hill

4. Creating Themes

The researcher will now have a list of groups, with tentative titles and a descriptive summary, or quotes from the participant which describe the theme, which has brought together all the different elements of the participants' narrative. The researcher will look across the groups to see if there are any that seem to be different elements of an overarching experience. These become minor themes of a major theme which encapsulates the theme.

The final stage is to turn the grouped meaning units into themes and to title the themes so that they capture an aspect of the experience of freedom. Van Manen (1990) describes how important the art of writing is in Hermeneutic Phenomenological Research and this is also true for Existential Phenomenological Research. The art required by the existential researcher is to capture the meaning of the words and anecdotes of the participants and transform them into themes that capture the meaning of the phenomena under investigation.

Physical Dimension Themes

Sudden emergence and connection

- Freedom suddenly appears as a feeling of connection

Death is the ultimate limit

- Approaching death is a horrible feeling but then there is nothing and freedom is over

---

5. Final Analysis

The above steps will be repeated for each dimension. Bringing the four dimensions together in the final analysis enables a spatial understanding to be gained about the experience of a phenomenon, in this case the experience of total freedom. The full analysis of Bonnie's interview produced the spatial themes shown in Table 6.3.

Each dimension provides a different facet and demonstrates a holistic view of the experience. For Bonnie it can be seen how the experience of freedom creates a tension between the personal and social dimensions. The analysis showed how other people and societal expectations can restrict the experience of total freedom and that for Bonnie freedom was a personal and private experience which emerged from her being herself. The physical dimension brought to light the feeling of freedom and how it suddenly arises in the moment and how death is always in the background as an ultimate limit and end of freedom. The spiritual dimension highlighted how freedom was an otherworldly experience, a miracle or a dream. It connected Bonnie to something greater than herself and came about through curiosity and openness to the world and what might be possible.

Table 6.3 Example of a full analysis of the four dimensions

Physical Dimension	Social Dimension	Personal Dimension	Spiritual Dimension
Sudden emergence and connection	Societal rules restrict freedom	Freedom is personal	Connecting to something greater
Death is the ultimate limit	Expression creates freedom	It is up to me	Being curious
	Freed from the gaze of others	Finding my way	Otherworldly

Another way of looking at the experience from the four dimensions is to look at the various ways in which freedom had been experienced, the examples that the participant had brought and how they can be viewed through the four dimensions of existence. For example, if we chart Bonnie's experiences of freedom over the four dimensions they would be diverse and multiple as shown in Table 6.4.

From this table we can see that Bonnie experienced more freedom in the social dimension and her experiences of freedom were connected to her relationship with other people, in terms of how free she felt, but also how others impacted her ability to experience freedom. Each dimension contained a paradoxical element, which served as an enabling or limiting factor. This aspect will be elucidated further in the next chapter.

The spatial heuristic is the one most often used in SEA research at NSPC and it has been applied to a range of topics as can be seen below:

Charlotte Macgregor: An Existential Formulation of Transformative Experiences in Nature

John Bennett: 'A Good Night Out' (Voices of 'Binge' drinkers). A Phenomenological Investigation of Binge Drinking Women in Yorkshire

Table 6.4 Summary of Bonnie's experiences of freedom in the four dimensions

Four Dimensions	Types of Freedom Experienced
Physical	Connecting with nature
Social	Lockdown
	Language and humour
	Leaving school
Personal	Being oneself
Spiritual	Otherworldly

Valerie Landenberg: A Community-Based Experience of Permanent Exclusion from Secondary School: An Existential Reflection
Natalie Fraser: An Existential-Phenomenological Exploration of How Inner Dialogue Is Experienced by Rape Survivors

However, the spatial heuristic is just one of the lenses through which the participants' experience can be filtered, and the next chapters will demonstrate how further heuristics can bring to light other facets.

Chapter 7

The Filter of PARADOX

Introduction

Life is not straightforward, and as we have already seen (Chapter 5) our relationship with time means there is always a dynamic forward motion to our lives, which inevitably brings change with it. Life therefore involves inherent tensions, and these are inescapable. There is a temptation in research, as in life, to believe that we might be able to capture an experience in a finite and definitive way, to pin it down like an object to examine. But this is like trying to seize hold of water, as it slips through your fingers. Any human research must therefore account for both the onto-dynamic nature of human existence but also the fact that it is essentially paradoxical, i.e. that its opposing forces are an essential part of its being.

Existence Is Absurd and Ambiguous

Being is paradoxical and there is no being without nothingness. And because of this, human existence, which is a form and an expression of being, is also paradoxical. As soon as a human being has been born this human being is certain to die at some point in the future, though we don't know when this will happen. In between our birth and our death, we are given time to create a life. We live with this constant paradoxical tension and uncertainty. Tillich (1952) believed we needed the 'courage to be', the courage to create a life for ourselves in the face of the threat of non-existence. It was this element of uncertainty in existence that Camus took up in his philosophy. He wondered about the absurdity of existence, in terms of its finiteness, and posed the question of 'whether life is or is not worth living' (Camus, 1955: 11) and whether suicide was an option to consider, if life was so meaningless. Camus explored the notion of the absurd in relation to existence. He summed this up as:

> A stranger to myself and to the world, armed solely with a thought that negates itself as soon as it asserts, what is this condition in which I can have peace only by refusing to know and to live, in which the appetite for conquest bumps into walls that defy its assaults? To will is to stir up paradoxes.
>
> (Camus, 1955: 25)

For Camus the absurd is a paradox, for as soon as it is recognised there is no way of unknowing the absurdity of existence. Either we live in ignorance of the reality of the finiteness of human existence, or we are aware of that reality and then are confronted with its absurdity. The absurd is contradictory and emerges out of confrontation, a confrontation with our existence. He states that 'the Absurd is not in man . . . nor in the world, but in their presence together' (Camus, 1955: 34), highlighting the contradictory aspect of absurdity which is created between the individual and the world. Camus concludes that:

> It was previously a question of finding out whether or not life had to have a meaning to be lived. It now becomes clear on the contrary that it will be lived all the better if it has no meaning. Living an experience, a particular fate, is accepting it fully.
>
> (Camus, 1955: 53)

Camus therefore believed that individuals needed to accept the meaninglessness of life in order to keep going and find meaning in it, much like his hero Sisyphus, in his well-known essay 'The Myth of Sisyphus' (Camus, 1955). According to Camus, Sisyphus, who was condemned to push a boulder up a mountain for eternity because he had offended the Gods by putting people to death as a tyrant, only for it to roll back down again each time, would have been able to find meaning in his plight. Sisyphus, by facing the absurdity of his situation, would be able to become a hero, by making the boulder and his task of pushing it uphill day after day his own, thereby overcoming the meaninglessness of the struggle. Camus concludes that 'there is no fate that cannot be surmounted by scorn' (Camus, 1955 [1942]: 109).

De Beauvoir took a different position to Camus. She made a distinction between absurdity and ambiguity, stating that:

> to declare that existence is absurd is to deny that it can ever be given a meaning; to say that it is ambiguous is to assert that its meaning is never fixed, that it must be constantly won.
>
> (1970: 139)

Rather than seeing existence as Camus did as fundamentally meaningless as soon as the absurdity of life was revealed, de Beauvoir believed on the contrary that meaning or values are always present because despite the absurdity of life or its ambiguity, freedom is an essential aspect of life. De Beauvoir goes on to highlight the ambiguous nature of human existence, which is related to its changeable and uncertain condition; she states 'between the past which no longer is and the future which is not yet, this moment when we exist is nothing' (1970: 6). De Beauvoir contends that because the future is open and not determined in advance it reveals further possibilities: 'The fundamental ambiguity of the human condition will always open up to men the possibility of opposing choices' (1970: 128).

Individuals are always faced with opposing choices, either/or, and through this openness and freedom to choose they can have the potential to win as well as lose: 'Nothing is decided in advance, and it is because man has something to lose and because he can lose that he can also win' (1970: 35).

Despite their differences both Camus and de Beauvoir recognised the paradoxical nature of human existence. They showed that individuals are constantly confronted by opposing or contradictory choices and that life can be both meaningful and meaningless at the same time. As Camus remarked, 'In the midst of winter, I found there was, within me an invincible summer' (Camus, 1948 [1947]: 181).

Paradox of Existence

Of all the existential philosophers, Kierkegaard probably understood the tensions that existence brings the most, and his first book was about paradox. He recognised that freedom and choice create anxiety and that these experiences are central to our existence as human beings. Kierkegaard highlighted the ultimate paradox faced by human beings:

> It is perfectly true, as philosophers say, that life must be understood backwards. But they forget the other proposition, that it must be lived forwards.
> (Kierkegaard, 2008: 167)

The freedom to choose our future is always a choice in which we can never know in advance what the consequences of those choices will be. We are compelled to choose; even deciding not to choose is a choice. Whether a choice is a good one or not can only be determined in retrospect. The paradox for having to live our lives forwards, without certainty of what will happen, creates what Kierkegaard calls *Angst*, or existential anxiety. He described this famously as follows: 'anxiety is the dizziness of freedom' (Kierkegaard, 1944 [1844]: 61), showing that both anxiety and freedom are ontological aspects of our human condition. We are faced with the challenge of trying to create a sense of security for ourselves whilst at the same time being at the mercy of the unfolding of life which cannot be known in advance. Kierkegaard summed up the paradox individuals face as: 'I see it all perfectly; there are two possible situations – one can either do this or that. My honest opinion and my friendly advice is this: do it or do not do it – you will regret both' (Kierkegaard, 1987: 152). So, whilst human existence involves freedom and choice it also involves regret and guilt for the choices that were not taken up. In choosing, you must always reject other possibilities.

Self as Synthesis

Kierkegaard believed that it was not just existence that was paradoxical but that human beings were essentially paradoxical too. He argued that there is no fixed concept of the self, no personality or identity to be examined and described, or to be assessed or classified, rather the self is a synthesis of tensions that individuals face as part of their human condition. He offers a different perspective on the self that it is less about the personal qualities of an individual and more about how a self is created through an individual's way of approaching the intrinsic tensions of existence. He describes this in his book *The Sickness Unto Death* (Kierkegaard, 1980 [1849]: 11):

> The human being is spirit. But what is spirit? Spirit is the self. But what is the self? The self is a relation which relates to itself, or that in the relation which is its relating to itself. The self is not the relation but the relation's relating to itself. A human being is a synthesis of the infinite and the finite, of the temporal and the eternal, of freedom and necessity. In short, a synthesis. A synthesis is a relation between two terms. Looked at in this way, a human being is not yet a self.

A sense of self is formed from how an individual relates to the relations of three tensions explicated by Kierkegaard. These tensions are between the infinite and the finite, between possibility and necessity and between the temporal and eternal. The tension of the infinite and the finite relates to a person's ability to rise above their situation and their world and imagine a radically different one (infinite; i.e. seeing things in new ways), whilst at the same time being wholly aware of the world as it actually *is* (finite; i.e. full of limitations and boundaries and respecting the facts of life). There is also a tension between the many possibilities that are available in the future that can be created through imagination and the reality of the present moment. There is always a tension between a sense of a future 'me' which emerges out of possibility and what remains necessary taking into account who I am right now. Despite believing that individuals change and indeed choose to change, Kierkegaard sees there are limits to how we can change and in what ways. The final one of the three tensions concerns how individuals live in time. Here the temporal aspect of existence represents the changing self, which is situated in time and gets older, whereas the eternal aspect represents the constancy of the self, its continuity or the ideal of a true self. Therefore, Kierkegaard believed that the self changes and responds to circumstances and yet it must at the same time remain itself.

Therefore, in the same way we have the freedom to choose how to live our lives, the tension that is created in the synthesis of choosing ourselves also involves anxiety, as Kierkegaard explains:

> This is an adventure that every human being must go through – to learn to be anxious in order that he might not perish either by never having been in anxiety or by succumbing in anxiety. Whoever has learned to be anxious in the right way has learned the ultimate.
>
> (Kierkegaard, 1944 [1844]: 155)

Kierkegaard emphasises the paradox that we all face and have to address at various points in our lives. In his book *Sickness unto Death*, he describes how venturing out in the world may seem dangerous, but 'by not venturing, it is so dreadfully easy to lose . . . one's self' (Kierkegaard, 1980: 35), highlighting the inevitable tensions of life. This is a very similar view to Sartre's definition of the self as that which we express in our actions. If we do not engage with the world, according to Sartre (1956), we cease to exist. It is action that brings us to life and that creates value in the world.

Poles of Existence

Deurzen (2010 [1997]) elucidated how the work of Kierkegaard, de Beauvoir, Sartre and Camus demonstrates how the inevitable tensions and paradoxes of existence create the dynamic power of life. The anxiety that is experienced when faced with polarities and opposites, when one is confronted by a choice or a conflict, can be seen as an energy which compels an individual to move forward. As Camus pointed out, once we are aware of how absurd existence is there is no way of not knowing this. Equally there is no way of standing still, of keeping the status quo going. Life thrusts us forward whether we like it or not. Kierkegaard teaches us that rather than trying to avoid this existential anxiety we should embrace the energy that it creates and channel it into creativity. Creativity in this sense concerns the human ability to be an active agent in the world, an ability to make choices and to create possibilities out of those choices. Deurzen states: 'Life can be defined as the activity of movement between these opposites'. She goes on to say, 'without this tension, that involves us in continuous aspirations and desperations, ups and downs, tos and fros, there would be no human existence at all' (Deurzen, 2010 [1997]: 99). This movement between opposites, or the poles of existence, is a key element of onto-dynamics. We are pulled towards or pushed away from things, people, situations or emotions. This movement is closely connected to a person's values as we aim for movement towards what is important to us.

Whilst Kierkegaard identified three basic ontological tensions that human beings must contend with, de Beauvoir demonstrated how opposites can reveal something about its opposite pair. She noted that we cannot have the concept of good without the concept of evil, each side of the polarity is needed to understand something of the whole dynamic between polar opposites. Similarly, Heidegger (1962) noted how human beings move between modes of authenticity and inauthenticity, where true authenticity is only achieved momentarily and never completely until the moment of death, when our life is finally complete. Deurzen concurs when she says: 'Perfection, no matter how desirable, is nothing but death: death is perfection. For it is only when we die that life is completed. While we live, life is imperfect and incomplete' (Deurzen, 1998: 13).

Life, therefore, always contains conflicts, tensions and contradictions. As Kierkegaard noted we are always caught between what we might want in our lives and the realities of what we can have. Deurzen (2010) highlights the basic polarities of life that we all face, such as life and death or love and hate. Human beings face polarities on all four dimensions of existence, the most basic of which are to do with our ultimate desires and fears, as can be seen in Table 7.1.

Table 7.1 Dimensions and tensions of human existence (Deurzen, 2010: 141)

	Desires	Fears
Physical	Life	Death
	Pleasure	Pain
Social	Love	Hate
	Belonging	Isolation
Personal	Identity	Freedom
	Integrity	Disintegration
Spiritual	Good	Evil
	Purpose	Futility

The aim in recognising and being aware of polarities is not to move away from the pole of our fears and towards the pole of our desires, instead it is to acknowledge that both are contained in each moment. That in order to have life there has to be death and to have pleasure we also have to know what it is like to experience pain. Pleasure without pain would not be experienced in the same way. The same can be said for pain without pleasure. The poles of existence reveal something that would not be possible without knowledge of both. Understanding, therefore, comes from both sides not just from one. Holding the tension of polarities is to live creatively with paradox.

Table 7.2 sets the four dimensions of life against The Four Worlds of Existence. This reveals the many tensions of human existence and thus the broad dynamic play of contradictions and conflicts we are faced with. Living always involves working with such opposites and learning to work with dynamic tension instead of trying to have one's desires is a good strategy. This is not about finding compromises, but about making room for the whole spectrum of existence. The tasks of living

Table 7.2 Paradoxes and tensions

World	Umwelt	Mitwelt	Eigenwelt	Uberwelt
Physical	**Nature:** Life/Death	**Things:** Pleasure/Pain	**Body:** Health/Illness	**Cosmos:** Harmony/Chaos
Social	**Society:** Love/Hate	**Others:** Dominance/Submission	**Ego:** Acceptance/Rejection	**Culture:** Belonging/Isolation
Personal	**Person:** Identity/Freedom	**Me:** Perfection/Imperfection	**Self:** Integrity/Disintegration	**Consciousness:** Confidence/Confusion
Spiritual	**Infinite:** Good/Evil	**Ideas:** Truth/Untruth	**Spirit:** Meaning/Futility	**Conscience:** Right/Wrong

concern survival, affiliation, identity and meaning-making (Deurzen, 2010), all of which can be experienced in many varied ways. Table 7.2 contains a summary of some of the tensions most of us experience.

Hegel's Dialectics

SEA research needs a dialectical approach, where opposing sides are examined (see Chapter 4). This is an important aspect for the research dialogue, but it is equally important as part of the analysis process.

Nineteenth century philosopher Hegel created a dialectical method which expanded Plato's work with dialogue, which was about finding a way beyond contradictory statements towards truth. Hegel argued that the whole of nature and history progressed through dialectical opposition and synthesis.

A dialectical movement is composed of three phases: a thesis, an antithesis and a synthesis:

First moment   This is about positing a certain idea.
Second moment   This is about positing the opposite to this idea.
Third moment   This is about bringing together the opposing forces into a forward movement that comprehends but transcends both previous moments.

In the beginning we might have a moment of understanding which becomes fixed or determined, so it becomes a dogma. Quite often this is the usual way in which human beings generate their understanding. For example, in a first moment we experience other people as caring and loving and come to believe human beings are good. Then in a second moment we discover the opposite is true and human beings can be hateful and unfriendly and we have a reaction to our previous belief, which we now consider to have been false. Ultimately, in a third moment, we come to recognise that both the thesis and the antithesis were false and only relatively true. We discover that human beings are complex and we arrive at a dialectical understanding of others, where we allow for the whole frame of possibility, holding the paradoxical tension. Hegel saw that in that first moment of determination the intention is one-sided. Therefore, in the second moment the opposite needs to be considered and we end up with the tension of contradiction of polar opposites. Then we need to be able to come to the moment where we overcome that tension, as we arrive at the *Aufhebung*, which literally means both to cancel (or negate) and to preserve at the same time (Standford Encyclopaedia of Philosophy, 2016). This third moment involves grasping both the first and second moment together which allows for a greater understanding to be gained, as we hold onto the paradoxical tension and see the dialectical forward movement with which we grasp the whole dynamic experience and transcend it.

For example, in Arnold-Baker's research on motherhood (2019) she found that the mothers she interviewed described how they had not been changed by the experience of becoming a mother, they felt that they were still the same person. But they also described how their lives had completely changed. The mothers, therefore, were faced with a paradoxical position of feeling the same and being different, in the same moment. To only consider one side of the experience, such as they didn't feel any different, and not the other, that their lives had completely changed, meant that the whole experience and the tension it creates would not have been drawn out. By drawing out the implicit tensions a deeper understanding can be found. Deurzen shows how this can be used in therapy, but the process is equally pertinent for research:

> In this way the focus of the analysis shifts from the explicit to the implicit. While always starting from the obvious, from what is actually there, the search is on to reveal the implied essence and meaning and to assist the client in a process of reconnecting with what is of true significance to her/him.
> (Deurzen, 1998: 148)

Application of the Lens of Paradox

As this chapter has demonstrated any research into our experiences of human living must account for their paradoxical and contradictory elements. Not to do so would mean not taking into account the complexity of human life. It would only ever present a one-sided view. If we are to gain a deep understanding of phenomena and experiences in our everyday living, we need to highlight their complexities, paradoxes, contradictions, tensions and conflict.

This means going back to the transcripts of the research dialogues to apply the lens of paradox to the participants' words. To do this the transcripts are read through again with paradox and contradiction in mind. The existential researcher should keep the following questions in mind while reading the transcript:

- What tensions are being highlighted in the participant's discourse?
- What paradoxes are they being faced with?
- Where is the conflict?
- What contradictory statements have they made?

Identifying paradoxes means keeping in mind the whole of the transcript and identifying areas where the participant has contradicted themselves or has highlighted a tension or conflict.

In our research on freedom, we searched for meaning units or capta which highlighted the paradoxical nature of total freedom. The first thing to come to light after we applied the filter of paradox to the participants' transcripts was that two of our participants right at the beginning of the interview stated that there was no such thing as total freedom.

> At first, I suppose my reaction was 'but it's never total [laugh] is it?'
> (Bonnie)

Olga concurred when she stated:

> I can't imagine anyone being totally free, it is not possible.

Therefore, despite free will being an ontological condition of human existence (Kierkegaard, 1987, Sartre, 1956 [1943], de Beauvoir, 1970 [1948], Heidegger, 1962) our participants noted that they always experienced limits to their freedom. Freedom was never totally free. This is a particularly important finding in existential literature and one the Black existentialists (Fanon, 2021 [1952] and Etoke, 2023) have also stressed. Perhaps the notion of total freedom or absolute free will is not possible. That freedom is always limited, not just by how we might choose to limit it ourselves from a moral or ethical position as de Beauvoir urges in her book *The Ethics of Ambiguity* (1970 [1948]), but by our situation and the actions of others. It seems that ontologically we may have the possibility of total freedom but our ontic experience of it is that freedom is always limited both by ourselves and by others. As Olga stated, 'the loss of freedom came from the outside world, not me'.

Interestingly, the concept of *free will* has been taken up by two biologists recently who published books on this area in 2023. Sapolsky's book was titled *Determined* (2023) and Mitchell's book was titled *Free Agents* (2023). Johnson (2024) who reviewed both books highlighted how the authors took opposing positions on whether or not freedom can be total. Mitchell contends that free will is possible whilst Sapolsky takes an opposing position. Their points of contention revolve around the fact that freedom or free will always occurs within a context and therefore is never totally free. There are always things that are outside of our control which we cannot change, whether this is our environment, our situation, our history or our bodies. Therefore, from that position freedom is always limited. Mitchell on the other hand sees free will from a position of being able to make active choices, to pause and reflect rather than act in a reactive way. These are not new ways of thinking about freedom – Frankl (1964) addressed both positions in his work and believed that however limited we are in terms of our freedom we always have the freedom to choose the attitude we want to take towards what is happening to us. The work done by Deurzen (2010 [1997]) has often been about explicating the complexity of human existence and uncovering its many layers, and as with the concept of freedom, uncovering the nuances helps us to gain a deeper understanding, whilst holding the tension of the contradictions.

Therefore the paradoxical aspects of a phenomenon, in this case freedom, can reveal important aspects of its experience, which can be examined from both a descriptive phenomenological position and from an existential perspective.

After re-reading the transcript keeping paradox and contradiction in mind, meaning statements are highlighted or brought together. Each highlighted statement is checked to ensure that it is related to the phenomenon under investigation. For our research, paradoxical statements which were not connected to the experience of freedom were not included. For ease of presentation, the statements were then grouped according to the four dimensions of existence, and this also allowed for further analysis to be undertaken. The paradoxes faced by each of the participants are laid out below, highlighting their own individual paradoxical experiences of freedom.

The Filter of PARADOX   123

For Olga one of the paradoxes in the physical dimension revolved around how money and finances were at the same time a limit to freedom but also enabled freedom by allowing new possibilities and options to be present in her life. Another paradox in that dimension concerned a sense of home. Olga did not feel like she had a home, being a child of a migrant family and an immigrant herself. Place did not hold security for her. But a lack of security in a place gave her the freedom to explore and discover; it did not limit her freedom by being tied to one location.

In the social dimension the paradox concerned her fight for freedom, particularly in the context of Brexit. She fought against Brexit because of the value she placed on the right for free movement, for the freedom to travel and live in different countries, but also for the love of London where she had chosen to live. Olga fought even though she knew they would not win. The fight for freedom was the important thing, even though it felt like a tragedy and a foregone conclusion.

The paradoxes faced on the personal dimension concerned her emotions and feelings. The experience of freedom was both exciting and scary at the same time, but the fear did not stop her from embracing her freedom.

In the spiritual dimension Olga felt that not belonging to a home, a city, a system or a country gave her the freedom to face something greater than just one place. It enabled her to encounter the universe and the cosmos.

Each of the paradoxes experienced by Olga in the four dimensions represented a movement between two poles: between security and insecurity, between belonging and isolation, between fear and excitement and between right and wrong.

Table 7.3 Olga's paradoxes of freedom

Dimension		
Physical	**Finances Dictate Freedom**	
	Lack of money is a prison	Financial freedom is hard won and allows new options
	A Sense of Home	
	Home is not the place where you live	No security means you are not tied to a place
Social	**Fighting for Freedom**	
	Fighting for the love of a place, and for the right for freedom	Knowing that it is a fight that will be lost
Personal	**Embracing Freedom**	
	Feeling very excited about everything	Feeling very scared
Spiritual	**Belonging**	
	Belonging to a system restricts freedom	Not belonging allows you to encounter the cosmos and the universe

For Bonnie the physical dimension also highlighted the limits of freedom, but where finances had been the delimiter for Olga, death was the ultimate limit for Bonnie. She found that she wanted to enjoy her space and her life despite the fact she would die.

The focus in the social dimension was around the paradox of how society impacted a person's freedom. Whilst there were some positive aspects of society and culture that came from living in particular countries, there were also restrictions to freedom through societal rules and requirements.

In the personal dimension Bonnie discovered that the COVID pandemic stopped her doing the things that she loved but she also realised at the same time that she loved not having the responsibility to do those things. Freedom came with responsibility and not having to face responsibility also felt like a freedom paradoxically. Bonnie also noted how her attitude was also contradictory, painting things in a negative light but also being open to seeing wonderful things at the same time. This was also echoed in the spiritual dimension where she felt that an unknown future meant she was always holding the possibility that something wonderful or something terrible could happen and she didn't know which.

The movement between polarities for Bonnie were between life and death, between social restriction and expansion, between being open and closed to what is being experienced and between good and bad in the future.

Luke on the other hand experienced a paradox of velocity in the physical dimension. He discovered that when he slowed the pace of his life down, he found that he was able to make sense of things more quickly. Like Bonnie, not

Table 7.4 Bonnie's paradoxes of freedom

Dimension		
Physical	**Limit and Enjoyment of Freedom**	
	Everyone is going to die	No harm enjoying my space
Social	**Society's Impact on Freedom**	
	Positive aspects of society	Societal rules restrict freedom
	Limits of Freedom	
	Fortunately	Unfortunately, we are all forgettable
Personal	**Outside Restrictions on Freedom**	
	Stopped doing the things I love	Loved not having the responsibility of doing them
	Freedom to Choose an Attitude	
	Painting things in a negative light	Being open to see wonderful things
Spiritual	**An Unknown Future**	
	Something wonderful is going to happen	Something terrible will happen and I don't know

having responsibility for material things gave Luke a sense of freedom, despite those material things, such as a car, having the potential to give him freedom.

In the social dimension Luke faced the paradox of holding onto previous experiences of freedom which came from other people, places and cultures but at the same time was not able to hold onto that experience. He found that he needed to keep finding ways of experiencing his freedom.

In the personal dimension he shared a similar paradox with Olga in that embracing freedom through travelling and putting himself in unknown situations was potentially scary and risky, but to go into those situations in that way would mean that it would alter the experience of freedom. Holding fear and assurance together in the same moment changes the experience.

Table 7.5 Luke's paradoxes of freedom

Physical	**Velocity in the Experience of Freedom**	
	Slowing life down	Allows meaning to be created quicker
	Material Things	
	Having a car gives you freedom	But carries the responsibility of looking after it
Social	**Carrying the Experience of Freedom**	
	After a number of years, it is still with me	But it is not with me still
Personal	**Freedom to Keep an Openness**	
	Going into the unknown can be scary	But if you go into those situations fearfully then it is not the same experience
	To Be Settled	
	The word settled	Is unsettling
Spiritual	**Attachment to Freedom**	
	Travelling has enabled an experience of total freedom	Becoming attached to the idea of freedom through travelling can be restrictive
	Freedom and Constraints	
	Freedom feels constrained if there are a lot of rules	Following rules frees up choices and gives a lot of freedom
	Despair and Hope	
	Looking at the world pessimistically throws optimism and hope away	Hope brings meaning and creative solutions

Table 7.6 Overall paradoxes of freedom

Physical	Social	Personal	Spiritual
Life/Death	Belonging/Isolation	Fear/Excitement	Good/Bad
Security/Insecurity	Restriction/Expansion	or Courage	Right/Wrong
Fast/Slow		Open/Closed	Despair/Hope

The paradoxes that were faced in the spiritual dimension were between wanting to experience freedom without becoming attached to the idea of freedom. Being able to hold onto pessimism and optimism at the same time. Where one without the other creates difficulties. If too pessimistic then it reduces freedom and possibilities. If too optimistic then the realities of life are not taken into account.

Luke was moving between the poles of fast and slow, between belonging and isolation, between fear and courage and between despair and hope.

The three individual analyses when combined together highlight the underlying existential tensions that are faced in an experience of freedom. Of course, this analysis can only ever be a snapshot of the experiences of these three participants. We cannot make greater claims about the experience of freedom for all, especially as the small sample was limited to white, Western participants. For a more in-depth analysis care needs to be taken to consider a broad range of participants for the sample. A recent example of how this can be achieved was highlighted by our graduate Stella Duffy (2024) who carefully ensured a cross-section of participants in terms of ethnicity, class, sexuality and maternity in her research into the experience of the menopause.

The combined existential paradoxes experienced by all three participants across the four dimensions can be seen above in Table 7.6. The overall analysis of the paradox of freedom shows how freedom is always limited. The limits are created by death and the security an individual feels, either financially or through their sense of home. Without security, freedom may be experienced in an adverse way, or a person may feel imprisoned by their lack of security. Olga describes feeling 'devastated' when she experienced financial restrictions on her freedom. Other aspects that impact freedom come through how society and other people can restrict or expand the experience of freedom. How it might be encouraged or discouraged and how belonging and isolation play a part in how free one might feel, to be or do something different. How a person manages the tension between fear and excitement will impact the experience of freedom too and whether a person is open or closed to freedom's possibilities. Freedom involves holding the tension between good and bad as it is revealed in an unknown and uncertain future. This unknown future also creates a tension between despair and hope; falling into either side of this polarity brings potential difficulties for an individual.

The application of the filter of paradox to research explicitly highlights the tensions and contradictions that an experience brings. It brings the dynamic nature of existence to the fore and in this way allows us to capture human reality more accurately. It is rare in life that an experience or phenomenon has only one meaning.

SEA explicitly seeks to draw these out. Through looking at the contradictory elements of a phenomenon the truth is uncovered. Heidegger (1962) describes this when he says 'the *Being-true* (*truth*) of the assertion must be understood as *Being-uncovering*' (Heidegger, 1962: 261). He believes that *Being-true* is a way of being-in-the-world. However, despite this truth is often hidden or disguised. Heidegger notes 'Truth (uncoveredness) is something that must always first be wrested from entities. Entities get snatched out of their hiddenness' (1962: 263). Therefore, according to Heidegger, truth is always a process of uncovering something that is hidden. If we take 'facts' at face value, from our understanding, as they first appear, then we remain at what Hegel would describe as the 'first moment'. We are not going beyond what is already known to us and available as understanding to a person. The truth as Heidegger sees it may still remain hidden. It is only by looking at the alternative positions that a deeper understanding will be found. Clarifying the paradoxical aspects of life helps individuals to find a purpose and direction in life. It allows them to see life under the guise of the onto-dynamics of existence. This will be explored more fully in the next chapter where the filter of purpose will be considered.

Chapter 8
The Filter of PURPOSE

Introduction

While it is possible to do a piece of SEA research by simply applying the lenses of time and space, including the four dimensions and their paradoxes, we make our scrutiny a lot more complete when we add a specific lens to zoom in on purpose and intentionality. If we really want to enliven our understanding of the existential situation of the person we are in dialogue with, we will get a clearer and more vivid picture of their lifeworld and experience, by filtering our capta through the lenses of purpose (this chapter) and passion (next chapter).

Purpose and passion are intrinsically connected (Deurzen, 2009, 2010 [1997], 2015 [1998]). Though there are many theories about emotions, the existential theory is that as human beings we are always orientated towards the world in a particular way. We are always disposed to the world in a certain mood. We are affected by everything we experience, do and see and this affectation can be captured in feelings, sensations, thoughts and intuitions. Heidegger (1962) spoke about our state of mind, *Befindlichkeit*, which literally means the way in which we find ourselves in the world. He also spoke about our attunement to the world, the mood with which we resonate with what is happening around us. In some ways this is an extension of our intentionality, the fact that our consciousness is always engaged and directed towards something in the world in a particular way, as we described in the theoretical chapters. What we are most preoccupied with and orientated towards is what matters to us most. Our feelings are an expression of what matters to us. They are triggered by our position in the world in relation to the things that we value. Even Martha Nussbaum, after carefully considering many emotional theories, including those of Athenian philosophers (Nussbaum, 1994), gradually came to view emotions as intelligent responses to the perception of value. In her book *Upheavals of Thought* (Nussbaum, 2001), she writes:

> Emotions, I have said, view the world from the point of view of my own scheme of goals and projects, the thing to which I attach value in a conception of what it is for me to live well.
>
> (Nussbaum, 2001: 49)

It is therefore vital for our Structural Existential Analytic research to probe for a person's values, beliefs and ideals, before we turn to their feelings and emotions. Value plays a pivotal role in existential praxis. The way a person acts is motivated and inspired by what it is they value in life.

While we can learn to be reflective about our mode of being and worldview, most of us initially are plunged into our intentionality in a non-reflexive manner. Therefore, it is very powerful to bring this state of mind and mood into awareness in our existential research. It is about connecting the dots of a person's awareness and their feelings about the world. These feelings and their state of mind are directly connected to the focus of their attention and the purpose they are pursuing, without even being aware of it. Though they may be blind to this purpose, their entire being will be straining in a particular direction and away from certain other directions. This is not as easy as to describe what attracts and what repels a person. It can only be formulated by tracing the threads of awareness of inner experience, mood and background preoccupations and feelings. The purposes we pursue get most of our attention and intentionality. What we want to become or achieve in life defines our orientation in the world. Some people have obvious plans and desires and longings and goals. But these are not necessarily aligned with the hidden life projects that matter to a person.

This is why it is so important to track these streams of feelings to discover a person's original project, as Sartre called it (Sartre, 1968 [1960], 1982 [1960]). When a person becomes aware of the life choices they are making by voting with their feet, instead of by deliberately setting themselves in a certain direction of travel, their intentionality becomes owned in a way it cannot be when a person pursues or surfs on surface values. Whether or not a person is able to progress towards the things they value determines how good they feel about themselves and their life. If they feel confused about their values and project, they may feel out of touch with themselves or stuck in a rut or dissatisfied with life. There are many people who are getting brainwashed into pursuing life goals that they feel they ought to pursue, because other people have suggested to them these are important. Young people may pursue their parents' values and the goals that the parents set for them from when they were very young. Teenagers may suddenly shift their value system towards a revolutionary and rebellious reactive set of values, because their peers have introduced them to an alternative lifestyle. Social media is a clear example of how we can be exposed to a system that highlights other people's values and ways of living which become internalised as an ideal to pursue. When people begin to actively contribute to society, they tend to, once again, absorb the values of their working environment.

If they feel they are on a path towards a worthwhile life goal it will be a very different matter than if they have just taken on board the values that were fed to them passively. To feel you are on the way towards a value is highly engaging, whereas feeling your values are slipping away or taboo or even unclear can be very upsetting. The way we engage with our intentionality gives us direction but also determines the attitude we take towards the experiences we have. In other words, our intentionality and the extent to which it is in line with our values determines our mood, our values and our meanings. Roy Baumeister in his book *Meanings of Life* (Baumeister, 1991), did a meta-analysis of many studies on what gives meaning to people's lives and he found that connecting up to the things you value creates meaning. He also found that going towards four basic ways of being increases the sense of living a worthwhile life. These were as follows. Firstly, it was about the sense of efficacy, which meant to feel effective in the physical world. Secondly it was about having a feeling of value, as in being of value to the world around you. Thirdly it was about having an inner sense of self-worth and being a good person. Finally, it was about having a sense of purpose. Therefore, the filters of values and feelings are a significant part of a full SEA piece of research. These will really provide in-depth information about what matters to the person. It will enable researchers to explore a participant's intentionality, their assumptions, their values and their purpose and objectives. We shall demonstrate what an important source of understanding of a person's experience this is. As always clear examples will be given of how to apply these filters.

Values

Values are the things, ideas, objectives, experiences or ways of being that are important to you and that matter to you so much that you care for them more than for anything else. A value is something you are willing to give something else up for. That is how value is determined: how much you prize it, compared to something else. Values are the things you prefer and that you are willing to work hard for. Ultimate values, such as love of life or God or the planet or land or your loved ones, are things you may even give up your own life for. The value of something is determined by how much you are willing to sacrifice for it. Values are a minefield of confusion as some are dictated to us by our culture, society, religion and education and others are picked up from peer groups, fashions, trends and the media. Some values form an archaic part of our instinctive behaviour, such as the desire to avoid spilling blood or to maintain our bodily integrity. Other values seem to be biologically engrained in our personal DNA, such as food preferences or our greater or lesser liking for crowds, or sports, or ideas, for example. Some values are like human universals, such as love and peace, truth, justice and freedom. They are at the foundation of most world religions but are also shared by atheists. Other values are very specific to individuals. Some are lifelong and some are temporary. There are many different ways of interpreting the same values. To learn to find our way through values is a huge challenge. When we do SEA research, we need to content ourselves with a method that can only tackle values and emotions at a certain level of depth. We cannot spend ten years in existential analysis with the people we interview. We are committed to finding out how people are disposed towards certain values and experiences and how they negotiate difficulties in relation to their values. But we have to do so in a limited and structured way rather than being flooded by the full complexity and force of the waves of a person's moral and emotional seascape.

It helps to link the idea of values with the four dimensions, because that brings some order into the many categories we are dealing with. There are very concrete physical values, such as pleasure or health or even life itself. Social values are things such as kindness and generosity or love. Personal, psychological values are for instance sensitivity or self-reliance, or curiosity. Examples of spiritual values are peace or truth or grace. Most of us have many values and there is a surprising amount of worldwide and religious agreement on some of the basic values, as mentioned above. This doesn't guarantee that people manage to live by their values. The fact is that values are often in contradiction with each other. So, I may feel that I should care for other people, in principle, but in practice my own needs will have to come first, for if I don't take care of resting and feeding and clothing myself, I cannot care for others either. Negotiating values is complex and many people find it much easier to stay within a particular religious framework that dictates how they should make decisions and live their lives. This is also not a guarantee of them living up to those standards. People are often very confused about their values.

Nietzsche (1974 [1882], 1961 [1883], 1969 [1887]) famously spoke about the need for human beings to re-evaluate all their values.

> Let us therefore *limit* ourselves to the purification of our opinions and evaluations and to *creation of our new tables of values* . . .
> (Nietzsche, 1974 [1882]: 335)

This is easier said than done, though Nietzsche's work shows us a path towards this kind of raising of awareness. As we have said several times, the human condition is a dynamic one that we can never control. Existentially and onto-dynamically speaking, for every value we have there is an opposite that is generally experienced as a threat, although it may just be the absence of the value. We have looked at this in our chapter on paradox and dialectics. For the value of being attractive there is the feared threat of being ugly. For the value of being a virtuous person there is the threat of being a bad person. It is tempting for people to champion the positives and malign the negatives. But as we have seen in the previous chapter, to learn to move forward dialectically we have to accept that life requires us to make room for the tensions of life. So we learn to develop our negative capability, as Keats called it, i.e. our capacity for tolerating uncertainty and negativity, taking on board the ways in which the absence of the good is sometimes a blessing. We need the dark to sleep and darkness helps us appreciate the value of light. We learn to feel less threatened by negatives and to find our way with all the colours of the emotional spectrum as we become more dialectically aware. As a researcher you have to manage a certain amount of neutrality in this respect, rather than judging your results in simplistic ways. You are phenomenologically observing a process, rather than rating people. You are not judging people's values and emotions, but understanding how these move them in their lives. The objective of your research is not to engage with your participants' values and certainly not to encourage them to challenge and change them. You can only do SEA research if you have learnt to be aware of both sides of the equation and appreciate that life is always a process of balancing contradictory forces, in finding an equilibrium.

Differentiating Values, Beliefs, Aspirations, Principles and Ideals

When your participant speaks about what matters to them or what they care about, or worry about, it is easy to get caught up in their narrative and lose track of the unspoken values that lurk behind their words.

Values can easily be obfuscated by a person's expressions of their beliefs and assumptions or even their opinions. In our research on freedom for instance we found that though all participants said they valued freedom, their ideas about what freedom was differed considerably. This was even true in terms of their shifting definitions of freedom throughout their own narratives.

When we interviewed each other as part of our pilot project, to formulate our interview questions, we became more acutely aware of this. So, for instance our initial search for freedom in our lives was in both our cases deeply inspired by the desire to be rid of pressures and tensions that had been imposed on us as teenagers. We sought to live in a way that was without such pressures, obligations and duties, to find our own way in the world. But as we encountered various situations of freedom of this type, we discovered that we sometimes felt lost, as we no longer had ground under our feet, or other people around us who needed us or cared for us. This altered our belief in what it means to be free and we discovered that freedom can often coincide with lack of identity or loss of social integration. This can even lead to a feeling of disintegration and loss of meaning (Yalom, 1980). Both of us found that with new engagements in the world our identity and confidence were once again built up. But we also found that the process of seeking freedom had led to the possibility of discarding a previous value system and renewing our values. Core values, like love, truth and peace and justice and freedom were also altered, though they remained in place. Whereas previously we might have thought that such values would remain exactly the same over time, we discovered that each of these principles of human existence became more specific after difficult experiences of loss of identity. Love may have been confused with commitment and loyalty previously, where it turned out to be more about truly seeing another and wanting the best for them. Truth was obviously expanding with every year of one's life, as more facts of reality were learnt and more experiences led to greater understanding of what was true and false. Similarly, the ideas of peace (world peace) were much more nuanced after discovering the limitations of a life devoid of conflict, leading to a much more complex understanding of how the movement towards peace is only possible when we remain open to diversity, disagreement, contradictions and conflicts. Freedom itself turned out to be a very moveable feast too. We could be free from worries only at the cost of loss of purpose. We could be free in terms of our physical freedom only at the price of working to earn our keep and have shelter and food available to us. We could be intellectually free only after much study and thought. In other words, values have a way of expanding and changing along the way of our investigation. Our values are initially wrapped up in our beliefs, assumptions and opinions about the world. They become purified as we learn more about their many aspects, connections and implications (Deurzen, 2025).

Similarly, if people hold strong principles, or ideals, such as 'all my decisions should be uniquely based on the principle that freedom is more important than anything else', it is difficult to investigate that value in a person's life, because it has become an obligation and a duty and a dogma rather than a value. This was something our participant Luke discovered when he said:

> but then because over the last 9/10 years I've done a phenomenal amount of travelling, it's been brilliant, but then I started to question it and think 'ooohh am I getting attached to the idea of travelling?' and is it, is it, it's not quite a material thing but it's almost like a dependency on the travelling to get my freedom.

Values are vectors of attraction, but there are many of them. If a person becomes wholly directed towards one particular value, they are no longer existentially dynamic. They have become machine like, robot like, and are no longer making decisions based in choice and uncertainty. They may even have become blind to the consequences of operating with certain values rather than others. It is important that a person has some doubt and openness towards the impact of their values on their life. They need to be able to let themselves be challenged by the reality of living with their values, for this is how they find knowledge and wisdom.

Different Layers of Value

It is possible to remind yourself of the different layers of value that people are operating with, before we attach them to the four dimensions of existence. Figure 8.1 illustrates the layers that a person is engaged with in the world, where 1 and 2 purport to the physical aspects of life, 3 and 4 relate to the social dimension, 5 and 6 to the personal dimension and 7 and 8 to the spiritual dimension. Observing how much of participants' discourse is related to these different layers of values can be very enlightening.

1. *Cosmic values.* We are all cosmic creatures, part of an immense universe, in which certain values are dictated to us, whether we like it or not. These are the values we have discovered through physics, and it is likely that our understanding of these fundamental values will change over time as we discover more about the universe. Right now we know that as humans we are

exposed to time, space, the strong and weak nuclear forces, the electromagnetic forces and the forces of gravitation, speed and light. How we relate to these affects our everyday existence. We can ignore them, or we can let ourselves be lifted up by this belonging to something greater than ourselves. Religions speak about the cosmos in a very different and more mystical way, as they address God.
2. *Natural values.* We are also natural creatures and are inserted into a physical environment that dictates many other aspects of what is possible or impossible for us. In our physical reality we are subjected to numerous physical needs: for shelter, for food and water, for safety, for sleep and for affection, sexuality and procreation. Out of these basic needs values are generated. We know for instance that if a person is suffering hunger and thirst their value of survival will override any social or cultural values that may stand in the way of them obtaining food and drink or feeding their children.
3. *Cultural values.* As social animals, human beings are constantly reminded of the obligations they have towards the groups they belong to. There are many cultural values that are shared around the world, but some are specific to certain national or social backgrounds and most of these values evolve over time. We can for instance gather whether a person operates within an agricultural or industrial or cosmopolitan ethical framework. Cultures that live close to the land will tend to value things like work, thrift, selflessness, industry and dignity, and will loathe waste, dissipation, poverty or egoism. In our research on freedom, it became obvious that those people who are closely working with their herds of cows or goats or horses consider the feeling of freedom to be mostly about feeling free to roam around on their farm with their animals. Care for the animals will outstrip any desire for holidays or time off from the farm. This is something many mothers of newborn babies also feel. Their freedom will be tied up with being close to their child, because they value being free to attend to the child's needs over freedom from having to tend the child's needs. This shows again how important it is to examine how values operate in a person's life, for the same values can lead to very different life choices.

Human values evolved through history and are different according to the resources we use (Morris et al., 2015). Other examples of societal values are the opposition between the values of the enlightenment with those of medieval or more religiously based societies. Enlightenment cultures tend to pursue values like democracy, intelligence, knowledge, reason and progress. Such societies will tend to loathe ignorance, thoughtlessness, dictatorships and irrationality. Industrial societies are likely to favour other kinds of values, like efficiency, profit, centralisation and obedience.

It will also be obvious that some societal values are compatible with progression, such as science, evolution, improvement, change and practicality. Whereas other societal values will favour conservatism, such as steadiness, reliability, hierarchy, respect and predictability.

4. *Familial values.* These are the values we grow up with and they are often the same as our cultural or social values, except if the family has migrated, so that there may be important tensions between the cultural values of the society they live in and the family values which maintain the heritage of the culture of the past of the family. There are also many professional values that become like familial values, as professional groups can easily become like a family. Accountants for instance often have values around accuracy and clarity, integrity, confidentiality and objectivity, and obviously around accountability and trustworthiness. The values of craftsmen, like cobblers or potters or basket weavers, are very different and are often related to aesthetic values and creativity, experimentation, mastery and excellence. When families transfer particular professions to their children, the familial values are usually particularly strong. This may or may not be appreciated by the next generations.
5. *Personal values.* These are the values we have harvested throughout life and have kept as our personal trophies and commitments. They are usually a combination of familial, cultural, religious and natural values. But sometimes it is possible for people to acquire a whole new set of values because of a particular cultural phenomenon that revolutionises a person's outlook. So, many sixties' children adopted the hippy values of the era, without having been taught these by their elders. They shifted their value system to a philosophy that singled out peace as a central value, in a world that was still very concerned about war, both the war in Vietnam and the Cold War. Around this value of peace making were other values like love and freedom, or even equality of people of different cultures or shades of skin and of different genders. It was very much about awareness raising of inequality and campaigning for this to be addressed. Many young people were at odds with their parents over this sudden shift in values. Parents were often perturbed that the new generation was not taking the need for learning and working as seriously as the post-war generation had done. But circumstances had changed and work and learning and studying for a career seemed outmoded for a while. This changed again in later generations. And individuals who had adopted hippy values often replaced these with the very much more profit-orientated values of the following decades, where money began to become a value that people were after, along with success, achievement and ambition.
6. *Inner, hidden values.* There are the secret inner values that we tend to hide from other people and sometimes even from ourselves and that are rarely based in fashions or maintained by societal pressures. In our research on freedom some of our participants spoke of such inner values that they wanted to test out in the real world. Bea wanted to get away from being dictated to by the society she left behind. Olga wanted to find out if there were other people she could feel close with in terms of her spiritual search for meaning. Bonnie wanted to be free floating and experiment in her life, without being told off by authority figures. All of the people interviewed shared the sense that their secret yearning for a life more in tune with their sense of themselves would

make them happier and more at ease in the world. Any piece of SEA research should aim to mine such deep-seated personal feelings, rather than just staying at the surface. They are often in conflict with some other values that we are trying hard to conform to.

7. *Spiritual values.* These are the values that inspire us. They are the values that we project onto the gods, or that we hold responsible for living a good life or being a good person. Whilst they may be religious values, they may also be values that rise above religious allegiance, such as truth and love, respect of life, property and justice, which are values that are broadly shared by most of humanity. These are the values by which we judge other people. For though we accept that different people hold different values, we recognise that these spiritual values are non-negotiable. Even so, some societies manage to bypass such values temporarily. An example of this is the post-truth society that was known in the noughties and teens of the twenty-first century, when there was a strong trend towards deconstructing and relativising everything.

For a while it was fashionable to contend that truth was always open to interpretation, or at least had two sides to it. This makes it nearly impossible to opt for permanence in one's values, for they become relative instead of steady and reliable. In fact, they stop being values at all. The same is true during times of war when the idea of killing and ending human lives is suddenly acceptable and desirable, as long as it is the enemy we kill. Such times are utterly confusing in terms of a person's spiritual values, as they undermine the absoluteness of such values.

8. *Ultimate values.* These are the ontological values that are non-negotiable. They are the values that we discover are still in place even when everything else is being destroyed in life. When we are meditating or contemplating on our lives or when we are facing up to failure, loss or death we uncover this rock bottom of value. One of these values is that of infinity and eternity, the recognition that life was there long before you and will continue long after you. Another one of these values is that of being. This is the realisation that things exist and that life is something mysterious and undeniable in the world that cannot be extinguished even by the evillest of human actions. When we are sunk into that inner black hole, where truth is the only thing that remains, we are confronted with this bottom line of ethical awareness. Though everything may be in question, some incontrovertible truth remains. Death as a reality will always present itself as the ending of whatever we have been concerned about to date. Tolstoy's story of *The Death of Ivan Illyich* (Tolstoy, 2008) is a good example of someone who realises that their ultimate values are more in line with their neglected spiritual values and family values, than with the personal values they had lived with all their lives. This was very much in line with Tolstoy's own experiences, as discussed in his book *Confessions* (Tolstoy, 1983 [1886]). Often when we are exposed to a situation that challenges our values and reveals ultimate values to us, we return full circle to the cosmic values we start with.

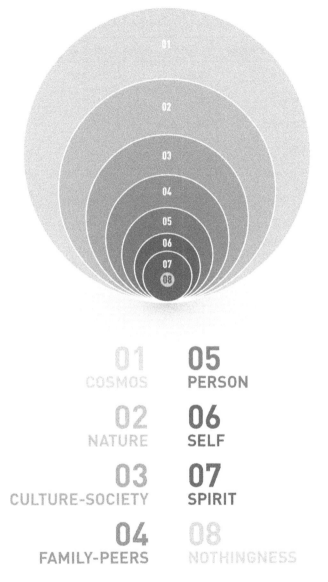

Figure 8.1 Layers that a person is engaged with in the world (Deurzen, 2025)

Existential Tables of Value

Table 8.1 (Deurzen, 2010, Deurzen and Adams, 2016) shows an outline of values at the four dimensions of human existence, alongside their opposites. As we saw in the chapter on paradox, it is vital to remember that life is never about seeking positivity or festering in negativity. It is always about dealing with the tension of

Table 8.1 Positive purposes and negative concerns and minimal and optimal goals on the four dimensions (adapted from Deurzen, 1998)

Dimension	Positive Purpose	Negative Concern	Minimal Goal	Optimal Value
Physical	Health	Illness	Fitness	Vitality
	Pleasure	Pain	Safety	Wellbeing
	Strength	Weakness	Efficacy	Ability
	Life	Death	Survival	Existence
Social	Success	Failure	Skill	Contribution
	Belonging	Isolation	Kinship	Loyalty
	Acceptance	Rejection	Recognition	Cooperation
	Love	Hate	Respect	Reciprocity
Personal	Identity	Confusion	Individuality	Integrity
	Perfection	Imperfection	Achievement	Excellence
	Independence	Dependency	Autonomy	Liberty
	Confidence	Doubt	Poise	Clarity
Spiritual	Good	Evil	Responsibility	Transparency
	Truth	Untruth	Reality	Authenticity
	Meaning	Absurdity	Sense	Value

opposites. The energy of life comes from the interaction of polarities, exactly like batteries allow power to flow between a positive and a negative side. The paradox is that we gain more vitality when we are aware of illness and mortality than if we deny these things and exclusively pursue health and fitness. We move from value to a sense of meaning when we gain insight into the way in which the forcefield of life works. As we live and experiment and learn about life, we gradually acquire more skill and understanding of how it all works.

It helps in SEA research to have an instrument to guide us in observing where a person has been landed in their quandary, or where they are situated in the world in relation to a particular issue. It can be good to be aware of minimal goals and optimal goals as compared to positive purposes and negative concerns.

Application of the Lens of Purpose

In a research project we are never in the business of improving our participants' lives or influencing them directly in any way. Despite this, many participants of SEA research give the feedback that they found the dialogue therapeutic and that it led to them having a better grasp of what was happening to them. Although we don't challenge our participants about their lives, we inevitably encourage them to reflect on where they are positioning themselves. In this process it does help if we understand how life works and in particular it matters that we understand about values and emotions. This is particularly necessary when we come to the attribution of meaning to our findings and we write up our results, interpreting our data and making sense of it all. We can only learn the deep lessons of what we are investigating by applying our philosophical understanding to it.

So, for instance in our freedom findings, we found that there were several people who sought freedom at some point in their life because they wanted to release themselves from certain social pressures upon them to conform to the expectations of society and family. To seek out freedom from conformity is a search for a situation in which temporarily there are no rules and no obligations. What we found was that when people were able to establish this kind of temporary pause in their lives, removing themselves from all commitments and organisations that would impose the same rules, they fell into a kind of hole. After richly enjoying that heady sense of freedom Alice for instance felt out of touch with her family and began to realise she valued some things from the past, though she was glad to be rid of other aspects of her previous life. Bea, who moved to a foreign country, rather like Olga had also done, found herself initially disconnected from the world around her, in a place where she was isolated and didn't feel she belonged anymore. So, though she had found that much desired liberty, she was now paying the price with the loss of other values she had not known were also important. It is therefore important to get a picture of how the whole value system shifts for a person and how they are able to learn more about values they have previously only known superficially. Bea said that she had found physical freedom to do as she wished, but that the thought that nobody cared about whether she was unsafe in that process was a bit of a shock to the system. Olga's freedom was very physical, it was about independent travel and sexual liberation. She felt she achieved this completely, but also discovered new values in the process. One of which was about belonging to the cosmos and feeling totally at ease in it, trusting it to keep her safe.

Any piece of SEA research will throw up such differences, since interviewing people about their most secret beliefs and values is always going to show up more distinct personal aspects and fewer shared values.

This is why SEA research has not only grown out of the practice of existential therapy but why it helps for SEA researchers to be a trained therapy practitioner. Understanding how a person's emotional experiences are directly related to their values is crucial when we start recording which values our participants are chasing and which troubles they appear to be trying to keep at bay. As psychotherapists doing research, we will find it easier to spot values in people's discourse than if we have not been trained to do so. We will also have facilities for challenging a person's narrative about a value.

For instance, let's say you are interviewing someone about their desire for freedom and they say to you that their idea of freedom is to have achieved perfection in the way they deal with their emotions and with their relationships, because it is their feelings and the intimacy with others that plagues them and makes them feel most unfree. While you will be recording their words and gestures, you will also wonder whether they are truly thinking this through. You may ask a supplementary question, without influencing their view, saying something like: 'Do you believe that human perfection is possible or desirable?' This will open up their very closed view about freedom and they may find that there is a lot more to explore before they have finished with this issue. If you said: 'Have there been times you have felt free when things weren't perfect?' this would also prompt them to further investigation of what they truly believe about freedom and what their experiences are. So, these kinds of interventions are helpful and will probe the issues under investigation more deeply.

Summary of Work with Values

1. Listen for values that are expressed in the interview and probe for contradictory or confirmatory evidence.
2. When you have transcribed your interview, read through it one time finding the values that are explicit, such as 'I really don't like people who lie' or 'I always wanted to travel and be free'. Then read through it a second time to find the values that are implicit. So, when someone keeps returning to the notion that she should not do certain things, or have certain things, ask yourself if the value expressed here may be 'modesty' or 'reticence'.
3. Keep two lists of the values you have spotted, implicit and explicit, and list them under the different rubrics of The Four Worlds, in Table 8.1.
4. You may also search for the opposite to the values, so for instance if someone talks a lot about commitment in love and to a job, are they at any point speaking about infidelity or changing jobs?
5. Alternatively, you can use the list of eight different kinds of values or decide to catalogue values in any other way that is systematic and coherent.
6. Now you will need to connect the values with the emotions introducing them or showing up as these values are mentioned or implied. This will become clear in the next chapter.

Intentionality, Purpose and Value

For the piece of research we conducted on freedom for this book, we viewed the transcript through the lens of intentionality, purpose and value, looking at where in the transcript the participants referred to their values and where they were talking about their purpose or intentionality.

We found that Luke talked about this element the most out of the three participants whose interviews we worked on, whereas Olga expressed her values more than her purpose and direction in life and Bonnie a combination of the two positions.

Once the individual meaning units of purpose and intentionality had been identified they were grouped together in broad themes. Further work was undertaken to try and assimilate these various aspects into an overarching theme which captured the experience. For example, Luke talked about his experiences of travelling in various places in the transcript as it related to purpose and intentionality;

these were grouped together as shown in the box below and a theme title of *Urge to travel and completely change the environment* was created from the following meaning units:

> - I just want to travel
> - This real urge to travel, to really travel properly
> - We might never be able to travel again so I had to make peace with that a little bit
> - Sometimes felt this urge to do and go to places
> - I just need to change this, completely change my environment

This process was repeated for each of the meaning unit groups which culminated in the following themes being identified:

- Urge to travel and completely change the environment
- Planning a direction but remaining open to what comes
- Complete freedom emerges from responsibility and deliberateness
- Purpose comes from questioning life, being open to new possibilities and letting go
- Throwing myself into the future
- Releasing dependency on material, social and situational things

For Luke freedom was something that he discovered he had achieved over time rather than actively seeking it in the way that Olga had done. His journey started with an urge to change his environment and to travel and to see different places, people and cultures. But before he could take this leap, he needed to ask himself lots of questions about his life and what he wanted or what he didn't want. Questions such as 'What am I going to do?', 'This isn't it, is there more to life than this?', 'Do I start again?' and 'Throw everything away?' This process of questioning enabled Luke to connect to what he was feeling and his sense of purpose. As a result of this questioning, he felt compelled to act. This involved opening himself up to new possibilities and experiences and letting go of his current life.

Luke found that freedom required responsibility towards yourself, in finding a direction, a purpose to aim for, and this also required a deliberateness. Freedom needed to be chosen in a deliberate way, and to ensure it was maintained, personal responsibility held him to account. There was a paradox in his intentionality to travel in this free way, between needing to plan a direction, i.e. to go East, whilst also avoiding planning and letting experiences dictate the direction of travel. Part of Luke's purpose was to stop the element of planning which he felt had taken over his life.

Not having a plan, just a direction, meant that Luke was throwing himself into his future with one guiding principle, 'to say yes to everything'; this allowed for one thing to happen after the next, and being immersed in what was happening to him rather than planning what he was going to do. Part of this throwing himself into the future also involved releasing the dependency he had on things, material things, relationships and situations or places. This process even led him to question, in a paradoxical way, whether he had become dependent on travelling to gain his freedom and how freedom might actually come through how he thought rather than what he did.

When looking at Luke's values he stated that 'Freedom is my number one value'; this was echoed by Olga who also held this as her main value and who similarly attempted to attain her freedom through travelling. Luke's other values were:

- Having a sense of responsibility and professional integrity
- That it is good to question a lot of things
- A passion for the Far East and a love of Eastern philosophy
- A real sense of purpose from connection
- Wanting to experience different things and ways of doing things
- Valuing people who were calmer, happier and more genuine

The antithesis of what he valued revealed that:

- Money was not a motivator
- He didn't want to be pulled along by the system
- Ticking all the boxes of what society expects does not lead to happiness

Olga's intentionality themes were similar to Luke's:

- Her main motivator was to be free
- Wanting to encounter life in new ways, going ever wider
- Ensuring that she is living according to her values
- Needing to make good on her ideas

Bonnie's experience of freedom differed from the experience of both Luke and Olga. Bonnie did not experience her freedom through travelling; instead it came from more everyday life events. Bonnie's intentionality themes were:

- Weathering the storm
- Freedom emerges, it cannot be made to happen
- Trust yourself
- Being open to the future

One of the ways in which Bonnie's intentionality was revealed was the attitude she took towards difficult times or experiences. This involved her trying to find ways through the difficulties, which she highlighted when she said: 'I just get through this'. This attitude is a way in which she copes with the unpredictability of life and how she orientates herself in life.

Part of the unpredictability of life is that it is not possible to know in advance when you will have an experience of freedom. Bonnie describes how freedom comes from the inside out and that it 'pops up' because it is already there as a possibility and therefore freedom is an act of discovery; you discover yourself in the moment of freedom. Bonnie stressed that you cannot consciously make freedom happen and this is echoed by Luke when he describes how he became aware of his freedom through travelling and did not set out to have an experience of freedom. Olga on the other hand is more focused on how she directs herself towards experiences of freedom; this is a major ongoing goal for her and is very intentional.

Bonnie describes how freedom comes about through being true to yourself, trusting herself and also trusting the situation that will enable something to emerge. Again, this is how she orientates herself towards the world, as trust.

Likewise, Bonnie orientates herself towards the future in an open way, allowing herself not to know what will happen next, not getting bogged down with difficulties or wanting to know. This is linked to the other theme of trusting herself. Bonnie trusts that whatever she encounters she will be able to find a way through and will also have experiences of freedom.

As these illustrations demonstrate, looking at values, intentionality and purpose reveals differing aspects of the phenomenon under investigation. This particular piece of research also shows how looking at intentionality and purpose can highlight the processes and elements that lead to experiences of freedom. This will be discussed further in Chapter 10 when all the different lenses will be brought together.

Chapter 9

The Filter of PASSION

The Filter of Passion: The Emotional Compass

Existential therapy always zooms in on the deeply felt reality of a person. Existential research should do the same and bring out the emotional and ethical content of an experience, something so often left unsaid and unheard of in research. As we saw the importance of locating a person's values and beliefs in the previous chapter, we also saw how closely this is connected to the feelings people have about the things in the world that they experience. Values and beliefs help to identify what is important and meaningful for a person. They help a person move towards things that matter to them and away from things and experiences which are not important. Emotions and moods also help a person navigate their experiences. As for any navigation a compass is useful, and the emotional compass has been designed to show how emotions are connected to the values a person holds. The emotional compass applies just as much to sensations, to feelings, to moods, to thoughts as to moral intuitions.

Why Emotions Matter So Much

In everyday life, each word we say, each gesture we make and each action we undertake is a way through which we express our feelings and intentions about the world and our relationship to it. In an existential dialogue, a person is enabled to become aware of how they are situated in relation to their world and how they feel about the different aspects of their life that they are describing. They learn to recognise that things are never neutral. In the same way in nature, there is always weather, there is always emotion or mood in a person. To become aware of this is to see the links between the person and the world in which they find themselves and to note the way in which they experience this. They can begin to trace what they value, prize and want and what they devalue, fear or despise. They will begin to see how the paths they have taken and the choices they have made are an attempt to reach spaces and places that they will feel are both safe and worthwhile. To appraise yourself and your life is not something you learn to do very early on. Therefore, we cannot assume in an existential dialogue that the other person is familiar and conversant with their own values, feelings, evaluations and purpose.

Many people are confused about what it is that they want in the world and in life. They often chase things that they have come to believe that they should want, without necessarily doing so with any inner conviction or a deep sense of commitment. Values exist at all levels. As we have seen in the sections on paradox and values, the things we desire are often opposed to things we dread. A very simple way of understanding human emotion is to recognise that we feel good when we move towards the things that we want and value and we feel bad when we move away from them. Most people imagine that there is a state of happiness they could achieve if only they could remain or be united with the things they value so that they can stay in their comfort zone and be in a happy place. The reality is quite different. Life is in constant movement and is a dynamic process, not one state. Change is inevitable and inexorable. We cannot fix life and we cannot hold onto the things we value forever. We can only do our best to work towards certain objectives or ways of being, but circumstances and other people will affect and alter our situation continuously and therefore we find that the goalposts are constantly moved. As soon as you have obtained that job you so badly wanted, or you have bought that house that was going to make you happy ever after, or you have finally secured that relationship your heart lusted after so passionately, you will discover that things are not quite what they seemed. That job that was going to secure the income you craved turns out to take over all your time and attention and exhausts your available energy. It has also exposed you to colleagues who bring out unknown dark feelings in you, that you haven't even begun to formulate for yourself, let alone understand. That house you couldn't live without and that looked so perfect turns out to have far more structural defects than the survey seemed to describe, and you realise its neighbours are very noisy and keep you up at night. The partner you were so in love with, turns out to have some unpleasant habits and goes off with mates every weekend and isn't helping with the cleaning or the shopping, so you feel as if you have made a terrible mistake and you feel lonely and forsaken, but can't quite believe this yet. All these feelings are telling you something important about what you treasure and what is precious to you. For instance in the case of the job, perhaps you wanted the security or the status, or the challenge, or the income, or the opportunities the job brought you, but now you can see that along with those values that you have obtained you have also become connected to a situation that brings with it a whole raft of things you do not like. Similarly, the house you bought because you valued the idea of having your own safe space in the world, where you could do as you pleased, has brought awareness about the precariousness of property and the many demands it makes on you. With possessions come the responsibilities of care and this alters your feelings about your values. Gradually life brings home the reality that everything we want and achieve has a price and that we are never alone in the world, that situations evolve and bring new aspects to the fore, many of which we may not love. There will always be things going wrong, there will always be other people throwing their hat in the ring. There will always be uncertainties to contend with. Maturing is a process of discovering that wanting things is only the start and that our values become refined by experience. For instance, young people may just look for someone who will love them and be faithful, and they will discover that love is far more complex than that. It doesn't mean that love is not possible. If a partnership is truly mutual and based in a commitment to solving differences and conflicts together, the value of love will gradually expand. If you labour under the illusion that another person can meet all your needs, demands and expectations, you may end up feeling that love is impossible. Values often start out being rather simplistic, one-sided and naïve. We all go through our own version of learning that teenage dreams of solving all our problems by becoming rich and famous or by being loved and adored by people crash on the rocks of reality. Even popstars or film stars, footballers and media personalities discover that there are no superpowers, and all human beings have feet of clay. Not only do we all have to contend with mortality, illness, rejection and disappointment, privileges like wealth and celebrity bring their own unpleasant challenges such as loss of privacy, trust and intimacy. For every value we acquire we give up something else.

The existential reality is that every human being keeps moving around a continuous cycle of chasing values, losing values, feeling moments of happiness, and moments of sadness. The whole range of the emotional spectrum is available to each of us and we will feel these feelings whether we like it or not. Many people yo-yo from great emotional heights to deep lows without any understanding of what is happening to them and what the existential meaning of their emotions is. Many people are simply not aware of their hidden values. Clients who come for therapy are often as confused about themselves as they are unhappy. We should not assume that the people we interview in a piece of SEA research are necessarily conversant with the meanings of their feelings and values. Many ordinary folks go through life suppressing their feelings as much as they can, because most cultures teach us to do this. At the same time people know, at some level at least, that their emotions are essential to their vitality and to the intensity of their experience. They may not be clear though about how their emotions guide them towards what they care about and worry about and motivate them to do what needs to be done. Just like pain and pleasure guide us in the physical world to help us avoid what is dangerous and pursue what feels good, so happiness and sadness guide us in our life choices.

What makes things far more complicated is that we have many different feelings about many different things and people and events and memories and future plans and more things going on in our lives than we can compute consciously. In one moment of your here and now existence your mind is being confronted with thousands of impulses and reminders about the things that currently matter in your life. While there may be an internal hierarchy of values, it is hard to say how exactly you are going to prioritise your values and emotions. Your concern for your parents and other family members may for instance compete with your concern for your partner, friends, colleagues and peers. And all of these may contradict your impulse to do something that currently seems most attractive to you. It is impossible to do right by everyone all the time. It is impossible to serve all your values at once. There is a permanent film of past life playing at the back of your mind and you are constantly comparing what you are doing now to what you did yesterday, last year, ten years ago and what others are doing and what you might want to do tomorrow or next week, next year or in ten years. You are having to knit together your story minute by minute, with new information coming in every second from so many different sources, that it feels as if the input is out of your control. And yet you are having to make decisions and will do so, whether you are choosing your options deliberately or by default. We have seen how complex our values are and how many layers of them impact on our lives. Values will organise what you attend to first and foremost and what you ignore. Values will trigger the feelings that will guide the decision making that will lead and prompt your actions. Bear in mind that the story your research participant tells you is an attempt at making sense of a multi-faceted experience, which they may not have had a chance to reflect on very deeply previously. Go slow and bear with the feelings that are emerging and surfacing.

The Emotional Compass

It is important to be aware of the values, beliefs, aspirations and ideals of a person if you are going to try to make sense of their feelings. For the feelings are the energy expressing a person's dynamic striving towards what is of value to them and away from what threatens their values. Once we understand this, we can make good use of the instrument of the emotional compass (Deurzen, 2012 [1988], 2010 [1997]), which was designed to map the whole spectrum of human emotions along the natural cycle of our ups and downs. Emotions are the expression of where we find ourselves in relation to our values. Our feelings swing upwards as we move towards the possession of a value. Our feelings swing downwards when something or someone we value slips away and is lost. This illustrates how each emotion is a powerful marker of our position in the world, in relation to specific values. In this way emotions are also a reflection of where we would like to get to. They are the road markers and signposts on the journey of life as well as the source of particular qualities of energy needed at each juncture. Emotions only make sense when we understand them in connection with the values they refer to for a particular individual at a particular time in a specific situation. All of us are capable of each of these emotional states of mind and we encounter them every day in many ways, forms and shapes.

When we feel happily united with the things that we value (say a love relationship, a home, or something more abstract like our freedom for instance), we find ourselves figuratively on top of the world as we embrace our fate. This is represented at the top of Figure 9.1, as the space of happiness and flourishing. Here our feelings are high, and we feel at ease, as all seems well with the world. This usually turns out to be a rather fleeting experience which we cannot hold onto for very long. When we are feeling low and sad, we find ourselves at the bottom of our emotional world, out of touch with what matters to us. This is depicted at the bottom of Figure 9.1. At this opposite end of the emotional spectrum, we tend to experience life in a rather frozen state, feeling alienated and disaffected from our values. This is often referred to as a state of depression. The journey downward from happiness to sadness is the trajectory of disappointment and disengagement. The journey

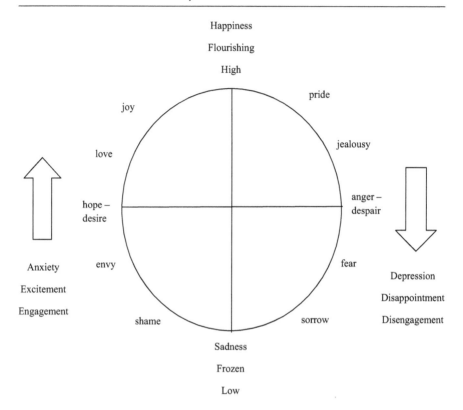

Figure 9.1 Compass of emotions

back upwards from sadness to happiness is the trajectory of engagement with a new value and this can bring excitement but is always fuelled by anxiety. When we are fully alive, we are constantly in one of these states or moods, somewhere along the emotional spectrum. We cannot live without feelings. We can only stop feeling something by moving into another feeling. We can however dim down or suppress our emotional tone.

It is easier to grasp the idea of the dynamic cyclical movement of our emotions when we divide the emotional compass up into four quarters, creating broader areas of the fundamental types of emotion. Besides the basic states of happiness and sadness, there are two types of emotions that bring us from happiness to sadness and two sorts of emotions that guide us back from sadness to happiness.

Imagine that the value you are seeking is placed at the top of the compass of emotions, in the place of happiness. Let's say that your value is 'freedom' and that you are currently pretty at ease with a large amount of freedom, as you have just gone on a year abroad and are pleased with this situation, doing a lot of what you like doing, such as surfing and working with animals. You feel in a great place, on a high.

The Filter of PASSION   149

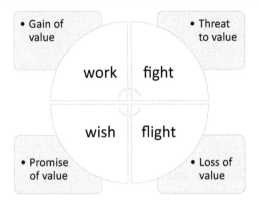

Figure 9.2 Four kinds of emotions

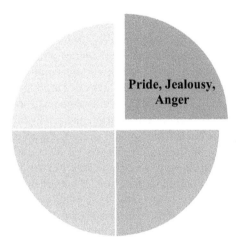

Figure 9.3 Threat to value: fight with pride, jealousy, anger

Everything seems pretty good and possible to you right now. But this won't last. Eventually you get back home and have to start on an admin job you don't really want to do, because you have to earn a living and save up to study for a career you want to invest in. Now you feel your sense of freedom is threatened. You move into the upper right corner of the diagram (Figure 9.3) into emotions of threat.

1. *Emotions of threat.* When you feel that your value is being threatened or thwarted, you will experience powerful emotions of threat. These generally

show up as defensive (pride), protective (jealousy) or aggressive feelings (anger). This may manifest in the first instance in a marked increase in your outward signalling of pride or confidence, as you try to hold onto your previous position and try to shore up the value you used to gain so much happiness from. Some people may call you confident, others may think you are a bit too proud or cocky or boastful and overconfident, and they may call you arrogant. Those who are more sensitive to your struggle may recognise that you are actually being defensive of something you instinctively fear is now under threat. As the threat to your value is becoming more serious you may feel an intense sense of jealousy, which is an attempt at guarding and protecting your value, holding onto what you love. Jealousy is like saying: don't touch my value for it's still mine. This works the same if your value is someone you love (like a partner), something you love (like your home), an idea you love (like freedom or truth) or something about yourself that you love (like your intuition, your creativity or your intelligence). If your possession of the value becomes completely untenable, and is suddenly no longer yours, you may find that threat so serious that your feelings explode into anger against anyone or anything that is threatening your value.

Not everyone's emotions run in the same pattern though. We all go down different paths and may find ourselves reacting in different ways at different moments. As we learn to recognise our values and emotions, we can alter the way it goes. Some people acquire certain emotional patterns that they get stuck in. Other people skip whole areas of emotion and may for instance swoop past pride and jealousy straight into anger, as soon as they feel threatened. Not everyone is good at doing pride and confidence. Some people are in permanent jealous competitive mode. It often means that they are insecure about the value they are defending. Others go from cockiness to anger in a flash. It depends a lot on how self-possessed you are in your enjoyment of your value and how entitled you feel to it. If you completely lack confidence in your claim to that value (especially if the value is a person or an object for instance), you may bypass this kind of emotion altogether and slide straight from the pleasurable illusion of possession to a despairing feeling of loss of value, which means that you skip through the whole section of threat to your values and you bypass the idea of fighting altogether, shifting down a gear into emotions of loss straightaway.

2. *Emotions of loss*. When you experience your value as being taken away from you altogether, and it is clearly no longer useful or possible to fight for it anymore, you will flee and slide into emotions of loss and sorrow. As your value is slipping away from you, you may first experience feelings of despair or despondency. While these make you vulnerable, they can sometimes have the effect of attracting compassion and trigger help and support from others, which can lead to a retrieval of the value in some cases. When this doesn't happen, you may glide downwards into experiencing fear at the reality of your injury and defeat and you may feel an inclination to remove yourself from the situation altogether.

Figure 9.4 Loss of value: flight in despair, fear, sorrow

Some people crash into fear so easily that they run away from challenges and losses immediately and give up, giving over to sorrow and despair very quickly when under threat. Evasion of your threats may provide a temporary solution and help you find a space of sanctuary in your state of surrender. This may help you to lapse gracefully into the now inexorable descent into sorrow and with it the process of grieving and letting go. If we bypass this phase and do not allow time to ponder our loss of value it will be much harder to find a way to transform our sorrow into a new beginning.

As you descend down the slippery slope of your emotional cycle, through the lower right quadrant, the loss may make you feel you are falling into an abyss of sadness, right down to the bottom of your inner world, where you will end up feeling lost, paralysed, frozen and cut off. This can buy you time to absorb the loss and do the necessary mourning, but it can also become a cold and lonely place where you get trapped and end up passively lingering for far too long.

The bottom of the emotional compass is a strangely steady low plateau kind of place where you are flattened against the rock bottom of your existence and experience a dazed feeling of time and space being suspended, temporarily. In this state of withdrawal from the world, you may become so numbed that you feel your emotions have flattened altogether and you may say that you feel nothing. Gravity helps you to stay there, and this makes it tempting to dwell there longer than necessary in inactivity and impassivity. But sooner or later you will experience acute feelings of emptiness and deprivation that will disturb you from your slumbers. Heidegger called this existential guilt, which he showed led to existential anxiety and the desire to re-engage with the world.

Life will always present new challenges and possibilities and eventually you will feel your need and dispossession sharply. You still need to care for yourself if you are to survive and you now must re-engage with new values, from your humble and lowly position of temporary deprivation. You will embark on the next quarter of the emotional compass with some hesitation. It takes effort to wake up from a depressed position and to take the risk of re-engaging with new values. It helps to be inspired in some way.

3. *Emotions of promise*. Now, from your sadness, which often goes with feelings of self-denigration, you move into the third kind of emotions, which are emotions of promise and an appetite for renewal of value in your life. These emotions are hard to contend with from your position of misery and gloom in your lowly frozen place. Initially you may just feel a sense of shame at having failed at everything or feeling deficient as a human being. As you feel so disenchanted with yourself and your position in the world, you are likely to start feeling envy for people who are in a better position and who hold something of value that you desire also. This means that slowly the green shoots of new longing and yearning are making themselves felt. Hopefully this will be forward looking and not just backwards looking with regret over what was lost. It is a good thing when you can renew your commitment to working for a lost value, in a new way, and this is how you ascend into the lower left quadrant of the cycle. In letting go of your past value, i.e. a lost spouse, or house, or sense of accomplishment, or pursuit of a certain goal, and find a new goal, a new partner, dwelling, commitment or value to work towards, your aspirations will be so the clearer and more realistic as you have derived meaning from your previous losses and begin to understand better how life works. You can see how to go about finding new purpose and you are ready to engage with the work of obtaining this.

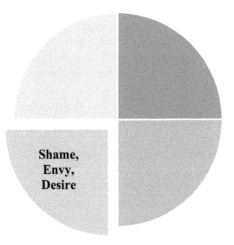

Figure 9.5 Promise of value: from freeze to shame, envy and desire

It is very common to feel shame and guilt in this aspirational phase of emotionality, as you will tend to struggle with not feeling good enough or regretting past mistakes and you may blame yourself for this, falling back to the frozen state at rock bottom occasionally. You may also see other people enjoying the value you aspire to with relish and your envy will sting you into action (or crash you back into the ground of your sadness if you give up on your own capacity or lack of strength, confidence or motivation). One of the real problems in finding and engaging with new purpose is that this goes with the activation of your ergotropic, sympathetic, active working mode again, whereas you could maintain a sleepier or nurturance-seeking trophotropic, parasympathetic mode of being whilst in your depressed state. The ergotropic mode kicks your system right back into the alertness of anxiety, readying you with the energy you need for action. This is uncomfortable and challenging, but also exhilarating if you don't pathologize the feeling of anxiety but recognise it as a burst of new energy and focus it on your new project. It is vital to have such focus and a realistic objective for that energy if you are going to push forward towards the next phase, entering into the upper left corner of the emotional cycle, which is that of the gaining of value.

4. *Emotions of gain.* In the upper left quarter of the compass of emotions, we are in that very demanding phase of movement towards something we truly value. This often feels like hard work and calls for our commitment and full engagement, even our dedication. Nothing is easier than to slump back down the compass into a feeling of inferiority or deficiency, giving up. It is not easy to learn to tolerate anxiety and it is hard to learn to use its energy in constructive ways, in order to do the work required for success in achieving something of value again.

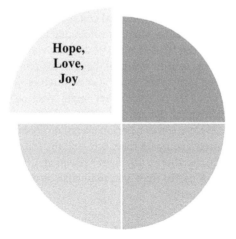

Figure 9.6 Gain of value: find hope, love, joy

The emotional experience here is always coloured by the sense of hope, which is the feeling of committing to a new future where there is possibility and where good things will come our way as we do what we can to obtain them. The extent to which we are willing to work for our values is the extent to which we will do the work of loving what we want and wanting what we love. Love is that feeling of going out of yourself, reaching towards what is valuable and attractive, good and desirable. It always takes work and devotion, and for it to endure we have to carry on doing that work, day after day, moment after moment. This explains why love should never be taken for granted, because it only survives as an emotion if it is maintained as a stance in the world and is realised in active and engaged commitment. Eventually such hard work will pay off in feelings of joy, which come from that wonderful sense of being all at once united with what we value and love. To achieve what we desired and worked so hard towards provides us with momentary pleasure and delight, perhaps even elation. This takes us to feeling on top of the world. It is as if we can take flight into happiness once more. As soon as we reach such happiness, we can be sure that it will turn into pride and jealousy or anger, as our value will inevitably be threatened by the predictable process of entropy and loss.

Putting all of this together, the whole compass of emotion looks like that shown in Figure 9.7.

It is important to understand that each emotion is the manifestation of a particular way of being in relation to a specific value and that what matters in the research is that we track the emotional experience in relation to the value in question. Each emotion is connected to a particular colour on the colour spectrum and is placed on the compass in the right position in relation to its opposite, which will also be its complementary colour. A lot can be done with this understanding that emotions are arranged like the colours of the rainbow and are all necessary for the full spectrum of light to shine in our lives. There are no good and bad colours and there are no good and bad emotions. Emotions move us along towards values and away from lack and need.

The emotional compass can be used in lots of different ways. As always, the creativity of the researcher and the specific needs of the research project will determine how to proceed. We have seen many interesting SEA research projects where researchers designed new ways of using the compass. They might focus on sensations rather than feelings, or they might compare the ups and downs of a particular person over time, tracing the dialectical development of a person's learning about a particular situation.

One researcher created a compass rose, bringing the four compasses of the four dimensions of existence together in one figure (Bennett, 2014).

There are a number of useful steps you may wish to take when using the emotional compass in SEA research:

1. Trace and record the emotions expressed in the dialogue.
2. It helps to video record sessions on zoom, so that you can remind yourself of facial expression, gestures, silences, tears, grimaces, tone of voice and breathing. Emotions are often visible even when not expressed in words.

The Filter of PASSION 155

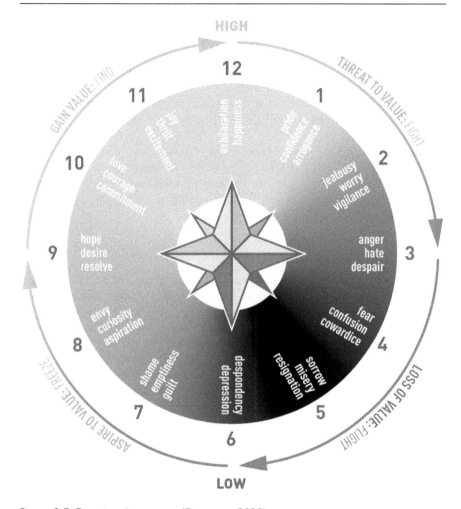

Figure 9.7 Emotional compass (Deurzen, 2025)

3. Determine initially whether the emotions observed are emotions of threat, loss, promise or gain or describe full possession or dispossession of value.
4. Track the specific values each emotion relates to and never assume there is one major value driving the participant, not even when you are investigating one (as was the case with our freedom research project).
5. Find a way to represent how these emotions were experienced by each of your participants. Some emotions may seem positive or negative according to circumstances. Jealousy might be experienced as vigilance and caution rather than as possessiveness and paranoia for instance.
6. Ask yourself whether emotions were side tracked by values other than those related to the topic under investigation. For instance, if a person is deeply bereft of a parent who has died but is just entering into a sexual relationship with a

highly desired partner, there may be tensions and contradictions in their emotional experience. On the one hand they are soaring towards joy, whilst on the other hand they are still despondent in their un-mourned loss.
7. Make a comparison of the emotional dynamic trajectories of all participants and see if there are any predictable patterns.
8. Work out how a person negotiated, understood, interpreted and learnt from their gains and losses of values.

All of this is complex and sophisticated, as our emotions are. It will become clearer when we return to Olga's interview on freedom. We shall illustrate how to work with passion and emotion in practice and how we used the lens of the emotional compass to establish more precisely what was going on for this participant in our SEA research project on freedom.

Application of the Lens of Passion: Illustration

At the start of the interview Olga is immediately engaged and emotionally present with the researcher. She expresses her interest in the topic of freedom and speaks about 'hard won financial freedom', thus defining freedom as the freedom from financial concerns initially and at the same time expressing her awareness of how hard this had been to come by. She says: 'I worked for a long time in a very unpleasant job to save lots of money' and looks and sounds pained at the memory. It is evident that she was indeed prepared to work extremely hard in a pressurised job to achieve this state of freedom. This shows that she has been through many difficult times and emotions in acquiring her value and that she is continuously aware that she will again lose this financial freedom, as funds run out. She tells the researcher that she had at the same time done a counselling course, preparing for a better future after her return from her world journey. She looks pleased about this and there is a sense of her pleasure at her own good planning. It seems like a flash of pride. She knows that this did not work out quite the way she planned, but she is still confident that she did the right thing to avoid having to work in a pressurised environment ever again. We may well wonder if she is telling the researcher that it is not just financial freedom she is aiming for, but freedom from unpleasant jobs altogether, which may mean that her value is more something like self-sufficiency or independence or autonomy. At this point she laughs. Humour comes from a place at the top of the emotional cycle. Humour is the release of tension that occurs when we suddenly grasp the loss of dignity and pretence that a human being has been holding onto, and their collapse into humiliation and humbling is exposed. When we see someone slipping on a banana skin, who previously was walking head held high, this is funny, whereas when someone elderly and frail and who was previously already bent over falls, it triggers compassion and pity, which comes from our identification with another's plight and pain in watching them falling to the ground. Fragility falling is painful, whereas pride slipping and falling is funny: laughter is a sudden release of tension. We can find our own plight funny too, as

Bonnie describes in her interview, if we are able to let go of our pride. But if we are wounded or hurt and we desperately wish to restore our dignity, then we won't find it funny and resent it greatly if others laugh. When Olga laughs, she is laughing at herself. She continues: 'I looked at my bank balance and I thought, OK, now is the time. I can support myself on my savings for a certain amount of time'. She takes her desire for independence totally seriously but is aware that it will only be a token or rather temporary independence. She seems at ease with this and does not sound bitter. She is super realistic in her expectations.

Two minutes later, as she continues to explain, she actually says this:

It was a limited freedom, right, it didn't last very long but . . . well there was so many things in my life that I wanted to do but could never do because I didn't have the money and uh and when I had a certain amount of money and had my and you know fulfilled my obligations to myself, educational obligations and so on, I thought OK . . . I always knew what I really wanted to do and I had done something like before in a time before but for erm 10 years before that er I wasn't able to do it and so I felt, um I am going to see if this um if this is possible in my life, if certain things are possible not just in general but in my life and I think as I as I then realised that many people do and I felt for a long time, I already felt, if I'm not already too old for it. Although I wasn't actually that old [laughter].

This time she is really laughing quite a lot at herself, as if she is afraid that her desire to buy her freedom is somewhat odd or objectionable. The laughter sounds more like embarrassment than joy and relaxation. She is self-conscious about her objective, aware of its relative value. She is questioning her own hope in her objective, humbling herself, taking herself back into the left lower quadrant of the emotional compass. This also has the effect of grounding her.

As she continues her story and tells the researcher how she went at the age of 40 around the world on her own, she is hesitant about her self-approval, until the researcher remarks that this seems a brave thing to have done and would have exposed her to a lot of frightening experiences. She now remarks: 'I wanted that. I wanted to encounter life in ways that I hadn't encountered it before or only a little bit', confirming that her journey was not just about realising the value of freedom, but also an affirmation and testing of independence and courage. Olga confirms this by saying that she was excited to welcome all that into her life, though she was also a bit scared.

She talks about going to California for three months on a work study programme and travelling in the desert in the Southern Hemisphere and then going to the Far East, a stop she had only put in because the travel consultant had recommended it as somewhere easy to get away from. She found it hard to get away from. She fell in love with a man she met and went back to live in that country for ten years. This changed her entire life and she did things there like directing an opera and writing books and becoming sexually liberated in ways she could not have previously imagined. Now she sounds amazed and a little overawed at the magnitude of the changes that were brought on. This isn't just about freedom anymore. It is about exploring what life is about.

She considers whether or not she would have had such experiences without the world travel, and believes the sexual experimentation could still have happened, but she would not have seen the world as she did nor discover that geographical freedom.

The researcher asks: 'Can you explain to me what that freedom feels like and what you discovered in the process?' and Olga launches into a whole new part of the story of her discoveries.

As we saw earlier, at this point she speaks of her cosmic discoveries. She describes her astonishment at discovering that the sun sets in the north in Australia and how the sun is right overhead in Bangkok and goes out like a light. Her discovery that her relationship to the universe was expanding in this way was perhaps the most important one she says, especially since she had been working night shifts in London. She says:

> It was the actual moment to moment experience sensory and also emotional experience of being in a different place.

She gives various examples, including the example of the sky reaching to the ground, when in the desert, referred to previously. Olga is completely absorbed by her own recounting of her experience, and she shines with excitement at her amazing discoveries. She adds other things, then talks about her surprise, which turned into awe and wonder:

> at first I was very surprised. I thought how can the stars be on the ground [laughter] again, I wasn't by myself, so I asked other people, did you notice this and they said they did, but it didn't produce the same effect on them I could see that and um, and for me it was like, at first I thought what if we fall off, the planet, and then I thought well clearly we're not, so it's going to work somehow and then, and then I thought, the world is so big I wish I could go there and I would like to live for a long time so I could encounter all these things and I want my little mind to be widened more and more and more, um, it was like sort of a metaphysical kind of experience really.

Her overwhelming feeling at this point was of being one with the cosmos and the galaxy in a way she had never felt before. 'Yeah, it was that kind of feeling, it was less about me really and more about encountering, yeah, I keep saying in a word, reality, because that is what it is'. At this point the researcher says: 'so, it's about merging with something transcendent and feeling a part of that and it sounds like that gave you an ultimate sense of awe and freedom at how huge it all is'. Olga replies 'And I didn't find it scary, I almost found it a bit comforting'. The researcher asks how that was comforting.

Olga explains:

I don't know I think for me, all my life I wanted to be free, this is one of my main motivators in life, um and for many other people too and when I was travelling, when I started travelling, even then, I encountered other people like me who were travelling for the same reason not the majority but there were quite a few. So, kind of 'seekers' or something like that, right? Er, comforting because all the, all the troubles on this planet, um that are so limiting, and which impacted me as well so much and everyone else too, they are really so insignificant.

It is as if she has found a place of peace with this idea. She has discovered that it isn't really freedom she was looking for. She was seeking to experience something beyond the confines of her normal troubled life and discovered that she is really part of something huge that transcends the ordinary difficulties and the limitations of life by far. It is as if she has discovered a new spirituality, rather than just freedom. This merging with the galaxy has given her new ground under her feet as well as that whole universe, full of stars to belong with. Far from this unsettling her, it has given her a feeling of perspective and belonging.

The interview goes on for quite a bit after this and considers different aspects of freedom, such as political freedom and political threats to freedom, as well as the realities of having to find stability in a certain country in order to be able to enjoy the freedom of a pension fund. But at these points Olga is talking about more pragmatic considerations about her life choices. The most emotional part of the interview by far was her account of her transcendental and spiritual sense of merging with the cosmos, somehow floating beyond her previous concerns and seeing her life in its widest possible significance.

This tells us a lot about Olga's depth of awareness of the discovery of spiritual freedom, whereas in other parts of the interview the topics of physical freedom (travelling to different places), social freedom (discovering different cultures), sexual freedom (discovering different people in intimate ways), personal freedom (loving becoming a theatre director again after a long time, being an author, falling in love), political freedom (escaping from political oppression by moving to a different country), financial freedom (working hard to save money so as not to have to work for a bit) and freedom of expression (using pseudonyms) are all discussed in some detail.

Olga has thought a lot about all these things and has much to contribute to our understanding of freedom, but the most poignant moment of the interview was her story about the moment that she lay in the desert at night, seeing the stars going all the way to the ground, and she felt no longer afraid, but able to let herself merge with the stars. This was a moment of personal transformation that altered her outlook on the world and life. These things are no longer just ideas, they are now part of her experience. Olga says: 'it was a very physical, literally a very grounding experience of lying on the desert. So, I think it was that I, the feeling that this was not just an idea, this is how it is'. When she speaks about this she comes across as having calmed all emotion and somehow having found peace. Rather than chasing any particular value, or fearing losing a value, she has come to terms with a felt sense of truth. Truth is grounding in this way and rises up in the background, above and beyond our values and emotions.

Figure 9.8 shows how Olga's emotional experience of freedom can be charted using the emotional compass. Her emotions move from Pride, Confidence and Humour to Fear and Devastation, towards Embarrassment and Curiosity which results in Excitement and Awe. As described above, Olga moves back and forth in her emotional experience, and up and down.

Luke's experience of freedom was predicated by feeling that he had lost his freedom. He had begun to notice that he was unhappy and it was confusing to him because on many levels he had a good life and one that he felt he should be happy with:

> I had a nice house, it was a nice you know, four bed town house, nice and that and I had a nice car, a nice sports car and I had a nice girlfriend. I had, I ticked all those boxes if you like and people looking in would say like 'oh wow Luke, you've got everything, you know, it's amazing.

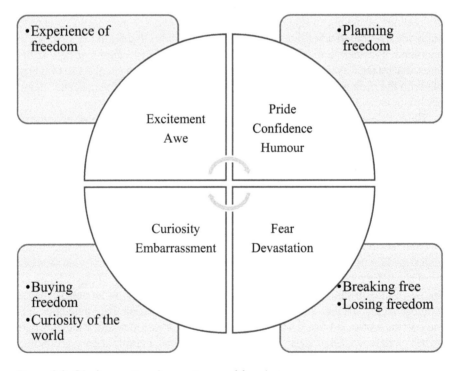

Figure 9.8 Olga's emotional experience of freedom

The feeling of unhappiness was the beginning of a process of re-evaluation that he undertook to look at his life and to try and discover the source of his unhappiness. One source was his relationship with his girlfriend, which ended, but another was feeling trapped within a system of corporate life that felt stifling.

After his experience of freedom, which came through travelling in the Far East, he also discovered that a loss of freedom came with the pace of life in the West, which was exhausting.

> I still felt it, I still felt the speed, the pace of society, the pace of life, so much faster and even when I was just leaving the house to go and I don't know, to go and buy some basic things at the shop, it was like oh ok erm right what time are the shops open, have I got my money, have I got my keys, have I locked the door, have I? It was like wow, oh wow that's 20 things I've had to do just to go, and basic, just to go and erm buy something. It was just, it was just, wow what's going on here?

A further loss of freedom came from an unexpected place when he did a graduate course that he felt would be very purposeful and rewarding but it actually led to a loss of optimism and hope for him, which related to the threat to his value of freedom. This threat to value became an actuality in that it led on to him feeling depressed and this made it difficult for him to access opportunities for freedom at this time. Therefore exhaustion, unhappiness and depression are all connected to a loss of freedom.

Luke's experiences of freedom were connected to his travelling. He describes his experience of complete freedom as:

> I had a friend that was living in Thailand at the time, so that gave me a destination to just to head towards, just somewhere to fly to and just to land. There was a little channel to direct, some direction. I mean to me, that was complete freedom. But I guess in a way, I'm trying to think in a way how it could be more complete, would I just go to the airport and just get on any plane maybe? I don't know [laughter] but that's quite interesting.

Luke spent time moving back and forth between the Far East and where he lived in the UK.

Returning to the UK, returning to the faster pace of life, where the 'world was coming at you', felt more difficult than living in a more 'by the seat of your pants' way that he was doing whilst travelling. He discovered that he needed bravery to combat those periods where he was moving between experiences of freedom and lack of freedom. Bravery enabled him to keep himself going before he was able to embark on another of what he called his 'freedom tours'.

Luke realised how important the experience of freedom had become to him, and how tied it was to his ability to travel. Lockdown during the COVID pandemic limited his ability to travel and therefore of any experience of freedom. During lockdown and since, Luke had to re-evaluate how freedom was tied up with travelling and how dependent he had become on it. This meant that he had to make peace with the possibility of not being able to travel in the same way again and the possibility of not being able to experience freedom in the same way. It meant that he started to think how he might find other ways to experience freedom, through travelling in the UK but also having freedom within his mind.

As part of this exploratory process Luke realised that the emotions he felt towards his experiences of freedom were about love and passion towards the environment that he was in. This was not just the physical environment, but an atmosphere that the environment had, which combined culture, society and other people. This love and passion were something he was seeking to recreate in other ways since that first experience.

Luke's emotional experience of freedom can be summarised as shown in Figure 9.9. The diagram shows how each of his emotional responses to freedom are related to value, whether that is a threat to value, a loss of value, a promise of value or a gain of value.

Both Olga and Luke spoke about the courage required of them in the process of aiming for freedom. Courage is closely related to mastering anxiety and persisting with the work of going towards your purpose and the things that matter to you. Both were also aware that the freedom values they had been pursuing developed over time. Initially they were felt as a freedom to get away from tension or particular ways of life. But gradually each of them began to develop an awareness of how much commitment and work was involved in staying with a process of freedom

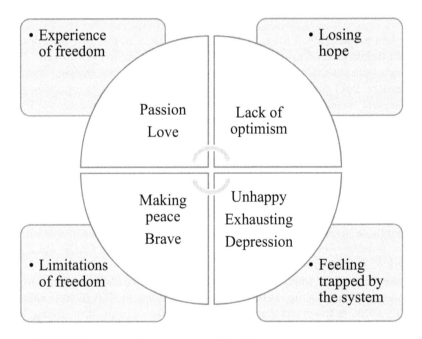

Figure 9.9 Luke's emotional experience of freedom

seeking. They also began to think about freedom in different ways. It is often the case that when we focus on the emotions our participants' experience, we discover deeper and more important aspects of their experience. For each of our participants freedom was redefined by the experience of seeking it and reflecting on it. They also seemed to articulate this more and more clearly as the process of our Existential Research Dialogue progressed towards its end.

Chapter 10
Synthesis

Bringing the Analysis Together

When we have meticulously trained each of our existential lenses on our participant's discourse in the Existential Research Dialogue (ERD), the ERD comes to life in new ways. As we make sense of the words at so many different levels, their meanings begin to light up and add value to each other. It is as if we have shone a number of different lights on the dialogue, from many different directions, and we see the connections between what is happening in the dialectic of time zone, in The Four Worlds of the spatial dimensions and in terms of the paradoxes and tensions all this throws up. We understand how the values and emotions are connected and how our research participants have approached the topic on which they have been interviewed. We will also be looking at how we can combine the findings of each of the participants to begin to look at underlying themes that are common to all. We will again illustrate this by what we did with our research project on the experience of freedom. As we have already stated earlier in this book, we are only using the responses from three participants, as well as drawing on our pilot interviews with each other, as we wanted to focus on quality not quantity. We are therefore, not able to make any wider claims about the human experience of freedom in a general way. But common themes may nevertheless enable us to get a sense of some of the elements that make up the concept of freedom. But first we will look at the analysis of Bonnie's experiences of complete freedom through the five SEA filters to demonstrate how the different filters bring different aspects to light. The full analysis for both Luke and Olga can be found in the Appendix.

Bonnie

The Filter of TIME

From the analysis it is clear that for Bonnie there was a temporal aspect to freedom. Freedom is and has always been a possibility in her life. Freedom comes from letting go of the past and being in the present moment through wondering and being open. Past experiences can act as a limiter to Bonnie's experiences of freedom in

Table 10.1 The filter of TIME

Temporal Dimension	Themes
Past	Freedom is always there
	Freedom in letting go of the past
Present	Freedom appears suddenly in the present moment through wondering and openness
	Freedom emerges from being oneself
Future	Death is an unwanted end
Eternity	Knowing freedom is not total; forever makes it total
Time limited	The limits of freedom are important, and death is the final limit
Living / moving in time	More freedom with age

the present, and the future. When Bonnie can orientate herself in the present, by letting go of limiting past experiences, and taking an attitude of wonder and openness, she is able to be herself. This attitudinal orientation means that freedom has the ability to suddenly appear. It can be a surprise. Surprise arises when a new element suddenly comes to the fore and imposes a new experience on us out of the blue. This often occurs in the upswing from the lower left to the upper left quadrant on the emotional compass. It is the complement to the experience of humour, which we described above as occurring in a sudden movement from the upper right to the lower right quadrant. In other words, surprise is a sudden tension, whereas humour is a sudden release of energy.

Whilst freedom is an ever-present possibility for Bonnie there is an ultimate limitation which comes through death. There is something about knowing that freedom cannot be total forever which makes it total freedom for Bonnie. As she describes:

> then I thought maybe the fact that I don't know, it's like something that will evaporate, it won't last, makes it so incredibly special. So, the context knowing deep down, this is not total forever makes it almost total.

The limits of freedom are important, whether the limits are created through time or through the ultimate limit of death, they do allow possibilities of freedom to arise. Bonnie found that she experienced more freedom as she aged and that was partly due to her having more confidence in being herself and being more open in the present moment and more able to have the experience of being able to let go of the past.

In the analysis of the filter of TIME, it was important to ensure that the focus of the analysis is always connected to the research question, and this will be discussed further in the section on Reflexivity below. Two further themes were highlighted in

Bonnie's capta on time which were *life goes on* and *what happens after the end?* However, these were not included in the final analysis as they were broader themes about her experience of living and confronting existence rather than specifically related to her experience of freedom.

The Filter of SPACE

The filter of SPACE gives us another perspective, a different lens to consider Bonnie's experience of freedom:

Table 10.2 The filter of SPACE

Four Dimensions	Themes
Physical	Sudden emergence and connection
	Death is the ultimate limit
Social	Societal rules restrict freedom
	Expression creates freedom
	Freed from the gaze of others
Personal	Freedom is personal
	It is up to me
	Finding my way
Spiritual	Connecting to something greater
	Being curious
	Otherworldly

The analysis of Bonnie's experience of Space has already been discussed in some detail in Chapter 6.

In the physical dimension the main theme concerns how Bonnie's freedom emerged out of a connection with the physical environment, whether that was through a connection with nature or that the physical environment that she was in enabled an experience of freedom to emerge, such as being on a train for four hours. There is an inevitable cross over between the physical dimension and the filter of Time, as time can also reside in the physical dimension and this accounts for the theme *Death is the ultimate limit* which appears in the physical dimension and is a theme in the filter of Time. There is also an element of the temporal filter in the theme *Sudden emergence and connection*, which shows how there is a temporal element to the experience of freedom in the physical dimension. The themes in the physical dimension demonstrate how time, temporality and the environment interact to create freedom.

In the social dimension the main themes concern how the impact of others and society can limit or enable freedom. Societal rules, for example, will always have an impact on one's experience of freedom. The experience of freedom that Bonnie had feels closer to de Beauvoir's (1970) ideas of the ethics of freedom, that our freedom is always in relation to other people than to Sartre's (1956 [1943]) concept of freedom which is a theoretical affirmation of personal freedom as being-for-itself.

Bonnie was highlighting this tension of how personal freedom can be attained. Bonnie elucidated that freedom is more possible away from the gaze of others but that language, which is shared with others, enables freedom to be expressed, so that it reveals freedom in a sense. Freedom, therefore, appears to be something to be navigated in the social dimension to come into its own.

The personal dimension reveals how the process of the experience of freedom comes into play. Bonnie states how *Freedom is personal*, there is no universal experience of freedom in the same way there is no universal experience of meaning. But Bonnie also emphasises how it is also *Up to me* whether she experiences freedom or not. This brings a different perspective on freedom and one that will be discussed further below when we look at bringing all three analyses together. Like the physical dimension there is an interplay between the filter of time and the filter of space here. Bonnie describes how freedom is always a possibility (filter of Time: Past/future) but how she accesses freedom in the present moment requires something to come from her. The attitude of wonder and openness that was highlighted in the temporal dimensions is one that is personal to her. This attitude has been cultivated over time and has come out of her experiences. What she has learnt from the past is how experiences of freedom have come into being. This is an interesting understanding when we look at it in terms of existential philosophy. Bonnie is acknowledging that freedom, or free will, is an ever-present possibility, but how we enact our freedom or allow our freedom to emerge is a choice that has to be made by the person in the present. This echoes Frankl's (1964) ideas that we have to decide on the attitude we take towards what we are experiencing, and it seems the same is true for freedom. Bonnie's final theme in this dimension, *Finding my way*, shows that the experience of freedom is a process, that moves over time, and requires fine tuning and reflection.

In the spiritual dimension Bonnie's themes are *Connecting to something greater*, *Being curious* and *Otherworldly*. The theme of *Being curious* is also linked to the personal dimension as well as the temporal dimension theme of wonder and openness. This theme relates to how Bonnie approaches the world of her experiences and how she understands and makes sense of them. The spiritual dimension is the dimension of our values and beliefs, our meaning and understanding, or purpose and motivation. Bonnie values being curious and open to experiences. Bonnie starts each day wondering what life will bring her that day. She understands that this orientation in her life has enabled her to have experiences of freedom but also it allows her to be open to new possibilities that may have been closed off with a different attitude. She gives the example of needing to find work and how one experience led to another which resulted in her working in a theatre. Being curious enables her to find ways in which she can enact her freedom. In this way the personal and spiritual dimensions are coming together and interacting with each other.

Another element of Bonnie's experience of freedom was reflected in the themes *Connecting to something greater* and *Otherworldly*. Both of these themes are related to something outside of Bonnie's experience and also outside of the usual range of possibility in the world. Some of the experiences of freedom that Bonnie

Table 10.3 Bonnie's experiences of freedom

Four Dimensions	Examples of the Experience of Freedom
Physical	Connecting with nature
	Train travel
Social	Lockdown
	Language and humour
	Leaving school
Personal	Being oneself
Spiritual	Aging

had felt out of this world, that they belonged to a different realm or a different dimension. Bonnie described it as follows:

> that moment for me, and everything else seems to blur away, it's clear, that's the clear bit and even sitting on the train for the four hours, you know, [husband] and the cats, were out of it, blurry, gone, the children, everything, so it's really wonderful.

This sense of relishing the moment was also echoed in her early childhood experience of kissing the grass. Bonnie was talking about how she is fully present in her moments of freedom, so that it takes her out of her everyday living and life and connects her to something greater than herself: nature, the planet or even the universe.

The filter of space highlights different aspects of the experience of freedom, as it shows up in the world, how others impact it, how a person might enable it and how they make sense of it. This gives a greater depth to the experience under investigation. A further way of analysing the experience of freedom through the filter of Space is to look at the types of experiences that led to freedom and how they connect to the four dimensions (see Table 10.3). Each of the experiences brings another aspect into view.

The Filter of PARADOX

We now turn to the filter of Paradox. The previous two filters highlight the themes and structures of the phenomenon under investigation. The filter of paradox highlights the tensions and the paradoxical nature of the phenomenon. There are of course some overlaps with other filters, and this is inevitable because life does not occur in neat boxes and analysis is just a way of structuring experiences so that their meaning can more easily be grasped, described and obtained. Bear in mind that statements are only paradoxical to the extent that they are opposites and both true and that they are applied to the same experience.

Synthesis 169

Table 10.4 The filter of PARADOX

Physical	Limit and Enjoyment of Freedom	
	Everyone is going to die	No harm enjoying my space
Social	Society's Impact on Freedom	
	Positive aspects of society	Societal rules restrict freedom
	Limits of Freedom	
	Fortunately	Unfortunately, we are all forgettable
Personal	Outside Restrictions on Freedom	
	Stopped doing the things I love	Loved not having the responsibility of doing them
	Freedom to Choose an Attitude	
	Painting things in a negative light	Being open to see wonderful things
Spiritual	An Unknown Future	
	Something wonderful is going to happen	Something terrible will happen and I don't know

The tension that is experienced by Bonnie in the physical dimension is between the ultimate limit of freedom, i.e. death, and how that focuses her back on what is happening in the present, how she can enjoy her space, her life, and what opportunities of freedom can be present for her. It is the ultimate limit of freedom that makes freedom possible.

In the social dimension the tension is connected to the impact that others and society have on the experience of freedom. Societal rules can limit and take freedom away, but society and other people can also enable freedom. During lockdown, for example, freedom of movement was prohibited and that was experienced as a loss of freedom, but it also enabled freedom too, which we will explore further below. A further tension in the social dimension connects to the tension in the physical dimension, death means that we are all forgettable and this can be experienced as a limitation of freedom but at the same time it can enable freedom, freeing Bonnie from the expectations of others and allowing her to be herself and a forgettable being.

In the personal dimension the lockdown experience highlighted the tension of how responsibility intersects with freedom. On the one hand lockdown limited the experience of freedom but on the other hand it also took the responsibility of certain aspects of life away which was freeing. Not having to be responsible, for a particular way of living, for expectations and towards other people. The personal dimension also highlighted the tension created in the attitude we take to life. Bonnie shows that she has a choice in how she can respond to what is happening to her, either painting things in a negative or positive light, choosing to hold onto things or 'delete' them behind her as she goes. Both positive and negative attitudes are held in each experience.

In the spiritual dimension the paradox centred around the tension between knowing and not knowing. Bonnie holds the tension of how she faces an unknown future, as we all do. Once again, this orientation towards her future is guided by her attitude and the tension she experiences in the personal dimension, something wonderful or something terrible might happen, she doesn't know which but keeps a curious attitude towards whatever might happen. Again, holding the tension between all the likely outcomes that can occur in each moment.

The Filter of PURPOSE

The next filter to be applied concerns Bonnie's intentionality and her sense of purpose. This analysis identified the following aspects:

- Being open to the future
- Weathering the storm
- Freedom emerges, it cannot be made to happen
- Trust yourself

The filter of Purpose highlights different aspects of Bonnie's experiences. This filter could sit within the spiritual dimension as purpose and intentionality are part of the spiritual dimension, but it is also useful to separate this aspect out to bring greater depth to the analysis and to focus on values and intentionality specifically.

Some of these elements have been already elucidated in the other filters such as *Being open to the future*. The Purpose filter highlights a further depth in the process Bonnie goes through in her experience of freedom. The first element is *Weathering the storm*, which highlights how she is able to hold the paradoxical tensions that she experiences whilst facing an unknown future. Bonnie talks about 'weathering the storm', allowing herself to go through difficult experiences, and how she tries to put things in place to help her when she feels out of control or no longer in control of her freedom. Bonnie gives an example of rearranging ornaments on a shelf or rearranging a cutlery drawer when she is experiencing difficult things that are outside of her control. 'Weathering the storm', is part of the attitude Bonnie has developed to help her navigate the negative aspects of freedom, the limits of her freedom, especially when it is expressed as insecurity or uncertainty. This is also linked to the next theme of *Trusting yourself*, which underpins everything and holds it all together for Bonnie. Her curiosity, wonder and openness, the attitude she takes to difficult experiences and how she 'weathers the storm' are all connected to this belief in herself. Bonnie trusts herself to find a way, she trusts that

Synthesis 171

she can get through difficult times and even though she doesn't like it, she trusts that life will go on without her when she dies. This trusting of life leads to trust in herself and is also linked more concretely to her experience of freedom. She trusts that if she adopts this attitude of curiosity and openness then freedom will emerge in the moment and present itself. Bonnie cannot force it to happen because when she does, freedom does not emerge, there is something about how Bonnie creates a space for freedom, in how she interacts with her environment and herself that enables the possibility of freedom to present itself and manifest in her life

The Filter of PASSION

The final filter is that of Passion and this filter concerns the emotional flavour of freedom. As described in Chapter 9, emotions and values are linked and in the same way that people move about in the temporal dimensions there is movement in the emotional dimension as well.

As can be seen in Figure 10.1, the threat to value, in this case freedom, is seen in the top right-hand quadrant. Bonnie describes her emotional response to her freedom being restricted as hatred. Her experience of being at school was an example of when she felt the most restricted in her freedom and how she hated this experience:

> I never liked school, I hated school, but early on from Kindergarten, because I was in [country], after three weeks in Kindergarten I already decided, ok this is awful, but you've got to do it.

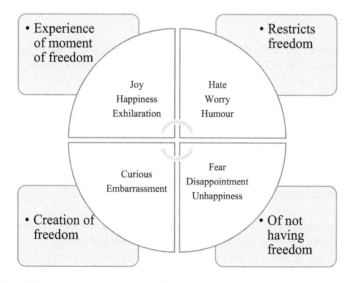

Figure 10.1 The emotional aspects of Bonnie's experience of freedom

Bonnie experiences feelings of hatred when there are threats to her freedom, which is a central value to her. But she also describes how worry can threaten the experience of freedom. If she becomes too worried about what others think, or what might happen to her or her family, then this affects her capacity to experience freedom. Bonnie used to worry about what people thought of her but saw the impact it had on her ability to be free. As a result, she has worked hard to free herself from that worry and now does not allow what others might think to matter to her.

There was also a worry for Bonnie about whether she is going to be able to experience freedom or how she is going to use her freedom, or free time, because it has the effect of distorting that freedom. As Bonnie says it 'messes up the whole thing'. If she does have expectations about how she might create freedom or use her freedom, then Bonnie feels disappointed in herself for not allowing it just to emerge and arise from the situation. The hardest element of worry for Bonnie is in relation to others whom she cares about, where things are outside of her control, like their happiness, and that worry also causes a restriction in her experience of freedom. As she describes: 'that the restriction of freedom comes from worrying and not being able to do something about it'. Bonnie has developed ways of coping and overcoming these situations by focusing on what she can do, such as clean the oven, tidy a drawer or organise a shelf. She finds activities to do where she does have control and is therefore able to reconnect to her freedom. This is a wonderful example of paradox: where control and structure create their opposite of freedom.

Bonnie has developed another process to enable her to overcome feelings of worry and hatred that might impact her experience of freedom, and this is her use of humour. Bonnie describes how she uses humour as a way of reality checking, of not taking herself or her situation too seriously:

> but it happens privately, my father had it, he would burst out laughing suddenly and he would be making himself laugh and I have that. I secretly fall about laughing at the ridiculousness of myself.

Humour is also used to keep her grounded in life, which helps her to keep orientated towards what she values and believes. Bonnie describes it as:

> I don't lose anything myself, I remain my values and everything. I somehow, rising up, it's and er, my biggest, closest friend is my humour, without that I don't think any of this is possible.

Humour is the antidote to worry for Bonnie, it enables her to move into this attitude of openness and curiosity and hold the inevitable tensions in life.

Bonnie's use of humour helps her to move away from 'getting really bogged down by the poor me, poor me'. She also notes that she has found a specific way of dealing with situations that make her sad, so that she doesn't get bogged down.

One is her use of humour; the other is how she is able to forget about the situations she finds difficult or upsetting. Bonnie describes it as:

> not even remembering awful stuff, or arguments with people, you know, where you, it deletes behind me kinda, after a while I can't remember, what was that about? Why I didn't like that person, or I can't remember, it's gone. So that is a freeing.

Bonnie is describing how freedom would not be possible without humour, that she would be too caught up in hatred and worry to enable her to orientate herself in a new way, with a different attitude which enables her to see possibilities.

The bottom right-hand quadrant concerns the Loss of Value and here we can see the emotions that Bonnie has experienced when her experience of freedom has been lost. She feels fear, disappointment and unhappiness. The fear that she experiences has a similar impact to worry. Fear is a limiter of freedom, if she is afraid then freedom is not a possibility, but it is also connected to feelings of a loss of freedom. Fear that freedom might not be possible again, or that there is no way out of a situation. Bonnie's greatest fear is centred on the limitation of freedom that is created by death and our finiteness as mortal creatures. In the same way that she deals with difficult situations, Bonnie finds ways of avoiding thoughts of death and how death is the actual death of freedom. Instead, Bonnie focuses back on life's possibilities, reminding herself that she is not there yet and, in doing so, she reminds herself of the opportunities and perhaps even the duties of the freedom still available to her:

> The thought is of course horrible, but I know at the same time I'll find a way as, meanwhile I am ticking along still, unless I die before him. And of course, we know obviously that anything can happen. But I think, thinking about the limit, the big death limit, back to how the freedom is highlighted the older I get must play a part in it. Must play a part, you know, knowing that, hold on girl you know, you're no way over the line, over the hill.

Disappointment for Bonnie is connected to trying too hard to create moments of freedom that invariably mean that freedom is not experienced. When she tries too hard to be free, she feels disappointed in herself, that she hasn't trusted herself to just allow the freedom possibilities to present themselves in any given situation. Unhappiness is connected to her use of humour, as described above. Unhappiness has the power to restrict the experience of freedom, and Bonnie has found that humour is a way in which she can move herself from one mood to another. This echoes Heidegger's (1962) idea that emotions are like moods and we are always in a mood, we are always attuned to the world in a particular way. There is a dynamic movement from one mood to another as we encounter situations, others and ourselves and the only way to get out of one mood is to get into another.

The bottom left-hand quadrant is connected to how one might aspire to a value and in this case how Bonnie moved towards creating freedom. School represented an interesting paradox for Bonnie in that it restricted her freedom with its rules, but her particular school was very liberal and allowed the children to respond however they wanted to the learning provided. It was up to her to decide what she was going to learn and achieve. The thought of not achieving and coming out of school without a piece of paper felt embarrassing and that proved to be the motivating factor. She was learning not because she was told to but because she chose to, and in doing so she demonstrated, or proved, something both to herself and to others. Therefore, embarrassment towards herself and other people helped Bonnie to create some freedom in her life and overcome what felt like restrictions to find agency for herself.

The overriding emotion throughout Bonnie's narrative was that of curiosity. Bonnie approached life in a curious way, she had an openness to others, the experiences she had and to the future. Curiosity was also a vehicle through which freedom was attained. As Luke described in Chapter 8, he wanted to move away from planning his life too tightly and Bonnie expressed the same. Freedom was never achieved through planning; it came out of connection, possibility and opportunity. Of letting things emerge. In order to be able to live in this way, Bonnie needed to trust herself and this came hand in hand with curiosity. She trusted her ability to face whatever life threw at her and to find a way, by looking at the possible avenues of freedom that were available to her.

The final quadrant in the top left-hand corner concerns gaining value and for Bonnie this related to how freedom felt. Bonnie's first experience of freedom occurred when she was a child, and she had the experience of bending down and kissing the grass. In that moment, a spontaneous moment of freedom, Bonnie felt happiness and joy and enthusiasm for life. She describes it as:

> I mean and so every now and then I get this, this freedom rush [laughter], yeah, it can also happen, and I know I'm now combining joy, happiness, whatever you want to call it. All these words close down so much. I'm combining that because it's exhilarating, it's . . . Oh . . ., and I smile, I'm sure I smile.

Bonnie finds it difficult to find the words to describe this feeling of freedom when it occurs, but it is exhilarating, and she seems to be expressing a love for life and connection at that moment. She also feels joy in moments of freedom; it can be a joy of being herself, or being able to enjoy a coffee, or just the joy of the experience as it is unfolding.

In this chapter we have focused on one of our participants, Bonnie, to show how the different filters come together in the analysis. We have demonstrated how the filters interact and intersect to produce a deep understanding of the experience, which in this case is the experience of freedom. The next step in any analysis will be about bringing the narratives from the different participants together to find similarities and commonalities in their experiences. There will inevitably be aspects of each participant's experience which will be unique to themselves so the aim of the next step of the analysis is to draw out what is present in all their narratives and to note differences and contradictions at the same time. Below you can find the final analysis for our research into the experience of freedom.

Final Analysis

In the following tables we are bringing together the different findings from all participants, showing them as accumulated findings for each filter and each category of experience.

Table 10.5 Themes for the filter of TIME

Past	Desire for freedom is always present
Present	Freedom suddenly appears and is fleeting and comes from movement in time
Future	Freedom is limited by age and death
Eternity	Freedom is always a possibility to work towards Total freedom might only be possible outside of the bounds of human existence
Time-limited	Freedom is limited in time and is temporary
Moving in time	Opportunities for freedom are always present

Table 10.6 The filters of SPACE and PARADOX

Four Dimensions	Themes
Physical	Connection to the physical world is an important part of freedom Death is the ultimate limitation of freedom
Paradox	Life versus Death Home versus Insecurity Freedom versus Responsibility
Social	Society and others can restrict freedom Sharing connections and finding a tribe can create freedom
Paradox	Individual versus Society
Personal	Freedom is a personal encounter with the whole self
Paradox	Avoidance versus Encounter
Spiritual	Curiosity, awe and wisdom in encountering the world and universe
Paradox	Known versus Unknown Closed versus Open Bound versus Expansive

176 Structural Existential Analysis

The filter of PURPOSE:

- Freedom is the main motivation
- Deliberately finding ways to encounter freedom through experiences
- Developing a trusting, open and questioning attitude creates freedom
- Freedom is not arrived at through planning, but through connection, possibility and opportunity
- Sometimes you have to make room for freedom by creating time away from your usual work/duties

This final analysis shows some of the commonalities that our participants experienced in their freedom. The analysis showed that although the possibility of freedom was always present it can be limited, either by death or the limits of human existence or by other people. Freedom becomes possible through connections with nature and the physical environment or to a connection with something greater than us, the cosmos for example. Freedom comes about through the attitude a person takes to be themselves, to be curious and trusting and emerges out of the moment. The experience of freedom evokes feelings of excitement, awe and joy and the loss

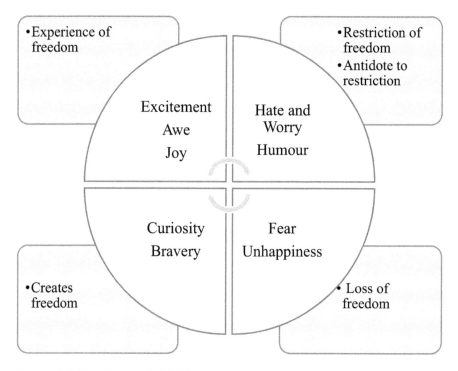

Figure 10.2 The filter of PASSION

of freedom creates fear and unhappiness. Whereas existential philosophers have been concerned to describe the ontological aspects of freedom and free will, our research aimed to detail the ontic experience and to question whether absolute or total freedom is possible.

The findings of the research that we conducted into total freedom surprised us. We had thought that an experience of being totally free, where the way ahead was so open that your life could go in many different directions might be overwhelming to a person. But we did not find that to be the case with our participants. Of course, with a larger sample, with participants coming to the research from different contexts and situations this may have arisen. Although as our participants reminded us it might not be possible to be totally free. It is this aspect of the research, where the focus narrows to how we as researchers engaged with our own process (transcendental reduction), that is elucidated in the next chapter.

Chapter 11

Returning to Phenomenological Principles

Structural Existential Analysis involves looking at an experience in its many layers, from different perspectives using different lenses. Each lens or filter draws different aspects out and taken together they allow for a deeper understanding of the experience or phenomenon being investigated. There is flexibility in how the methodology can be used. Whilst we have demonstrated how a full SEA analysis can be conducted, doctoral students who are limited by word count and time might decide to focus on a couple of the filters for their analysis. Existential researchers might also want to look at how time intersects with space across the four dimensions as one of our graduates, Elizabeth Feigin, did in her research on coming out in orthodox Jewish communities (Feigin, 2021).

Feigin (2021) explored the experience of coming out in the Orthodox Jewish Community and wanted to examine how it was experienced over time in the four dimensions of experience. She therefore combined the temporal dimensions with the spatial dimensions to track spatial experiences over time, as can be seen in Table 11.1.

Another graduate of ours, Farasat Sadia (2020) chose to highlight the emotional experience in her research into fathers' experience of living with new mums who have been diagnosed with Postnatal Depression (PND). Farasat employed Deurzen's emotional compass (Deurzen, 2012, 2016) in her analysis to show the emotional rollercoaster that her participants experienced whilst caring for their partners who had PND after the birth of their first child. It showed up very clearly how intensely and deeply these fathers were plunged into the experience of threat and loss of value.

SEA has also been successfully blended with other phenomenological approaches such as Interpretative Phenomenological Analysis (IPA) and Van Manen's Hermeneutic Phenomenology. Landenberg, a graduate of NSPC blended SEA with IPA in her research into the experiences of children who had suffered permanent

Table 11.1 Feigin's (2021) consolidated 16-point table

	The past (before coming out)	The present (the moment of coming out)	The future (after coming out)	Temporality (present moment of vision)
Physical World (things)	- Orthodox Jewish Observance - Journey of Sexual Discovery - Realisation of Being Gay - Suffering	- Stuck-ness - Sexual Exposure	- Religious Restrictions - Shame - Emotional Expression	- Physical Intimacy
Social World (people)	- Jewish Social Scene - Perception of Being Gay - Lack of Gay Role Models - Fear of Rejection & Judgement by Others - Secrets & Isolation	- Comfort of others - Unknown Response - Strategy	- Relief: Pleasantly Surprised - Gay Community - Improved Relationships - Rejection, Disappointment & Frustration	- Safety of the Environment - Paradox of Orthodox Judaism & Being Gay - Challenging the Silence: Having gay, non-sexual reference points
Personal World (Self)	- Personal Relationship with Judaism - Mental Health & Despair - Realisation of Gay Identity - Alternative Identity/ Overcompensation	- Personal Acceptance - Personal Shame and Other Pain - Personal Relief	- Belief - Personal Struggle	- Loss & Discovery - Hopes & Reality - Personal Connection / Distance to Judaism
Spiritual World (ideas)	- Praying the Gay Away	- Religion as a Challenge - Faith in Oneself	- Health - Less Observant - A Distance - Faith in Others	- The Problem with Jewish Orthodoxy - Relationship with God - Ongoing Questions - Ultimate Identity Acceptance

exclusion from school. Landenberg (2020) demonstrated the similarities and differences between the two methodologies as shown below:

Research Methods

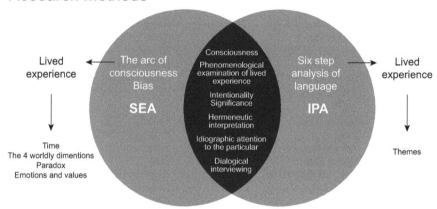

Figure 11.1 Landenberg's (2020) diagram of how to blend SEA and IPA

A number of pieces of research conducted at NSPC have also successfully blended Van Manen's Hermeneutic Phenomenology, or a heuristic methodology with SEA (Arnold-Baker, 2015, Garland, 2019, Sadia, 2020, Christophy, 2017).

Reflexivity, Epochē and the Three Reductions

Reflexivity, the epochē and the three reductions are intrinsic to any piece of phenomenological research but especially to the methodology of SEA. Chapter 2 goes into the theory behind the need for reflexivity and the use of SOAR. In this section we will be discussing how epochē, SOAR and the three reductions have been applied to the research and analysis that we conducted for this book.

SOAR must be applied in both the dialogue stage and the analysis stage and is really a reminder of reflexivity throughout the research process. We have discussed how it is applied in the ERD stage in Chapter 4, which is an important stage as it is the level of data capture. Existential researchers need to be aware of their own sphere of bias and orientation to the world at this and at every other stage of the SEA research. We can never come to anything completely neutral, naïve or bias free so the role of SOAR and the three reductions is to help us keep track of how our bias may influence the research. In this way our bias becomes the active edge of our observations without it interfering with our observations, as we are aware of the shape of the lens through which we are looking at the phenomena under consideration.

It is important during the existential dialogue and the analysis to be aware of your own state of mind. Existential therapists are used to doing this, tracking their own thoughts and reactions whilst attending to their client's words and being. They know how invaluable their own state of mind and responses can be, in providing them with direct observations of the process and of valuable illustrations of the client's way of being-in-the-world and their effect on other people. To hold your bias in awareness requires you to be aware of two conversations at the same time. You are listening to what your participant is working out and you are also listening to your own response to this and figuring out whether your response is something for you to filter out, or whether it provides you with important new information that needs to be taken into account. What you are hearing and thinking as the researcher is part of the process. For it allows you to seek for the essence of your participant's experience and to ask supplementary questions that will allow this to come through in what your participant is formulating. It is not easy to listen to yourself and to apply the phenomenological reduction to your thoughts, whilst at the same time fully attending to the participant's words. This is a skill that needs developing over time and can often feel difficult to master at first. Using SOAR can help keep track of what the researcher needs to attend to during the interview and analysis process, and SEA researchers need training in tracing their own.

S: State of mind
O: Orientation
A: Attitude
R: Reaction

As we discussed previously it is helpful to have your own thoughts, beliefs and assumptions on the topic recorded before beginning the research, but this is not a one-off task, it is one to be repeated throughout the research process. A research diary is a useful way of capturing the different aspects of SOAR, both before and after a research dialogue but also during the analysis process. This is essential as the existential researcher will be using themselves as a tool for the analysis. It is the existential researcher who will be guiding the participant to articulate in an ever more in-depth, expansive and profound way what their true experience of the phenomenon under investigation has been and is now. The existential researcher will also be delving into uncovering the meaning of the participant's words and experiences during the analysis. For the piece of research we conducted for this book we divided the dialogue and analysis stages, which worked extremely well. Emmy conducted the dialogues and Claire conducted the analysis. Having more than one person involved in the existential research is a useful way of ensuring bias is minimised or at least challenged by the dual aspect approach to the material. Claire was able to note the differences in each interview; in some there were a lot of interactions between the participant and Emmy, and in others less so. This was interesting to reflect on. It is harder to reflect on your own impact on the participant if you are the sole researcher. Having more than one pair of eyes scrutinising the process helps in locating prejudice and bias at all levels. The dialogues with more interactions were typically centred on eliciting more descriptive understanding, clarifying and checking, asking more exploratory questions. The dialogues that had fewer interactions were a response to how the participant was narrating their experience and how they were already giving a full and descriptive account. During the analysis Claire was able to look for any potential bias that had crept in through the dialogues and decide how that might be included or not in the analysis. She was also able to take a fresh and more objective look at the material, including the impact of the researcher's words.

It might not be possible to have a co-researcher involved in your research if it is a doctoral piece of research and this makes the role of the primary supervisor so the more important. Sometimes a secondary supervisor looking at the work less frequently can also show up forgotten text or implications or note that the researcher has focused more on certain elements than on others. The process of analysis, and the findings, need to be discussed and interrogated to ensure bias is kept at a minimum and that full use is made of the details that have been gathered, so that the meaning of the experience or the phenomena under investigation are fully considered and are extracted as cleanly and as thoroughly as possible.

The Three Reductions

We have described above how the three reductions can be used in the existential dialogue; we will now focus on how they are used in the analysis process.

The Phenomenological Reduction (Epochē)

The phenomenological reduction comes to the fore during the first stage of the analysis when the researcher is beginning to work with the transcript and starts to identify meaning units and how they might be clustered together. In therapeutic terms this is very similar to the process of doing a dream analysis. We gather the materials and the story of the dream and then suspend our desire to want to rush to interpretive conclusions about the meaning of the dream. Instead, we discipline ourselves to look at the dream themes in a detached, structural and systematic manner, simply stating and listing them phenomenologically. It helps to teach yourself to be restrained and cautious at this stage, holding back from drawing any conclusions as yet.

1. *Suspend your assumptions and track, observe, and bracket your bias, watching your own intentionality and intentional arc.*

    This is just as important in the analysis stage as during the dialogue stage, especially when you are analysing the second or third or later transcripts. It is tempting to find themes that you have already uncovered in the previous analysis, so it is important to keep this as a potential bias in your mind and treat each participant's transcript as if it were the first. There is often a worry for novice researchers that no common themes will be uncovered. This worry needs to be put to one side. It is more important to delve into each participant's experience than to worry about how all the participants' experiences might be brought together. If diversity is shown up rather than similarity, this is also a finding.

2. *Describe what you observe and experience. Don't analyse or interpret.*

    This is important in the existential dialogue stage as it helps to get a full and descriptive account of the experience under investigation. But it is also important in the first stage of the analysis, where the researcher is working to highlight meaning units and cluster them together. At this stage there is no analysis or interpretation, it is about arranging the data into a format that orders, organises and structures the capta, to allow for analysis to take place in the next stages. It involves keeping an open mind to what might come next. The existential researcher needs to try not to pre-empt their own analysis. Analysis is a process which takes time, care, dedication and attunement. Each stage of the analysis helps to fine tune the understanding and involves a deeper immersion into your participants' experience.

3. *Horizontalise your observations, by seeing their context and situation: note the limit of your observations.*

    Horizontalisation is important in the research dialogue but also in the first stage of the analysis. There will always be limits. When reading through the transcript you will often discover that what might have been inferred in the dialogue may not have been captured in words in the transcript as you imagined it. The researcher will find half-finished sentences or ideas that weren't fully formed or expressed. You become aware that as a listener you had imagined extra meanings, where none were expressed. You cannot make up for these lost meanings. It is good practice for existential researchers who wish to improve their dialogue skills to carefully read through the transcript of their first dialogue or pilot study to highlight for themselves where there were lost opportunities and how they could have probed further. The Existential Research Dialogue is an art that takes quite a lot of practice. Learning to detect hidden meanings, and probing to expose them, requires skill and experience. New researchers learn to see how and where they might have cut the participant off, or where they made assumptions about what the participant was saying rather than asking them to describe it themselves. The more the existential researcher engages with their own process the better the dialogue and the analysis will become. Give yourself time to master the Existential Research Dialogue, by using your understanding to facilitate the other's exploration rather than by imposing your own views or double guessing meanings that weren't expressed. Self-reflection is of the essence here. It may help you to create a peer research group in which you give each other feedback on your blind spots in the dialogue.

4. *Equalise your experience and pay attention to every aspect of it, instead of allowing certain things to stand out or be given more weight.*

    Equalisation happens both in the existential dialogue as well as at the first stage of the analysis. The researcher is not looking to prioritise one aspect over the other. The researcher withholds from jumping to quick conclusions about the significance of one detail over another. Everything the participant says is taken as equally important and relevant to the research. No decisions at the first stage of the analysis should be taken in regard to how the content of the participant meets the research question. Every aspect of the participant's experience is considered equally and is allowed its full weight in meaning.

5. *Verify your observations, by checking from different angles, or at different times, or by asking others to confirm your observations.*

   This is an important part of the processing of the dialogue that has been recorded. Checking back with the participant that their words have been accurately recorded, grasped and understood is one way in which this can be done. But it can also be done by looking at the experience from different perspectives with a colleague or supervisor. This can happen at the end of the analysis process when the final analysis has been completed. This can be sent to participants to check that the analysis has captured the meaning of their experience. If this is not possible, some discussion about the accuracy and fairness of the material should happen with a third party.

The Eidetic Reduction

The eidetic reduction comes into its own during the second stage of the analysis, when the existential researcher starts to look at the meaning units and what they are communicating about the experience under investigation. At this point in the analysis, it is important to keep the research question in mind to ensure that the focus remains on the topic of the investigation. This helps in not getting caught up and side-tracked in the participant's narrative.

1. *Pay attention to the noemata: the objects of your intentional arc.*

   Once the first stage of the analysis has been completed and meaning units have been grouped together according to the filter or filters being used, the second stage is to start to see what the essence of the meaning units is and how they express something in relation to the research question. This stage involves clustering meaning units according to the experience they reveal, which in the case of the research for this book was freedom. The participants gave lots of examples of times in their lives that they experienced freedom or times when they had lost their freedom. In the analysis it is important to think about what the participants were actually saying about freedom in these examples. What was the essence of that experience, relationship, situation that allowed them to feel something in relation to freedom. This is about tracking the quality and deeply felt meanings of words, rather than about correctly structuring and categorising words or concepts. The examples that the participants give are the noemata, they are the objects of their experience. What you are doing now is to extract deeper meanings from these. This is only possible if the Existential Research Dialogue has touched on deep meanings rather than remaining at the surface. Therefore, in the dialogue and in the analysis, attention needs to be placed on what has happened in the examples given and how they highlight aspects of freedom. As we have seen above this means asking a lot of 'what was this like for you', or 'what did this mean or represent for you' or 'what was the experience of this in that moment' kinds of questions. We cannot inject meanings into our participants' words after the fact.

2. *Be aware of their many facets and different aspects, seeing as many adumbrations (Abschattungen) as possible.*

   For this stage in both the dialogues and the analysis, the existential researchers are focusing on how the experience can be looked at from different angles and different perspectives. Two of the participants in our research on freedom talked about experiencing freedom through travelling. As the researchers we thought about what it was about travelling that enabled that experience of freedom to be felt. This was especially poignant since both of us spoke also of geographic movement as the trigger of our own freedom experiences. This made it even more important not to fall into the trap of equating freedom with freedom of movement. So we wondered what conditions needed to be in place for an experience of freedom to occur. Was freedom possible in other areas of our participants' lives? How did freedom materialise for them and in what ways? These questions were usefully held in mind in both the existential dialogue as well as during the second stage of the analysis. They stopped us jumping to conclusions and sharpened our investigation of how freedom might be experienced when a person is still, at peace or stagnating.

3. *Look for essences behind the appearances (Wesenschau).*

   An important part of existential research is to draw something out about the experience that is hidden and not immediately accessible at surface level. If the analysis stays at the level of the surface presentation of the noemata or purely at the level of description, then important details of the experience will not be elucidated. This is about not taking things at face value. The existential researcher will ask themselves what is behind this example? What is the participant trying to communicate? What was their deeply felt lived experience? What were the essential parts of this experience? In our research into freedom, it became clear through the analysis that the way in which participants connected to the natural world and their environment was an essential part of their experience of freedom. This needed to be teased out by looking at what each example was expressing. We were amazed at the vivid descriptions they had given us, about kissing grass, or merging with stars, or going on freedom tours, and we aimed to do justice to the richness of that imagery. We understood how much this meant to our participants.

4. *Pay attention to the genetic (or historical) constitution of the entities you observe, as everything is dynamic and in flux over time.*

   Whether this is addressed explicitly or implicitly, participants will talk about their past, present and future in relation to their experience. In our research on freedom, participants gave examples of previous times in which they experienced freedom or were deprived of it. They described what freedom felt like in the present moment and they reflected on how they might experience freedom in the future or how the future might limit their freedom. There is a movement back and forth in time in the participants' narrative. The filter of Time is useful in capturing this element more fully and more explicitly, and as has been shown in Chapter 10 in the final analysis examples the filter of time highlights different aspects than a purely descriptive thematic analysis would achieve. In our research we were discovering something about the dynamic nature of freedom. It was clear that the freedom journey of all participants, including ourselves, was one of historical change. Freedom became easier to recognize, when examining the way it showed up at different times of life, in very different ways and in different circumstances.

5. *Aim to grasp the universal qualities in what you observe, taking the view from the infinite.*

   This part of the eidetic reduction is most relevant to the final stage of the analysis when the themes from different participants are brought together in order to highlight any universal qualities. This part of the analysis involves looking across the themes of the different participants to see where they may be expressing similar aspects of the process. In our research on freedom, each participant gave their own experience of freedom which emerged in lots of different ways. But they all had in common this understanding that freedom is one aspect of the journey of life and is a dynamic process rather than something that can be obtained or possessed. The aim of the reductions is to look beyond the examples in order to come to the themes or the essence of the experience. What makes freedom, freedom, for example? Once this has been done for each of the participants, the task is to look for the universal qualities across the participants. What is shared? What is essential to this experience or phenomenon?

The Transcendental Reduction

The transcendental reduction focuses on the transcendental ego, i.e. it tracks how the observer's understanding of the observation and of what is observed affects our personal understanding. This means that there comes a point where as existential researchers we need to draw conclusions and come up with interpretations of what we have observed so carefully. This also draws on tracking the internal process of the researcher during the research and how this may have helped or hindered participants to elicit their own process during the existential dialogue.

1. *Focus on the process of your awareness, on the ego cogito itself, the subject of your intentional arc.*

   This part of the transcendental reduction is about shining a light of awareness on yourself as an agent and reflective subject of the investigation, and if you have the facility to do so, also of the subjective experience of your participants. How are participants connected to their experience as a subject in the research dialogue? How aware is the participant of their part in the experience of the research? Can they access different elements, such as their thoughts, feelings, reactions, emotions, behaviour? Have you, as a researcher, been able to follow all of these responses and have these reflected in responses of your own? How have you made sense of the thoughts, feelings, reactions and intuitions that were coming up for you during both the dialogue and the analysis? This was a rich area for us as we were able to have discussions about this process between us. We became aware of how emotional the material on freedom was for us and how we felt we were learning from our participants' experiences, sometimes in very new ways. The awareness that freedom was gradually becoming more and more described as a dynamic existential process than something that could be possessed or desired or controlled was profoundly meaningful to both of us.

2. *Through self-reflection find the transcendental ego, the thinking subject that is outside of this specific experience, seeking your connection with consciousness itself.*

As existential researchers we aim to hold the tension between self-observation and availability for the participant's experience to unfold as fully as possible. But once the dialogue has been completed, has been recorded and is under consideration, our personal responses and reflections become an essential part of the process. It is our own knowledge and careful work that is going to reveal hidden wisdom in our participants' words and experiences, and this changes us, as we become one with the meanings that were expressed. This takes us beyond our personal response into a transcendental grasp of universal meaning. This is something existential therapists are trained to do when working with clients, and it involves a great deal of reflection, both in what is happening for themselves as well as for their clients. In therapeutic circles this is often referred to as working with the counter transference, whereas the phenomenological reduction refers to the work with the therapeutic process and dialogue itself, and the eidetic reduction relates more to what some might call the transference, i.e. what is referred to at the deepest layer of the experience. Each of these moments is important. The first process is about helping the participant, through prompt questions and reflections, to articulate their own process in relation to the experience or phenomenon under investigation. How are they relating to what is happening to them or has happened to them? Both in the past, i.e. in the moment of the experience that they are describing, but also in the present, i.e. how are they making sense of it now, in the present moment with the researcher? And also in terms of future meanings that are affected by this new understanding.

The second process is to bring awareness to the essence of what is going on, and the third, the transcendental aspect, is about bringing the inner experience and understanding of the existential researcher to bear on the interpretation of the results of the investigation. How is the researcher understanding and making sense of what the participant is saying to them? How are their own experiences of freedom, for example, being brought to the surface while listening to their participants, and how is the researcher able to ultimately combine the careful observations of the participants' statements with their own knowledge and experience. How do they draw conclusions and learn from their observations? How are they making meaning out of their observations?

3. *Overcome solipsism in a movement towards inter-subjectivity.*
The process of qualitative research is inter-subjective. The participant's experiences, whilst their own, are also experiences of how they have connected and interacted with others to create their personal experience. Their decision to participate in research rather than in therapy, is also a choice for sharing their experience and making it available for meaning making in a communal, inter-subjective way. In the existential dialogue the narrative that emerges is co-created through the inter-subjectivity between participant and researcher. In the research for this book, if Claire had also undertaken an existential dialogue with the participants on their experience of freedom it would be different from the one Emmy had conducted. Even though the examples the participants gave might have been the same, there would be something in the inter-subjective space between participant and researcher that would create a difference. The way this research went was the outcome of the inter-subjective dynamic between Emmy and the participants, but it was shaped by Claire's vision of the structure of the meanings of freedom that were harvested. How and when the researcher intervenes, when and where probe questions are asked, and which element of the narrative is being clarified for example, guides the process in a certain direction. Existential therapists are taught to consider the impact their interventions will have on the course of the discourse in the therapeutic encounter, and this is also true for research. You could make research much more robust by having different researchers doing the same research with a number of different participants and combining the results. The discussions we had with each other about our findings were another layer of meaning making.

It is in the analysis which employs an element of hermeneutics, where the researcher is looking to make sense of what has been expressed and to grasp and understand all the meanings that can be collected from the capta. This is about filtering what has been harvested to get the goodness and richness out of the contributions of the participants' words. This too is a creative process, which is applied to the creation that has been brought about by the researcher and the participant. Each of these processes are inter-subjective and they aim to create inter-subjective meanings that are valid beyond the understanding of each participant. It was greatly strengthened for us by being able to dialogue about it, to get beyond personal meanings towards shared meanings.

One of the difficulties with reliability and validity in qualitative research is that it is not possible to completely replicate a piece of qualitative research because there will always be numerous inter-subjective elements to it. Both in the existential dialogue or interview and in the process of analysis. This is why reflexivity and the process of SOAR and the reductions are so important. They attempt to minimise the impact of the researcher, but the researcher will always have an impact on what or how an experience is narrated, and they will certainly have an impact on how that experience is analysed. This inter-subjective aspect accounts for the difference between Husserl's notion of phenomenology and how Heidegger, de Beauvoir and Merleau-Ponty understood phenomenology. If phenomenology is undertaken as a purely philosophical exercise involving one person, the philosopher, analysing a specific phenomenon, then the inter-subjective aspect is not so critical, though the problem of bias is greater than ever. As soon as we introduce another, as we do in research but also in therapeutic work, then inter-subjectivity has entered into the equation.

The inter-subjective elements need to be addressed and articulated. They are not an interference. They are part of the catalytic process. Existential phenomenology is also looking to grasp something that goes beyond the inter-subjective towards the universal. While we carefully account for the way in which our understanding is arrived at and hold the tension in a transparent way, we are also seeking to formulate new ways of thinking about the phenomena under investigation and this is a potential contribution to knowledge in psychology and philosophy.

4. *Find the horizon and limit of your own encompassing understanding around the point zero of your intentionality.*

One of the ways to address the limitations of the horizon of our understanding is to be clear about our limitations as researchers. Another is to have a dialogue about our findings. There may be elements within ourselves that stop us from truly understanding another or even a particular topic under investigation. It is not possible to completely understand another person however much we might try. These limits are important to recognise. Recording accurately how different participants, coming from different perspectives and life experiences, report on the same issue in different ways is as valuable as finding similarities and universal characteristics. We seek to go beyond anyone's personal horizon towards a wider and broader expanded horizon of the experience in question. We must also recognise that likewise our participants may experience limits in the way that they can understand and articulate their own experience, and that being confronted with our interpretations of their and other participants' contributions they may feel either gratified in having widened our joint understanding or they may feel as if they had wanted to say more and explain better what they meant.

5. *Check and verify your own perspective against that of multiple others, checking for truth value.*

As already mentioned, as SEA is not a quantitative piece of research that can be guided by mathematical principles, reliability and validity are important. Yardley (2008) and Finlay (2008) give good descriptions of how to ensure these elements are addressed in qualitative research. Checking your own perspective, however, is essential. We recommend that whenever you undertake SEA research you work with another in a joint way, as the authors have done on their piece of research. Or if you are a doctoral or master's student you need to work with your supervisors or team up with a colleague if you are undertaking some independent research. We favour research collaborations and research groups, in which we throw light on each other's findings and ways of working. It is important to talk through your findings with another to ensure that your understanding of the capta is also one that another could grasp and that makes sense, whilst also being warranted. In the same way that it is helpful for participants to be guided to look at other perspectives, the researcher too needs to be challenged in their analysis and interpretation to ensure that it is rigorous and valid. Sometimes this might be difficult if the supervisor or research partner has differing views about the way the analysis has been conducted or how an interpretation has been reached. But it is important to have this external scrutiny because the aim of the research is to uncover something hidden and expose some truth about our existence. This is easier to do when challenged and when shown different angles to what we have observed.

An example of how the three reductions, epochē and reflexivity can be conducted in a piece of research can be found in the box below. This excerpt (with permission) is from Natalie Fraser's (2021) doctoral research on how inner dialogue is experienced by rape survivors.

Example of the Process

Example of time theme emerging:

> after it happened, it got quite instantly into the darker and depressing . . . probably for the year after it happened it was very much like that. And then it's sort of slowly evening itself out.
>
> (Ely, line 34)

Analysis notes:

'*After it*' referring to the time after the rape. '*Quite instantly*' referring to the speed of time and a transformation during that time.

'*For the year after it*' referring clearly to the year after the experience of rape; '*it was*' referring to the emotional nature of the inner dialogue being described as having characteristically similar qualities for that specific time period.

'*And then it's*' + '*evening*'. Linguistic abbreviation of, '*And following that, it currently is*'. . . . nuanced reference to the present continuous experience.

Mindful Reflexivity Notes:

Careful observation of the difference between our experiences: her time is experienced in more clear and distinct phases than my own.

> Burning sensation in my heart both during and after the interviews when I reflect upon the long-term impact that rape has on the participants. I feel committed to changing this misconceived narrative about rape being understood and worked with as a single, physical event, and instead highlighting that rape is experienced as a long-term violation across all dimensions of existence.

Bringing It All Together – Seeking an Existential Understanding

The final stage of any piece of research is to bring the analysis together, and to uncover some potential universal themes about the experience or phenomenon you have been studying. The existential researcher will return to the existential literature to see how the research findings can be understood in terms of existential theory.

In the case of our own small research project on freedom this leads us right back to the classics. The concept of freedom or free will has been an area of interest for many existential philosophers or thinkers. Much of the focus previously has been on establishing, ontologically, how freedom is an intrinsic part of human existence and how our experience of freedom is connected to an experience of anxiety (Kierkegaard, 2000, Sartre, 1956) when we have to come to terms with the responsibility we hold for not only our choices but how we create and recreate both ourselves and our lives. Freedom has also been examined from the angle of how people are limited in their freedom either through physical imprisonment of some form or how we imprison ourselves to avoid the angst of embracing our freedom. What we were interested in finding out through our research was what the experience of total freedom was like, i.e. the opposite to limited freedom. As already noted, the research we conducted was in itself limited with only three participants and two pilot study participants. We cannot make any bold claims about the experience of total freedom in general, however it was interesting that even with these few participants there were some similarities in their experiences that were noteworthy and thought provoking. Of course, further research would need to be conducted to gain more meaningful findings. What we found, however, was that even though the participants believed they had had an experience of complete or total freedom there was a paradox for them in that they felt it could never be complete. Olga wondered whether total freedom would only ever be possible if our mortal lives were not so bound in time and space. She felt that maybe the closest anyone could come to that type of complete freedom would be if they had excessive amounts of money and could buy their freedom. Although she also noted that this type of freedom had its difficulties too. All three participants noted that total freedom was fleeting and temporary and whilst freedom is one of the ontological structures of human being it is not possible to live in a totally free way all the time, even in exceptionally free circumstances. Another interesting finding from this research which has not been found previously is that freedom comes out of a connection to our experience of the world in a physical way. All three participants talked about an experience of total freedom when they were connected at a deep level with nature and the world, and this connection allowed them to feel free in the moment, almost rising above themselves temporarily. A further finding that was shared by all participants concerned their mindset, and how they understood themselves and their position in the world and the attitude they took to their experiences. This finding confirmed Frankl's (1964) ideas of how we can create meaning and freedom in the most limiting of circumstances. Additionally, all three described how other people and society can limit the experience of freedom which confirmed de Beauvoir's (1970) ideas of how one must be mindful of the way in which our freedom impacts others.

The limitations of this book have also meant that we have only been able to scratch the surface of the rich findings of our research on freedom. We hope that the preceding chapters have given ample examples of how Structural Existential Analysis can be used and how the different filters can be applied together. SEA is a creative methodology and whilst it adheres to phenomenological and existential ideas and practices it also allows space for each existential researcher to adapt the method to suit their own purposes. This has been highlighted recently in the interest our doctoral students have shown in creating 'found' poems (Duffy, 2024) to creatively capture the phenomenon of an experience.

How SEA Compares with Other Phenomenological Methodologies

The main comparable methodologies which employ phenomenology and/or existential approaches are Descriptive Phenomenology, IPA, Hermeneutic Phenomenology (Van Manen, 1990), Ashworth's Fractions of the Lifeworld and Existential Phenomenological Research (Churchill, 2022). The first two employ a more phenomenological approach to research whereas the latter approaches combine existential analysis with phenomenology. SEA sits within this latter group. The existentials, or filters that SEA utilise – Time, Space, Paradox, Purpose and Passion – are grounded in existential philosophy and therapeutic practice. Van Manen (1990) in his methodology originally suggested four existential lifeworlds to consider – lived temporality, lived corporeality, lived relations and lived spatiality – although more recently he added lived things and technology and death, language and mood (Van Manen, 2017). Ashworth's (2003) methodology on the other hand highlights eight Fractions of the Lifeworld: selfhood; sociality; embodiment; temporality; spatiality; project; discourse; and moodedness. All three approaches use lenses or filters to access other perspectives and new ways of looking at the phenomena under investigation. None of the approaches use filters in a rigid way but rather as a tool to turn our attention to what is at hand and to also help in the structuring of the research and presentation of the findings. The filters help to draw out deeper existential understandings. Although Van Manen describes six steps in his analysis, he also cautions against a stepwise approach. Ashworth, similarly to SEA, takes a more structured approach to the analysis through the use of his different fractions.

The main criticism of existential phenomenological approaches is twofold. The first is that they are not sufficiently phenomenological in a philosophical sense (more has been written about this in Chapter 2). The second criticism to be levelled against these approaches is that the fractions or filters create artificial categories into which data are forced. However, as has been shown in this book, there is a need for an organising principle in any type of qualitative research and so long as the structure is held lightly and with curiosity and reflectivity then it can be a useful tool to organise and analyse the data to shed light on the existential elements the phenomena contain.

Fernandez (2024) explores how philosophers have taken a 'qualitative turn' towards qualitative research methods as can be seen in the work of Zahavi (2014a and b). However, he makes the point that the research produced by qualitative approaches that draw on existentials is on a par with philosophical research. Although there has been reluctance by philosophers to be interested in or use phenomenological qualitative studies, there is a case for them doing such applied research. Fernandez argues that existential phenomenological approaches add 'a new layer of depth, nuance and sensitivity to existing approaches' (Fernandez, 2024: 28). The increase in the development of the field of Existential Phenomenological Research demonstrates a need for researchers to go beyond the confines of thematic analysis and explore the existential dimensions that are contained in all human experiences.

We hope that our contribution to the field of existential research will be helpful to many young researchers in the field and that they will find new and creative ways to implement the ideas and methods we have presented. We are certain that your feedback and comments will help us to develop Structural Existential Analysis further.

Suggested Further Reading

Arnold-Baker, C. (ed.) (2020). *The Existential Crisis of Motherhood*, New York: Palgrave Macmillan.
Deurzen, E. van (2010). *Everyday Mysteries: A Handbook of Existential Psychotherapy*, second edition, London: Routledge. [1997].
Deurzen, E. van (2012). *Existential Counselling and Psychotherapy in Practice*, third edition, London: Sage [1988].
Deurzen, E. van (2013). Phenomenological Psychotherapy, in E. Neukrug (ed.), *Encyclopedia for Counselling and Psychotherapy*, Oxford: Oxford University Press.
Deurzen, E. van (2014). Structural Existential Analysis (SEA): A Phenomenological Research Method for Counselling Psychology, *Counselling Psychology Review*, 29(2): 70–83.
Deurzen, E. van (2014). Structural Existential Analysis (SEA) A Phenomenological Method for Therapeutic Work, *Journal of Contemporary Psychotherapy*, 44(3): 59–68.

Deurzen, E. van and Arnold-Baker, C. (2005). *Existential Perspectives on Human Issues*, Basingstoke: Palgrave Macmillan.

Deurzen, E. van and Arnold-Baker, C. (2018). *Existential Therapy: Distinctive Features*, London: Routledge.

Draeby, S., Deurzen, E. van and Lodge, R. (2017). A Comparison of Learning Outcomes in Cognitive Behavioural Therapy (CBT) and Existential Therapy: An Interpretative Phenomenological Analysis, *International Journal of Psychotherapy*, 21(3): 45–59.

Fernandez, A. V. (2024). Existential Phenomenology and Qualitative Research, in K. Aho, M. Altman and H. Pedersen (eds.), *The Routledge Handbook of Contemporary Existentialism*, Abingdon: Routledge.

Finlay, L. (2008). A Dance Between the Reduction and Reflexivity: Explicating the 'Phenomenological Psychological Attitude', *Journal of Phenomenological Psychology*, 39: 1–32.

Giorgi, A. (1994). A Phenomenological Perspective on Certain Qualitative Research Methods, *Journal of Phenomenological Psychology*, 25(2): 190–220.

Harkness, C. (2018). *The Nature of Existence: Health, Wellbeing and the Natural World*, London: Red Globe Press.

Moustakas, C. (1994). *Phenomenological Research Methods*, London: Sage Publications.

Van Manen, M. (1990). *Researching Lived Experience: Human Science for an Action Sensitive Pedagogy*, London: Routledge.

Willig, C. (2009). *Introducing Qualitative Research in Psychology*, second edition, Maidenhead: Open University Press.

Bibliography

Adams, M. (1998). Experience and Representation of Space, *Journal of the Society for Existential Analysis*, 9(1): 2–16.
Arendt, H. (2018). The Human Condition, second edition. London: The University of Chicago Press. [1958].
Arendt, H. (2020). The Freedom to be Free, London: Penguin, Great Ideas.
Arnold-Baker, C. (2015). *How Becoming a Mother Involves a Confrontation with Existence: An Existential-Phenomenological Exploration of the Experience of Early Motherhood*, Doctoral Thesis, Middlesex University / New School of Psychotherapy and Counselling. https://repository.mdx.ac.uk.
Arnold-Baker, C. (2019). The Process of Becoming: Maternal Identity in the Transition to Motherhood, *Existential Analysis*, 30(2): 260–274.
Arnold-Baker, C. (ed.) (2020). *The Existential Crisis of Motherhood*, New York: Palgrave Macmillan.
Arnold-Baker, C. (2023). What Is Existentialism? In C. Arnold-Baker, S. Wharne, N. Hakim Dowek, N. Gibson and J. Molle with E. van Deurzen (eds.), *Existential Therapy: Responses to Frequently Asked Questions*, London: Routledge.
Ashworth, P. D. (2003). The Phenomenology of the Lifeworld and Social Psychology, *Social Psychological Review*, 5: 18–34.
Ashworth, P. D. (2016). The Lifeworld – Enriching Qualitative Evidence, *Qualitative Research in Psychology*, 13: 20–32.
Ashworth, P. D. (2017). Interiority, Exteriority and the Realm of Intentionality: Implications for Phenomenological Psychology, *Journal of Phenomenological Psychology*, 48: 39–62.
Baumeister, R. F. (1991). *Meanings of Life*, London: Guildford Press.
Bennett, J. (2014). *'A Good Night Out' (Voices of 'Binge' Drinkers): A Phenomenological Investigation of Binge Drinking Women in Yorkshire*, Doctoral Thesis, Middlesex University / New School of Psychotherapy and Counselling. Eprints.mdx.ac.uk.
Berdayev, N. (2020). *The Philosophy of Freedom*, transl. Fr. S. Janos, Mohrsville, PA: FRSJ Publications.
Binswanger, L. (1946) The Existential Analysis School of Thought, In R. May, E. Angel and H. F. Ellenberger (eds.), *Existence*, New York: Basic Books.
Binswanger, L. (1963). *Being-in-the-World*, transl. J. Needleman. New York: Basic Books.
Booker, C. (2019). *The Seven Basic Plots: Why We Tell Stories*, London: Bloomsbury Publishing.
Boss, M. (1957). *Psychoanalysis and Daseinsanalysis*, transl. L. B. Lefebre, New York: Basic Books.
Boss, M. (1979). *Existential Foundations of Medicine and Psychology*. New York: Jason Aronson.

Boss, M. (2001). *Zollikon Seminars: Protocols, Conversations, Letters*, ed. M. Boss, transl. F. Mayr and R. Askay, Evanston, IL: Northwestern University Press.

Brooks, J., Morrow, R., Rodriguez, A., King. N., Smith, J. A., Langdridge, D. and Ashworth, P. (2015). Learning from the 'Lifeworld', *The Psychologist*, 28(8), August.

Brough, J. B. (1991) Translator's Introduction, in E. Husserl, *On the Phenomenology of the Consciousness of Internal Time (1893–1917)*, transl. J. Brough. Dordrecht: Kluwer Academic Publishers.

Buber, M. (2000). *I and Thou*, transl. W. Kaufmann, New York: Charles Scribner's Sons.

Bugental, J. F. T. (1981). *The Search for Authenticity: An Existential-Analytic Approach to Psychotherapy*. New York: Irvington.

Camus, A. (1948). *The Plague*, transl. S. Gilbert, New York: Knopf. [1947].

Camus, A. (1954). *The Rebel: An Essay on Man in Revolt*, transl. A. Bower, New York: Vintage. [1951].

Camus, A. (1955). *The Myth of Sisyphus*, transl. J. O'Brien, London: Hamish Hamilton, [1942], reprinted 1975, Harmondsworth: Penguin.

Camus, A. (2000). *The Outsider*, transl. J. Laredo, Harmondsworth: Penguin. [1942].

Christophy, C. (2017). *The Problem of Pain: A Heuristic and Structural Existential Analysis of Unexplained Physical Pain*, DCPsych Thesis, Middlesex University / New School of Psychotherapy and Counselling. Eprints.mdx.ac.uk.

Churchill, S. D. (2022). *Essentials of Existential Phenomenological Research*. Washington, DC: American Psychological Association.

Cromby, J. (2012). Feeling The Way: Qualitative Clinical Research and the Affective Turn, *Qualitative Research in Psychology*, 9(1): 88–98.

Danesh, A. H. (2019). *Exploring Iranian Political Refugees' Experiences in Britain, The Phoenix Rises from the Ashes: An Existential-Phenomenological Study*, Doctoral Thesis, Middlesex University / New School of Psychotherapy and Counselling. Eprints.mdx.ac.uk.

de Beauvoir, S. (1953). *The Second Sex*, transl. H. M. Parshley, Harmondsworth: Penguin. [1949].

de Beauvoir, S. (1966). *A Very Easy Death*, transl. P. O'Brian, New York: Putnam.

de Beauvoir, S. (1969). *The Woman Destroyed*, transl. P. O'Brian, New York: Putnam.

de Beauvoir, S. (1970). *The Ethics of Ambiguity*, transl. B. Frechtman, New York: Citadel Press. [1948].

de Beauvoir, S. (1984). *She Came to Stay*, transl. Y. Moyse and R. Senhouse, London: Fontana. [1948].

de Beauvoir, S. (1984). *Coming of Age*, transl. P. O'Brian, New York: Putnam. [1972].

de Beauvoir, S. (1996). *The Coming of Age*, transl. P. O'Brian, London: Norton and Co. [1970].

de Beauvoir, S. (2004). Pyrrhus and Cinéas, in M. A. Simons, M. Timmerman and M. B. Mader (eds.), *Philosophical Writings*, Urbana, IL: University of Illinois Press. [1944].

de Beauvoir, S. (2020). *What Is Existentialism?* London: Penguin.

Dennett, D. (2001). *Freedom Evolves*, London: Allen Lane, the Penguin Press.

Deurzen, E. van (2003). *Inauthenticity and Self-Deception in Heidegger's Being and Time in Relation to Psychotherapy*, London: City University.

Deurzen, E. van (2009). *Psychotherapy and the Quest for Happiness*, London: Sage.

Deurzen, E. van (2010). *Everyday Mysteries: A Handbook of Existential Psychotherapy*, second edition, London: Routledge. [1997].

Deurzen, E. van (2012). *Existential Counselling and Psychotherapy in Practice*, third edition, London: Sage. [1988].

Deurzen, E. van (2014a). Structural Existential Analysis (SEA): A Phenomenological Method for Therapeutic Work, *Journal of Contemporary Psychotherapy*, 45: 59–68.

Deurzen, E. van (2014b). Structural Existential Analysis (SEA): A Phenomenological Research Method for Counselling Psychology, *Counselling Psychology Review*, 29(2), doi:10.53841/bpscpr.2014.29.2.54.

Deurzen, E. van (2015). *Paradox and Passion in Psychotherapy*, second edition, London: Wiley. [1998].
Deurzen, E. van (2016). SEA: A Phenomenological Method for Therapeutic Work, in S. E. Schulenberg (ed.), *Clarifying and Furthering Existential Psychotherapy, Theories, Methods, Practices*, New York: Springer.
Deurzen, E. van (with Craig, E., Schneider, K., Längle, A., Tantam, D. and du Plock, S.) (eds.) (2019). *The Wiley World Handbook for Existential Therapy*, London: Wiley.
Deurzen, E. van (2021). *Rising from Existential Crisis: Life Beyond Calamity*, Monmouth: PCCS Books.
Deurzen, E. van (2025). *The Art of Freedom: Guide to a Wiser Life*, London: Penguin.
Deurzen, E. van and Adams, M. (2016). *Skills in Existential Counselling and Psychotherapy*, second edition, London: Sage. [2011].
Deurzen, E. van and Arnold-Baker, C. (eds.) (2005). *Existential Perspectives on Human Issues*, Basingstoke: Palgrave Macmillan.
Deurzen, E. van and Arnold-Baker, C. (2018). *Existential Therapy: Distinctive Features*, London: Routledge.
Deurzen, E. van and Arnold-Baker, C. (2019). The Case of Rahim, in E. van Deurzen (Editor-in-Chief) et al., *The Wiley World Handbook of Existential Therapy*, London: Wiley.
Deurzen, E. van and Iacovou, S. (2013). *Existential Perspectives on Relationship Therapy*, Basingstoke: Palgrave Macmillan.
Deurzen, E. van and Kenward, R. (2005). *Dictionary of Existential Psychotherapy and Counselling*, London: Sage.
Deurzen, E. van and Young, S. (2009). *Existential Perspectives on Supervision*, Basingstoke: Palgrave Macmillan.
Deurzen-Smith, E. van (1984). Existential Therapy, in W. Dryden (ed.), *Individual Therapy in Britain*, London: Harper & Row.
Dilthey, W. (1977). *Descriptive Psychology and Historical Understanding*, transl. R. M. Zaner, The Hague: Martinus Nijhoff. [1924].
Douglas, B., Woolfe, R., Strawbridge, S., Kasket, E. and Galbraith, V. (eds.) (2016). *The Handbook of Counselling Psychology*, fourth edition, London: Sage.
Dostoyevsky, F. (1999). *The Brothers Karamazov*, transl. C. Garnett, Signet Classic. [1880].
Dostoyevsky, F. (2003). *Crime and Punishment*, transl. D. McDuff, London: Vintage. [1866].
Duffy, S. (2024). *Grounding in Groundlessness, Being the Change: An Existential Phenomenological Exploration into the Embodied Experience of Postmenopause*, Doctoral Thesis, Middlesex University / New School of Psychotherapy and Counselling. https://repository.mdx.ac.uk.
Du Plock, S., and van Deurzen, E. (2015). The Historical Development and Future of Existential Therapy, *International Journal of Psychotherapy*, 19(1): 5–14.
Ellenberger, H. F. (1958). A Clinical Introduction to Psychiatric Phenomenology and Existential Analysis, in R. May, E. Angel and H. F. Ellenberger (eds.), Lanham, MD: Aronson.
Etoke, N. (2023). *Black Existential Freedom*, London: Rowman and Littlefield.
Fabre van Deurzen, E. (1975). *Quelques Reflexions Philosophiques sur certains aspects psychiatriques du refus de l'experience d'autrui*, Maitrise de philosophie sous la direction de Michel Henry, Montpellier: University of Montpellier.
Fanon, F. (2021). *Black Skin, White Masks*, transl. R. Philcox, London: Penguin Modern Classics. [1952].
Fanon, F. (1963). *The Wretched of the Earth*, transl. C. Farrington, London: Penguin Modern Classics.
Feigin, E. (2021) *An Existential Exploration of the Experience of Coming Out in the Orthodox Jewish Community*, Doctoral Thesis, Middlesex University / New School of Psychotherapy and Counselling. Eprints.mdx.ac.uk.
Fernandez, A. V. (2024). Existential Phenomenology and Qualitative Research, in K. Aho, M. Altman and H. Pedersen (eds.), *The Routledge Handbook of Contemporary Existentialism*, Abingdon: Routledge.

Finlay, L. (2008). A Dance Between the Reduction and Reflexivity: Explicating the 'Phenomenological Psychological Attitude', *Journal of Phenomenological Psychology*, 39: 1–32.
Føllesdal, D. (1969). Husserl's notion of noema, *Journal of Philosophy*, 6: 680–687.
Føllesdal, D. (1990). The Lebenswelt in Husserl. In L. Haaparanta, M. Kusch and I. Niiniluoto (eds.), *Language, Knowledge, and Intentionality: Perspectives on the Philosophy of Jaakko Hintikka* (Acta Philosophica Fennica, vol. 49). Helsinki: Haalka.
Føllesdal, D. (2006). Husserl's Reductions and the Role They Play in His Phenomenology, in H. L. Dreyfus, and M. A. Wrathall, *A Companion to Phenomenology and Existentialism*, Oxford: Blackwell Publishing.
Frankl, V. E. (1964). *Man's Search for Meaning*. London: Hodder and Stoughton. [1946].
Fraser, N. (2021). *You Are Not Alone: An Existential-Phenomenological Exploration of How Inner Dialogue Is Experienced by Rape Survivors*, Doctoral Thesis, Middlesex University / New School of Psychotherapy and Counselling. https://repository.mdx.ac.uk.
Fromm, E. (1941). *Escape from Freedom*, New York: Holt.
Fromm, E. (2001). *The Fear of Freedom*, London: Routledge Classics.
Fujii, L. A. (2018). *Interviewing in Social Science Research: A Relational Approach*, London: Routledge.
Gadamer, H. G. (1975). *Truth and Method*, transl. J. Weinsheimer and D. J. Marschall, London: Bloomsbury.
Gadamer, H. G. (1986). *The Relevance of the Beautiful and Other Essays*, Cambridge: Cambridge University Press.
Gallagher, S. and Zahavi, D. (2012). *The Phenomenological Mind*, second edition, London: Routledge.
Gallagher, S. (2020). *The Phenomenological Mind*, third edition, London: Routledge.
Garland, V. (2019). *'Being-in-the-World' as a Mother: Hermeneutic-Phenomenological Exploration of Lived Experiences of Eight New Mothers' Transition to Motherhood Within the Theoretical Frame of 'Four Dimensions of Existence'*, Doctoral Thesis, Middlesex University / New School of Psychotherapy and Counselling. https://repository.mdx.ac.uk.
Giorgi, A. (1994). A Phenomenological Perspective on Certain Qualitative Research Methods, *Journal of Phenomenological Psychology*, 25(2): 190–220.
Giorgi, A. (2009). *The Descriptive Phenomenological Method in Psychology: A Modified Husserlian Approach*, Duquesne: Duquesne University Press.
Giorgi, A. (2010). Phenomenology and the Practice of Science, *Existential Analysis*, 21(1): 3–22.
Giorgi, A. (2012). The Descriptive Phenomenological Psychological Method, *Journal of Phenomenological Psychology*, 43: 3–12.
Glaser, B. and Strauss, A. (1967). *The Discovery of Grounded Theory: Strategies for Qualitative Research*, Chicago, IL: Aldine.
Goodall, E. and Brownlow, C. (2022). *Interoception and Regulation: Teachings Skills of Body Awareness and Supporting Connection with Others*, London: Jessica Kingsley Publishers.
Heidegger, M. (1957). *Vorträge und Aufsätze*. Pfullingen: Neske.
Heidegger, M. (1961). *An Introduction to Metaphysics*, transl. R. Manheim, New York: Doubleday.
Heidegger, M. (1962). *Being and Time*, transl. J. Macquarrie and E. Robinson, New York: Harper and Row. [1927].
Heidegger, M. (1966). *Discourse on Thinking*, transl. J M. Anderson and H. Freund, New York: Harper and Row.
Heidegger, M. (1968). *What Is Called Thinking?*, transl. J. Glenn Gray, New York: Harper and Row. [1954].
Heidegger, M. (1969). *Identity and Difference*, transl. J. Stambough, New York: Harper and Row Torchbooks.

Heidegger, M. (1994). *Basic Questions of Phenomenology*. Bloomington, IN: Indiana University Press.
Heidegger, M. (1995). *The Fundamental Concepts of Metaphysics: World, Finitude, Solitude*, transl. W. McNeill and N. Walker, Bloomington, IN: Indiana University Press.
Henry, M. (1973). *The Essence of Manifestation*, transl. G. Etzkorn, The Hague: Martinus Nijhoff. [1963].
Henry, M. (1975). *Philosophy and Phenomenology of the Body*, The Hague: Nijhoff.
Henry, M. (1989). Philosophie et subjectivité, in A. Jacob (ed.), *Encyclopédie Philosophique Universelle*, Paris: PUF.
Henry, M. (1990). *Phénoménologie matérielle*, Paris: PUF.
Henry, M. (1993). *The Genealogy of Psychoanalysis*, transl. D. Brick, Stanford, CA: Stanford University Press. [1985].
Henry, M. (1999). Material Phenomenology and Language (or Pathos and Language), *Continental Philosophy Review*, 32(3): 343–365.
Henry, M. (2007). Phenomenology of Life, in P. M. Candler Jr. and C. Cunningham (eds.), *Veritas: Transcendence and Phenomenology*, London: SCM Press.
Henry, M. (2008). *Material Phenomenology*, transl. S. Davidson, New York: Fordham University Press. [1990].
Henry, M. (2009). *Seeing the Invisible: On Kandinsky*, transl. S. Davidson, London: Continuum. [1988].
Henry, M. (2012). *Barbarism*, transl. S. Davidson, London: Continuum. [1987].
Holzhey-Kunz, A. (2019). Philosophy and Theory: Daseinsanalysis – An Ontological Approach to Psychic Suffering Based on the Philosophy of Martin Heidegger, in E. van Deurzen (Editor-in-Chief) et al., *The Wiley World Handbook of Existential Therapy*, London: Wiley.
Husserl, E. (1927). Phenomenology, transl. and revised R. Palmer, for *Encyclopaedia Britannica*, www.hfu.edu.tw/~huangkm/phenom/husserl-britanica.html.
Husserl, E. (1931). *Ideas*, transl. W R. Boyce Gibson, New York: Macmillan. [1913].
Husserl, E. (1969). *Formal and Transcendental Logic*, transl. D. Cairns, The Hague: Martinus Nijhoff.
Husserl, E. (1970a). *The Crisis of European Sciences and Transcendental Phenomenology: An Introduction to Phenomenological Philosophy*, transl. D. Carr, Evanston: Northwestern University. [1938].
Husserl, E. (1970b). *Logical Investigations*, transl. J. N. Findlay, London: Routledge. [1900].
Husserl, E. (1973). *Cartesian Meditations: An Introduction to Phenomenology*, transl. D. Cairns, The Hague: Nijhoff. [1929].
Husserl, E. (1977). *Phenomenological Psychology*, transl. J. Scanlon, The Hague: Nijhoff. [1925].
Husserl, E. (1983). *Ideas Pertaining to a Pure Phenomenology and to a Phenomenological Philosophy*, First Book, transl. F. Kersten, The Hague: Martinus Nijhoff.
Husserl, E. (1985). Origin and Development of Husserl's Phenomenology. In *Encyclopaedia Britannica*, vol. 25, 15th edition, ed. J. L. Garvin, Chicago, IL: Encyclopaedia Britannica.
Husserl, E. (1991). *On the Phenomenology of the Consciousness of Internal Time (1893–1917)*, transl. J. B. Brough, Dordrecht: Kluwer.
Iacovou, S. (2015). *The Impact of Active Service on the Intimate Relationships of Ex-Servicemen, an Existential-Phenomenological Study*, Doctoral Thesis, Middlesex University / New School of Psychotherapy and Counselling. repository.mdx.ac.uk.
Jaspers, K. (1963). *General Psychopathology*, Chicago IL: University of Chicago Press. [1923].
Jaspers, K. (1971). *Philosophy of Existence*, transl. R. F. Grabay, Philadelphia, PA: University of Pennsylvania Press. [1938].

Jaspers, K. (1997). *General Psychopathology*, Vols. 1 and 2, transl. J. Hoenig and M. W. Hamilton, Baltimore, MD and London: Johns Hopkins University Press. [1923].
Johnson, J. (2024) Robert Sapolsky and Kevin Mitchell Diverge on Free Will: How can two experts on the brain disagree about free will? *Psychology Today*, www.psychologytoday.com/us/blog/cui-bono/202404/robert-sapolsky-and-kevin-mitchell-on-free-will?eml.
Kearney, R. (1986). *Modern Movements in European Philosophy*, Manchester: Manchester University Press.
Kierkegaard, S. (1940). *Stages on Life's Way*, transl. H. Hong and E. Princeton, NJ: Princeton University Press. [1845].
Kierkegaard, S. (1944). *The Concept of Dread*, transl. W. Lowrie, Princeton, NJ: Princeton University Press. [1844].
Kierkegaard, S. (1980). *The Sickness Unto Death*, transl. H. Hong and E. Hong, Princeton, NJ: Princeton University Press. [1849].
Kierkegaard, S. (1987). *Either/Or*, transl. H. V. Hong and E. H. Hong, Princeton, NJ: Princeton University Press.
Kierkegaard, S. (2000). The Concept of Anxiety, In H. V. Hong and E. H. Hong (eds.), *The Essential Kierkegaard*. Princeton, NJ: Princeton University Press. [1912].
Kierkegaard, S. (2008). *Kierkegaard's Journals and Notebooks*, Vol. 2, transl. I. McDaniel, Princeton, NJ: Princeton University Press.
Laing, R. D. (1959). *The Divided Self*, Harmondsworth: Penguin. [1970].
Laing, R. D. (1961). *Self and Others*, Harmondsworth: Penguin [1971].
Laing, R. D. (1967). *The Politics of Experience*, London: Tavistock.
Landenberg, V. (2020). *A Community-Based Experience of Being Permanently Excluded from Secondary School: An Existential Reflection*, Doctoral Thesis, Middlesex University / New School of Psychotherapy and Counselling. repository.mdx.ac.uk.
Lee, H. (2015). *To Kill a Mockingbird*, Vintage Classics. [1960].
Marion, J.-L. (2004). *The Crossing of the Visible*, Stanford, CA: Stanford University Press. [*La Croisée du visible*, Paris: Presses Universitaires de France, 1996].
Marion, J.-L. (2006). *The Erotic Phenomenon: Six Meditations*. Chicago, IL: The University of Chicago Press.
Marion, J.-L. (2008). *The Visible and the Revealed*, New York: Fordham University Press. [*Le visible et le révélé*, Paris: Les Éditions du Cerf, 2005].
May, R. (1967). *Psychology and the Human Dilemma*, New York: Norton.
May, R. (1969a). *Love and Will*, New York: Norton.
May, R. (1969b). *Existential Psychology*, New York: Random House.
May, R. (1977). *The Meaning of Anxiety*, New York: Norton. [1950].
May, R. (1983). *The Discovery of Being*, New York: Norton.
McLeod, J. (2003). Qualitative Research Methods, In R. Woolfe, W. Dryden, and S. Strawbridge (eds.) *Handbook of Counselling Psychology*, second edition, London: Sage.
Merleau-Ponty, M. (1964). *Sense and Non-Sense*, transl. H. Dreyfus and P. Dreyfus, Evanston, IL: Northwestern University Press.
Merleau-Ponty, M. (1968). *The Visible and the Invisible*, transl. Alphonso Lingis, Evanston IL: Northwestern University Press.
Merleau-Ponty, M. (1992). *Texts and Dialogues*, ed. H. J. Silverman and J. Barry, London: Humanities Press.
Merleau-Ponty, M. (2013). *Phenomenology of Perception*, transl. C. Smith, London: Routledge & Kegan Paul [1945].
Minkowski, E. (1970). *Lived Time: Phenomenological and Psychopathological Studies*, transl. N. Metzel, Evanston, IL: Northwestern University Press.
Mitchell, K. M. (2023). *Free Agents: How Evolution Gave Us Free Will*, Princeton, NJ: Princeton University Press.
Moran, D. (2002). *The Phenomenology Reader*, London: Routledge.

Moran, D. (2023). *Introduction to Phenomenology*, second edition, London: Routledge.
Morris, I., Seaford, R., Spence J. D. and Korsgaard, C. M. (2015). *Foragers, Farmers, and Fossil Fuels: How Human Values Evolve*, Princeton, NJ: University Center for Human Values Series, Princeton University Press.
Moustakas, C. (1994). *Phenomenological Research Methods*, London: Sage Publications.
Murdoch, I. (1970). *The Sovereignty of Good*, London: Routledge.
Nancy, J. L. (1993). *The Experience of Freedom*, Stanford, CA: Stanford University Press.
Nancy, J. L. (1998). *The Sense of the World*, Minneapolis, MN: University of Minnesota Press.
Nietzsche, F. (1961). *Thus Spoke Zarathustra*, transl. R. J. Hollingdale, Harmondsworth: Penguin. [1883].
Nietzsche, F. (1969). *On the Genealogy of Morals*, transl. W. Kaufman and R. Z. Hollingdale, New York: Vintage Books. [1887].
Nietzsche, F. (1974). *The Gay Science*, transl. W. Kaufmann, New York: Random House. [1882].
Nietzsche, F. (1982). *Daybreak*, transl. R. J. Hollingdale, Cambridge: Cambridge University Press. [1881].
Nussbaum, M. C. (1994). *The Therapy of Desire: Theory and Practice in Hellenistic Ethics*, Princeton, NJ: Princeton University Press.
Nussbaum, M. C. (2001). *Upheavals of Thought: The Intelligence of Emotions*, Cambridge: Cambridge University Press.
Page, M. J., McKenzie, J. E., Bossuyt, P. M., Boutron, I., Hoffman, T. C., Mulrow, C. D., et al. (2021). The PRISMA 2020 Statement: An Updated Guideline for Reporting Systematic Reviews, *BMJ*, 372: n71.
Plato (1997). *Complete Works*, ed. J. M. Cooper and D. S. Hutchinson, Indianapolis, IN: Hackett.
Plato (2005). *Phaedrus*, transl. C. Rowe, London: Penguin Classics.
Polkinghorne, D. E. (1992). Postmodern Epistemology of Practice, in S. Kvale (ed.), *Psychology and Postmodernism*, London: Sage.
Proust, M. (1973). *In Search of Lost Time, The Way by Swann's*, Vol. 1, transl. C. K. Scott Moncrieff and Terence Kilmartin, London: Penguin Books.
Ricoeur, P. (1966). *Freedom and Nature: The Voluntary and the Involuntary*, Evanston IL: Northwestern University Press.
Ricoeur, P. (1967). *The Symbolism of Evil*, transl. E. Buchanan, New York: Harper.
Ricoeur, P. (1974). *The Conflict of Interpretations: Essays in Hermeneutics*, transl. D. Ihde, Evanston IL: Northwestern University Press.
Romano, C. (2015). *At the Heart of Reason*, transl. Smith, M.B., Studies in Phenomenology and Existential Philosophy, Evanston IL: Northwestern University Press.
Sadia, F. (2020). *A Phenomenological Exploration into the Lived Experience of Fathers Living with New Mothers Diagnosed as PND*, Doctoral Thesis, Middlesex University / New School of Psychotherapy and Counselling. https://repository.mdx.ac.uk.
Sapolsky, R. M. (2023). *Determined: The Science of Life Without Free Will*, London: Penguin Vintage.
Sartre, J. P. (1956). *Being and Nothingness – An Essay on Phenomenological Ontology*, transl. H. Barnes, New York: Phil. Library. [1943].
Sartre, J. P. (1962). *Nausea*, Harmondsworth: Penguin. [1938].
Sartre, J. P. (1962). *Sketch for a Theory of the Emotions*, London: Methuen. [1939].
Sartre, J. P. (1963). *Saint Genet, Actor and Martyr*, transl. B. Frechtman, New York: Braziller. [1952].
Sartre, J. P. (1968). *Search for a Method*, transl. A. Sheridan-Smith, New York: Random House. [1960].
Sartre, J. P. (1969). Itinerary of Thought, *New Left Review*, 58: 48–66.

Sartre, J. P. (1971). *The Idiot of the Family*, transl. C. Cosman, Chicago IL: University of Chicago Press.
Sartre, J. P. (1982). *Critique of Dialectical Reason*, transl. A. Sheridan-Smith, London: Verso/NLB. [1960].
Sartre, J. P. (1992). *Notebooks for an Ethics*, transl. D. Pellaner, Chicago IL: University of Chicago Press. [1983].
Sartre, J. P. (2002). *The Roads to Freedom (The Age of Reason, The Reprieve, Iron in the Soul*, London: Penguin Classics.
Smith, J. A. (2018). 'Yes It Is Phenomenological': A Reply to Max Van Manen's Critique of Interpretative Phenomenological Analysis, *Qualitative Health Research*, 28: 1955–1958.
Smith, J. A., Flowers, P. and Larkin, M. (2009). *Interpretative Phenomenological Analysis: Theory, Method and Research*, London: Sage.
Smith, J. A., Flowers, P. and Larkin, M. (2022). *Interpretative Phenomenological Analysis*, second edition, London: Sage.
Spiegelberg, H. (1965). *The Phenomenological Movement*, The Hague: Martinus Nijhoff.
Spiegelberg, H. (1972). *Phenomenology in Psychology and Psychiatry*, Evanston, IL: Northwestern University Press.
Spiegelberg, H. (1975). *Doing Phenomenology: Essays on and in Phenomenology*, The Hague: Martinus Nijhoff.
Standford Encyclopaedia of Philosophy (2016). Hegel's Dialectics, in *Stanford Encyclopaedia of Philosophy*, https://plato.stanford.edu/entries/hegel-dialectics/.
Stein, E. (1964). *On the Problem of Empathy*, transl. W. Stein, The Hague: Nijhoff. [1921].
Stein, E. (2004). *Collected Works of Edith Stein*, Washington, DC: ICS Publications.
Strawbridge, S. and Woolfe, R. (2003). Counselling Psychology in Context, in R. Woolfe, W. Dryden and S. Strawbridge (eds.), *Handbook of Counselling Psychology*, second edition, London: Sage.
Thompson, E. and Zahavi, D. (2007). Philosophical Issues: Phenomenology, in M. Moscovitch, P. Zelazo and E. Thompson (eds.), *Cambridge Handbook of Consciousness*. New York: Cambridge University Press.
Tillich, P. (1952). *The Courage to Be*, London: Collins.
Tolstoy, L. (1983). *Confessions*, transl. D. Patterson, New York: Norton and Company. [1882].
Tolstoy, L. (2000). *Anna Karenina*, transl. R. Pevear and L. Volokhonsky, London: Allen Lane/Penguin. [1873].
Tolstoy, L. (2008). *The Death of Ivan Illyich and other Stories*, transl. A. Briggs, D. McDuff and R. Wilks, London: Penguin Classics.
van Deurzen-Smith, D. (2016). *Nurturing Artistic Creation: An Exploration into the Experience of Creative Inspiration Using the Four-Worlds Model*, Masters Dissertation, New School of Psychotherapy and Counselling.
Vanhooren, S. (2022). Existential Empathy: The Challenge of 'Being' in Therapy and Counselling, *Religions*, 13: 752, https://doi.org/10.3390/rel13080752.
Van Manen, M. (1990). *Researching Lived Experience: Human Science for an Action Sensitive Pedagogy*, London: Routledge.
Van Manen, M. (1997). *Researching Lived Experience: Human Science for an Action Sensitive Pedagogy*, London: Althouse Press.
Van Manen, M. (2014). *Phenomenology of Practice: Meaning-Giving Methods in Phenomenological Research and Writing*, London: Routledge.
Van Manen, M. (2017). Phenomenology in its original sense, *Qualitative Health Research: An International, Interdisciplinary Journal*, 27: 810–825.
Van Manen, M. (2018). Rebuttal Rejoinder: Present IPA for What It Is – Interpretative Psychological Analysis, *Qualitative Health Research*, 28(12): 1959–1968.

Van Manen, M. (2019). Rebuttal to Zahavi: Doing Phenomenology on the Things, *Qualitative Health Research: An International, Interdisciplinary Journal*, 29(6): 1–18.
Vlastos, G. (1991). *Socrates: Ironist and Moral Philosopher*, Cambridge: Cambridge University Press.
von Uexküll, J. (1921). *Umwelt und Innenwelt der Tiere*, Berlin: Springer.
Vos, J. (2021). Systematic Pragmatic Phenomenological Analysis: Step-Wise Guidance for Mixed Methods Research, *Counselling and Psychotherapy Research*, 21(1): 77–97.
Wardle, H., Rapport, N. and Piette, A. (2023). *The Routledge International Handbook of Existential Human Science*, London: Routledge.
Wharne, S. (2021a). Socratic Questioning and Irony in Psychotherapeutic Practices, *Journal of Contemporary Psychotherapy*, 52(3): 137–144. https://doi.org/10.1007/s10879-021-09514-7.
Wharne, S. (2021b). Empathy in Phenomenological Research: Employing Edith Stein's Account of Empathy as a Practical and Ethical Guide, *Methods in Psychology*, 5: 100053.
Willig, C. (2009). *Introducing Qualitative Research in Psychology*, second edition, Maidenhead: Open University Press.
Yalom, I. D. (1980). *Existential Psychotherapy*, New York: Basic Books.
Yalom, I. D. (1996). *Lying on the Couch*, New York: Basic Books.
Yalom, I. D. (2001). *The Gift of Therapy*, New York: Harper-Collins.
Yalom, I. D. (2005). *The Schopenhauer Cure*, New York: Harper-Collins.
Yalom, I. D. (2008). *Staring at the Sun*, London: Piatkus.
Yardley, L. (2008). Demonstrating Validity in Qualitative Psychology, in J. A. Smith (ed.), *Qualitative Psychology: A Practical Guide to Research Methods*, second edition, London: Sage.
Zahavi, D. (1999). Michel Henry and the Phenomenology of the Invisible, *Continental Philosophy Review*, 32/3: 223–240.
Zahavi, D. (2007). Subjectivity and Immanence in Michel Henry, in A. Grøn, I. Damgaard and S. Overgaard (eds.), *Subjectivity and Transcendence*, Tübingen: Mohr Siebeck.
Zahavi, D. (2014a). Contemporary Phenomenology at Its Best, *Europe's Journal of Psychology*, 10, 215–220.
Zahavi, D. (2014b). *Self and Other: Exploring Subjectivity, Empathy, and Shame*, Oxford: Oxford University Press.
Zahavi, D. (2018). Getting It Quite Wrong: Van Manen and Smith on Phenomenology, *Qualitative Health Research*, 29(6): 900–907.
Zahavi, D. (2019). *Phenomenology, the Basics*, London: Routledge.
Zahavi, D. (2021). Applied Phenomenology: Why It Is Safe to Ignore the Epoché, *Continental Philosophy Review*, 54: 259–273.

Appendix

Analysis of Luke's Experience of Freedom

The Filter of TIME

Temporal Dimension	Themes
Past	Always wanting freedom, not being tied to a system
	Freedom required preparation
Present	Movement and agency promote freedom
	Slowing down enables more
Future	Freedom limited to distinct periods
	Planning how to create further moments important
	Questioning how to live
Eternity	Freedom is a lifetime personal project
	Allowing the journey to unfold, an exponential learning curve as freedom evolves
Time limited	Freedom limited to periods of travel
Living / moving in time	Movement and agency important

The Filter of SPACE

Four Dimensions	Themes
Physical	The environment enables freedom
	Time slows and becomes one's own
	Detaching from material possessions is liberating
	Making peace with death
Social	Moving away from the fast-paced world that institutionalises
	Connection and support in building a tribe
	Energised by connection to purposeful people
Personal	Freedom came through reflecting on situation, exploration and led to liberation
	Throwing my whole self into the experience
	Feeling settled in my mind is home
Spiritual	Compelled towards curiosity: More to life than this
	Seeking spiritual environments: Nature, people and cultures
	Wisdom creates an opening and space for re-evaluation

The Filter of SPACE: Individual Experiences of Freedom

Types of Freedom Experienced in Each Dimension	Theme
Physical	Freedom of Direction
	Freedom of Time
	Financial Freedom
Social	Freedom from the System
Personal	Creative Freedom
	Freedom of Mind
Spiritual	Spiritual Freedom

The Filter of PARADOX

Physical

Velocity in the Experience of Freedom

Slowing life down	Allows meaning to be created quicker

Material Things

Having a car gives you freedom	But carries the responsibility of looking after it

Social

Carrying the Experience of Freedom

After a number of years, it is still with me	But it is not with me still

Personal

Freedom to Keep an Openness

Going into the unknown can be scary	But if you go into those situations fearfully then it is not the same experience

To Be Settled

The word settled	Is unsettling

Spiritual

Attachment to Freedom

Travelling has enabled an experience of total freedom	Becoming attached to the idea of freedom through travelling can be restrictive

Freedom and Constraints

Freedom feels constrained if there are a lot of rules	Following rules frees up choices and gives a lot of freedom

Despair and Hope

Looking at the world pessimistically throws optimism and hope away	Hope brings meaning and creative solutions

The Filter of PURPOSE

Intentionality
- Urge to travel and completely change the environment
- Planning a direction but remaining open to what comes
- Complete freedom emerges from responsibility and deliberateness
- Purpose comes from questioning life, being open to new possibilities and letting go
- Throwing myself into the future
- Releasing dependency on material, social and situational things

The Filter of PASSION

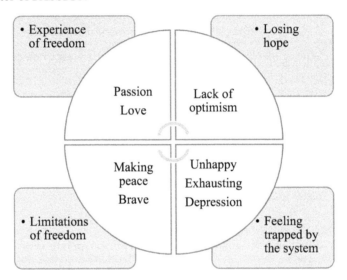

Analysis of Olga's Experience of Freedom

The Filter of TIME

Temporal Dimension	Themes
Past	Always needed freedom Smaller jumps into freedom
Present	Now is the time Freedom is fleeting and limited
Future	Limit of age
Eternity	Total freedom can only be experienced outside of mortal limits
Time limited	Freedom, life and the earth is very, very temporary
Living / moving in time	Number of times when life could have taken different directions

The Filter of SPACE

Four Dimensions	Themes
Physical	Embodied liberation
	Encountering and connection to the planet
Social	Freedom creates shared connection
	Others restrict freedom
	Fighting for freedom deepest value
Personal	Freedom comes from encountering myself in different ways which is liberating
	Freedom has to be created and takes a huge effort
	Freedom is a human right
Spiritual	Making good on ideas that changed life completely
	Awe in being connected with and beyond this planet
	Physical existence is temporary but being part of the cosmos is comforting
	Having too few or too many options can be problematic

The Filter of SPACE: Individual Experiences of Freedom

Types of Freedom Experienced in Each Dimension	Theme
Physical	Financial Freedom
	Sexual Freedom
Social	Political Freedom
	Freedom from the System
Personal	Creative Freedom
Spiritual	Cosmic Freedom

The Filter of PARADOX

Physical	**Finances Dictate Freedom**	
	Lack of money is a prison	Financial freedom is hard won and allows new options
	**A Sense of Home**	
	Home is not the place where you live	No security means you are not tied to a place
Social	**Fighting for Freedom**	
	Fighting for the love of a place, and for the right for freedom	Knowing that it is a fight that will be lost
Personal	**Embracing Freedom**	
	Feeling very excited about everything	Feeling very scared

Spiritual	Belonging
Belonging to a system restricts freedom	Not belonging allows you to encounter the cosmos and the universe

The Filter of PURPOSE

Intentionality	Main motivator was to be free
	Wanting to encounter life in new ways, going ever wider
	Ensuring that she is living according to her values
	Needing to make good on her ideas

The Filter of PASSION

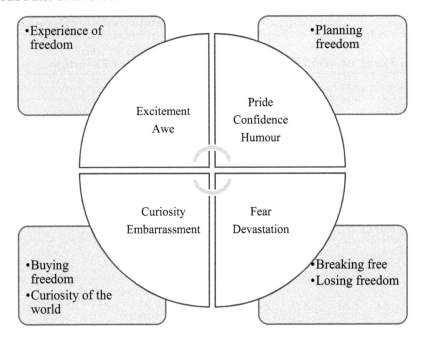

Index

Affectivity, 24–25, 30, 34, 43
 Befindlichkeit, 43, 128
Affective Turn, 68, 196
Ambiguity, 114–116, 122, 196
Anonymity, 66
Anxiety, 15, 52, 87, 101, 104, 116–118, 148, 151, 153, 162, 191, 200
 Existential, 116, 118, 151
Arendt, H., 3, 19, 22, 53, 195
Arnold-Baker, C., 1, 6, 13, 23, 61, 88, 89, 99, 100, 101, 102, 106, 109, 120, 180, 193, 194, 195, 197
Ashworth, J., 106–107, 192–193, 195
Aspirations, 118, 132, 147, 152
Assumptions, 5, 21, 27, 28, 33, 37, 50, 51, 56, 59, 61, 69, 71, 74, 75, 102, 130, 132, 133, 181, 182, 183
Authenticity, 24, 26, 30, 52, 101, 118, 138, 196
 Inauthenticity, 24, 26, 30, 52, 101, 118, 196
Awareness, 12, 14, 27, 29, 30, 33, 38, 40, 44, 45, 53, 55, 63, 70, 78, 83, 84, 86, 97, 102, 104, 129, 131, 135, 136, 145, 156, 159, 162, 181, 186, 187, 198
 Existential awareness, 5, 30, 48

Being, 5, 12, 14, 15, 24, 26, 30, 31, 44–50, 53–54, 57, 62, 74, 83, 86, 101, 102, 104, 112, 114, 129, 130, 136, 145, 153, 154, 169, 181, 196, 198, 200, 201
Being-in-the-world, 3, 5, 26, 30, 44, 45, 46, 48, 70, 97, 98, 99, 127, 181, 197, 198
Being towards death, 85
Being-with, 85, 97, 98, 100
Beliefs, 11, 31, 43, 50, 51, 61, 64, 71, 75, 101, 102, 104, 128, 129, 132, 133, 139, 144, 147, 167, 181

Bias, 5, 21, 33, 36–39, 42, 50, 51, 52, 81, 95, 108, 180, 181, 182, 189
Binswanger, L., 2, 52, 98–99, 102, 105, 195
Birth, 13, 61, 85, 103, 114, 178
Boss, M., 2, 26, 52, 195–196
Body, 30, 36, 47, 97, 100, 103, 105–106, 110, 119, 198, 199
Buber, M., 52, 62, 63, 196

Camus, A., 4, 16, 19, 52, 114, 115, 116, 118, 196
Capta, 71, 72, 76, 77, 78, 85, 107, 108, 121, 129, 166, 183, 188, 190
Change, 13, 14, 18, 30, 32, 34, 35, 36, 45, 52, 56, 58, 70, 73, 75, 82, 83, 86, 89, 92, 93, 114, 117, 120, 122, 125, 132, 133, 134, 141, 145, 157, 158, 186, 187, 197, 206, 207
Choice, 17, 52, 55, 61, 101, 115, 116, 118, 122, 125, 129, 133, 134, 144, 146, 159, 167, 170, 188, 191, 205
Cogito, 34, 35, 38, 186
Confidentiality, 66, 135
Consciousness, 14, 21, 24, 29, 31, 32, 33, 34, 35, 36, 38, 44, 46, 47, 48, 82, 83, 104, 119, 129, 180, 187, 196, 199, 202
Contradictions, 4, 6, 19, 47, 61, 73, 77, 88, 118, 119, 121, 122, 126, 132, 156, 175
Curiosity, 28, 41, 62, 111, 131, 160, 170, 171, 172, 174, 175, 176, 193, 204, 208

Dasein, 44, 45, 46, 85
Data, 2, 5, 7, 16, 35, 41, 48, 54, 56, 57, 59, 66, 71, 76, 81, 84, 107, 108, 109, 139, 180, 183, 193

Index

Death, 15, 26, 31, 36, 61, 74, 85, 93, 100, 103, 110, 111, 112, 114, 115, 117, 118, 119, 124, 126, 136, 138, 165, 166, 169, 173, 175, 176, 192, 196, 200, 202, 204
de Beauvoir, S., 3, 14, 16, 19, 22, 26, 27, 30, 45, 52, 61, 115, 116, 118, 122, 189, 196
Description, 5, 6, 12, 15, 21, 33, 50, 53, 54, 72, 76, 78, 84, 93, 106, 185
Deurzen, E. van, 1, 2, 5, 6, 13, 19, 23, 24, 28, 29, 32, 36, 37, 38, 53, 57, 61, 62, 64, 65, 68, 87, 88, 89, 99, 100, 101, 102, 105, 118, 119, 121, 122, 128, 133, 137, 138, 147, 155, 178, 193, 194, 195, 196, 197, 199
Dialectic, 7, 60, 61, 64, 88–89, 120, 131, 154, 164, 202
Dialogue, 4, 5, 12, 13, 14, 15, 16, 19, 20, 28, 30, 32, 35, 36, 60, 61, 62, 63, 64, 65, 68, 69, 70, 81, 82, 83, 113, 128, 190, 198, 200
  Socratic, 13, 60–61, 64
Dostoyevsky, F., 4, 16, 197

Ec-stases of time, 85
Eidetic, 25, 28, 32–35, 37, 83, 184, 186–187
Eigenwelt, 98, 100, 103, 104, 105, 106, 108, 119
Environment, 31, 33, 35, 65, 97, 98, 99, 100, 122, 129, 134, 141, 156, 162, 166, 171, 176, 179, 185, 204, 206
Embodiment, 56, 77, 99, 106, 192
Emotion, 2, 3, 6, 8, 18, 19, 26, 28, 30, 32, 35, 36, 39, 47, 48, 68, 69, 70, 71, 73, 75, 76, 84, 93, 100, 103, 105, 106, 107, 118, 123, 128, 129, 130, 131, 138, 139, 140, 144–60, 162, 163, 164, 165, 171, 173, 174, 178, 179, 180, 187, 190, 201
  Emotional Compass, 6, 68, 144, 147–148, 151, 152, 154–157, 160, 165, 178
Empathy, 16, 38, 39, 67, 68, 70, 75, 202, 203
  Ontic, 70
  Existential, 70, 202
Energy, 92, 104, 118, 138, 145, 147, 153, 165
Epistemology, 11, 12, 201
Epoché, 21, 22, 25, 32, 37, 81, 107, 108, 180, 182, 190, 203
Existential Research Dialogues, 7, 49, 51, 58, 59, 66, 67, 71, 72, 74, 75, 76, 77, 78, 84, 87, 91, 93, 120, 121, 138, 144, 154, 163, 164, 180, 181, 182, 183, 184, 185, 186, 187, 188, 189

Essence, 5, 13, 20, 21, 25, 33, 34, 35, 36, 38, 53, 57, 59, 63, 77, 78, 81, 83, 84, 95, 99, 101, 104, 121, 181, 183, 184, 185, 186, 187, 199
Eternity, 85, 88, 90, 95, 96, 115, 136, 165, 175, 204, 206
Ethics, 11, 66, 166, 201, 202
  Ambiguity of, 122, 196
Ethical, 25, 57, 87, 122, 134, 136, 144, 203
Existentiale, 43, 46
Existential Anxiety, 116, 118, 151
Existential Guilt, 151
Existential Therapy, 2, 8, 14, 42, 44, 48, 59, 60, 63, 64, 68, 69, 70, 71, 88, 139, 144, 194, 195, 197, 199
Experiential, 25, 29, 32, 35, 57, 84
Exploration, 5, 6, 7, 16, 20, 26, 27, 30, 31, 40, 43, 65, 71, 72, 74, 75, 76, 78, 81, 84, 90, 92, 97, 99, 106, 107, 113, 183, 195, 197, 198, 201, 202, 204
Exteriority, 24, 48, 195
Equalise, 37, 183

Fanon, F., 14, 53, 122, 197
Frankl, V., 2, 122, 167, 192, 198
Fusion of horizons, 12
Future, 30, 84, 85, 86, 87, 88, 90, 91, 93, 95, 96, 104, 114, 115, 116, 117, 124, 126, 141, 142, 143, 146, 154, 156, 165, 167, 169, 170, 174, 175, 179, 185, 186, 187, 197, 204, 206

Gadamer, H. G., 12, 22, 46, 49, 54, 63–64, 74, 198

Heidegger, M., 4, 5, 14, 15, 22, 24, 25, 26, 27, 29, 30, 31, 43, 44, 45, 46, 47, 48, 49, 52, 53, 54, 83, 84, 85, 97, 98, 99, 100, 101, 107, 118, 122, 127, 128, 151, 173, 189, 196, 198, 199
Henry, M., 4, 22, 24, 25, 28, 29, 30, 48, 52, 107, 197, 199, 203
Hermeneutics, 5, 7, 20, 21, 45, 63, 188, 201
  Hermeneutic circle, 46
Heuristic, 4, 5, 7, 17, 21, 25, 28, 31, 67, 78, 81, 106, 107, 108, 109, 112, 113, 180, 196
  Devices, 7, 31, 81
Horizontalise, 37, 183
Husserl, E., 1, 4, 5, 13, 21, 22, 23, 24, 25, 26, 27, 28, 29, 30, 31, 32, 33, 34, 40, 45, 46, 47, 48, 49, 59, 63, 68, 69, 82, 83, 84, 189, 196, 198, 199

Infinite, 38, 86, 93, 104, 117, 119, 186
Information Sheet, 65
Intentionality, 6, 8, 30, 34, 37, 38, 39, 49, 52, 63, 69, 73, 82, 83, 104, 106, 128, 129, 130, 140, 141, 142, 143, 170, 180, 182, 189, 195, 198, 206, 208
  Intentional Arc, 33, 34, 37, 38, 182, 184, 186
Interiority, 7, 21, 24, 25, 26, 27, 30, 32, 34, 48, 59, 195
Interpretation, 2, 5, 20, 28, 30, 45, 46, 48, 49, 63, 72, 136, 180, 183, 186, 187, 189, 190, 201
Interpretative Phenomenological Analysis (IPA), 64, 178, 194, 202
Introspection, 44, 48
Intuition, 21, 29, 46, 102, 150
I-Thou, 62–63

Jaspers, K., 2, 52, 68, 199, 200

Kierkegaard, S., 1, 4, 15, 52, 101, 116, 117, 118, 122, 191, 200
Knowledge, 1, 2, 5, 11, 14, 20, 21, 28, 29, 33, 37, 40, 41, 42, 43, 44, 45, 46–47, 48, 49, 52, 53, 57, 60, 61, 63, 65, 67, 68, 70, 71, 92, 119, 133, 134, 187, 188, 189, 198

Laing, R. D., 2, 3, 27, 200
Language, 24, 26, 27, 44, 63, 64, 68, 74, 85, 100, 103, 112, 167, 168, 180, 192, 198, 199
Lifeworld, 34, 55, 105, 106, 107, 128, 192, 195, 196
Literature, 4, 16, 19, 30, 51, 52, 53, 54, 57, 74, 122, 191
Lived Experience, 55, 57, 58, 64, 71, 77, 109, 180, 185, 194, 198, 201, 202
Logic, 11, 27, 41, 199

Maieutic, 7, 13, 21, 61, 64
Map, 1, 31, 44, 72, 86, 102, 106, 147
Meaning-making, 44, 83, 119
Member Checking, 78
Memory, 13, 20, 87, 91, 104, 156
Merleau-Ponty, M., 3, 14, 22, 26, 30, 31, 47, 48, 49, 52, 99, 102, 105, 106, 189, 200
Metaphysics, 11, 12, 26, 57, 198, 199
Minkowski, E., 86, 105, 200
Mitwelt, 98, 100, 103, 104, 105, 108, 119
Mood, 34, 39, 105, 107, 128, 129, 130, 144, 173, 192

Nietzsche, F., 4, 52, 131, 201
Noesis, 34, 35, 49
Noema, 25, 34, 35, 37, 49, 184, 185, 198

Observation, 2, 26, 28, 29, 33, 84, 92, 94, 186, 187, 190
Onto-dynamic, 6, 30, 48, 114, 118, 127, 131
Ontology, 11, 12, 57, 201
  Ontological, 1, 6, 11, 12, 25, 27, 43, 46, 55, 57, 70, 97, 116, 118, 122, 136, 177, 191, 199
Ontic, 2, 12, 57, 70, 122, 177

Paradox, 7, 8, 32, 55, 56, 73, 77, 81, 82, 115–117, 119, 121–127, 131, 137, 138, 141, 145, 168, 169, 170, 172, 174, 175, 179, 180, 191, 192, 197
Passion, 4, 7, 32, 40, 41, 81, 82, 107, 128, 142, 144, 156, 162, 171, 176, 192, 197, 206, 208
Past, 17, 30, 47, 58, 68, 82, 83, 84, 85, 86, 87, 88, 90, 91, 92, 93, 95, 96, 103, 115, 135, 139, 146, 150, 152, 153, 164, 165, 167, 175, 179, 185, 187, 204, 206
Perception, 6, 14, 26, 32, 44, 47, 69, 93, 98, 102, 128, 179, 200
Personal (dimension), 106, 108, 109, 111, 112, 117, 119, 123, 124, 125, 126, 130, 131, 133, 135, 136, 138, 139, 141, 159, 166, 167, 168, 169, 170, 175, 179, 186, 188, 189, 204, 205, 207
Phenomenology, 1, 4, 5, 7, 12, 13, 14, 21, 22, 23, 24, 25, 26, 27, 28, 29, 30, 31, 32, 37, 38, 39, 40, 45, 48, 49, 59, 69, 81, 82, 105, 106, 178, 180, 189, 192, 194, 195, 196, 197, 198, 199, 200, 201, 202, 203
Philosophy, 1, 4, 11, 12, 19, 21, 23, 24, 25, 26, 29, 41, 47, 52, 53, 60, 61, 82, 84, 98, 102, 106, 114, 120, 135, 142, 167, 189, 192, 195, 198, 199, 200, 201, 202, 203
Physical (dimension), 26, 30, 31, 35, 36, 39, 41, 42, 43, 47, 71, 72, 93, 96, 97, 99, 100, 103, 108, 109, 110, 111, 112, 119, 123, 124, 125, 126, 130, 131, 133, 134, 138, 139, 146, 159, 162, 166, 167, 168, 169, 175, 176, 179, 191, 192, 196, 204, 205, 207
Plato, 60, 61, 63, 64, 120, 201, 202
Pre-reflective, 46, 49

Present, 30, 43, 62, 83, 84, 85, 86, 87, 88, 90, 91, 95, 96, 103, 117, 164, 165, 167, 169, 171, 175, 179, 185, 187, 190, 204, 206
Project, 1, 2, 5, 7, 12, 19, 30, 32, 35, 45, 46, 48, 59, 65, 90, 93, 98, 99, 106, 107, 129, 132, 136, 138, 153, 154, 155, 156, 164, 191, 192, 204
    World-project, 98, 99, 107
Proust, M., 13, 14, 30, 201
Purpose, 6, 7, 8, 31, 32, 56, 62, 71, 72, 73, 77, 81, 82, 101, 102, 106, 119, 127, 129, 130, 133, 138, 140, 141, 142, 143, 144, 152, 153, 162, 167, 170, 176, 192, 206, 208

Radical, 24, 25, 26, 29, 117
Rapport, 65, 67
Reduction
    Phenomenological reduction, 21, 25, 28, 32, 33, 35, 36, 37, 55, 181, 182, 187
    Eidetic reduction, 25, 28, 32, 33, 34, 35, 37, 83, 184, 186, 187
    Transcendental reduction, 25, 29, 33, 34, 35, 36, 38, 49, 69, 177, 186
Reflection, 16, 26, 33, 38, 40, 47, 48, 61, 64, 68, 69, 101, 113, 147, 167, 183, 187, 200
Reflexivity, 17, 51, 165, 180, 188, 190, 194, 198
    SOAR - State of Mind, 5, 38, 42, 50, 62, 107, 180, 181, 188
Research Supervisor, 42, 50
Resonance, 3, 38, 68, 75, 78
Responsibility, 15, 52, 86, 101, 103, 124, 125, 138, 141, 142, 169, 175, 191, 205, 206
Ricoeur, P., 5, 20, 22, 29, 45, 201

Sartre, J. P., 4, 14, 15, 16, 19, 22, 26, 27, 30, 31, 45, 46, 47, 48, 49, 52, 61, 69, 88, 101, 118, 122, 129, 191, 201, 202
Selfhood, 27, 104, 106, 192
Smith, J., 22, 64, 71, 196, 202, 203
Social (dimension), 35, 36, 37, 39, 56, 71, 73, 88, 100, 103, 105, 106, 107, 108, 109, 111, 112, 119, 123, 124, 125, 126, 131, 133, 134, 135, 138, 141, 159, 166, 167, 168, 169, 175, 179, 204, 205, 206, 207
Socrates, 13, 40, 60, 61, 62, 63, 64, 66, 203
Space, 3, 6, 7, 8, 13, 26, 32, 42, 81, 82, 83, 84, 91, 92, 93, 94, 96, 97, 102, 103, 105, 106, 107, 109, 123, 124, 128, 134, 145, 147, 151, 166, 167, 168, 169, 171, 175, 178, 188, 191, 192, 195, 204, 205, 207
Spatiality, 47, 102, 105, 106, 192
Spiritual (dimension), 18, 35, 36, 56, 62, 73, 88, 99, 101, 102, 104, 108, 109, 111, 112, 119, 123, 124, 125, 126, 131, 133, 135, 136, 138, 159, 166, 167, 168, 169, 170, 175, 179, 204, 205, 207, 208,
Stein, E., 3, 22, 68, 69, 202
Subjectivity, 1, 11, 21, 25, 32, 41, 47, 203
    Inter-subjectivity, 26, 30, 38, 69, 188, 189

Temporality, 47, 52, 72, 86, 93, 106, 166, 179, 192
'The Look', 69
Tillich, P., 52, 114, 202
Timelessness, 85, 88, 93
Timeline, 86, 90
Tolstoy, L., 16, 136, 202
Transcript, 75, 77, 78, 95, 108, 121, 122, 140, 182, 183
Truth, 11, 12, 13, 15, 37, 38, 48, 60, 61, 62, 64, 65, 119, 120, 127, 130, 131, 132, 136, 138, 150, 160, 189, 190, 198

Uberwelt, 99, 101, 103, 104, 105, 107, 108, 119
Umwelt, 98, 99, 103, 104, 108, 119, 203
Universe, 74, 76, 93, 97, 98, 103, 123, 133, 158, 159, 168, 175, 208

Validity, 11, 52, 188, 189, 203
Van Manen, M., 22, 23, 25, 41, 50, 57, 64, 71, 72, 77, 78, 105, 106, 108, 109, 111, 178, 180, 192, 193, 194, 202, 203
Verification, 20, 28, 78

Wisdom, 40, 61, 133, 175, 187, 204
Wesenschau, 25, 38, 185
Worldview, 11, 12, 26, 27, 36, 37, 39, 63, 64, 73, 101, 129

Yalom, I., 2, 19, 52, 132, 203

Zahavi, D., 22, 25, 28, 49, 193, 198, 202, 203

For Product Safety Concerns and Information please contact our EU representative GPSR@taylorandfrancis.com
Taylor & Francis Verlag GmbH, Kaufingerstraße 24, 80331 München, Germany

www.ingramcontent.com/pod-product-compliance
Ingram Content Group UK Ltd.
Pitfield, Milton Keynes, MK11 3LW, UK
UKHW020411150325
456245UK00018B/279